BROKEN MEN

Broken Men

Shell Shock, Treatment and Recovery in Britain
1914–1930

Fiona Reid

www.bloomsbury.com/thegreatwar

BLOOMSBURY
LONDON • NEW DELHI • NEW YORK • SYDNEY

Bloomsbury Academic

An imprint of Bloomsbury Publishing Plc

50 Bedford Square	1385 Broadway
London	New York
WC1B 3DP	NY 10018
UK	USA

www.bloomsbury.com/thegreatwar

Bloomsbury is a registered trade mark of Bloomsbury Publishing Plc

First published in 2010 by Continuum
Paperback edition published 2011
Reprinted 2012

© Fiona Reid, 2010

Visit www.bloomsbury.com to find out more about our authors and their books
You will find extracts, author interviews, author events and you can sign up for
newsletters to be the first to hear about our latest releases and special offers.

British Library Cataloguing-in-Publication Data
A catalogue record for this book is available from the British Library.

ISBN:	HB:	978-1-8472-5241-8
	PB:	978-1-4411-4885-8
	ePDF:	978-0-8264-2103-6
	ePUB:	978-1-4411-6144-4

Library of Congress Cataloging-in-Publication Data

A catalogue record for this book is available from the British Library

Contents

To Danu and to Norry

Illustrations

Acknowledgements

Many people have helped me to complete this book. Professor June Hannam and Dr Mike Richards of the University of the West of England provided much valuable encouragement at an early stage, as did Dr Kent Fedorowich. I am also grateful to Professor Mark Connelly (University of Kent) for his useful advice and keen enthusiasm throughout. It would have been impossible to research or to write this book without the support of my colleagues at the University of Glamorgan. I would like to thank the History division as a whole for providing essential funds for research trips. In particular I am grateful to Dr Sharif Gemie and Dr Brian Ireland for reading early drafts of this work, and I very much thank Dr Jane Finucane for some essential technical assistance. Thanks are also due to colleagues in the English division at the University of Glamorgan, especially Professors Gavin Edwards and Andy Smith.

I am very grateful to Commodore Toby Elliott for allowing me full access to the Ex-Services' Welfare Society archives. These archives are held by Combat Stress, the charity that specialises in caring for veterans who have been traumatised by war service. I have quoted extensively from the written material and all the images in this book have been reproduced with Commodore Elliott's kind permission. In addition, I thank Ros Dunn for being so welcoming on my numerous visits to Combat Stress at Tyrwhitt House, Leatherhead. The staff at the National Army Museum have also been extremely helpful, especially Simon Moody who identified the papers of Edwin Blomfield for me.

When writing this book I consulted the letters, diaries and personal papers of many First World War combatants, medical officers and their families. Michael Dible gave me permission to use his father's papers and Thomas West allowed me to use his father's diary. I am deeply indebted to them both and wish to thank them for their generosity. Unfortunately I have not been able to trace all of the individuals whose words appear in this book, although I have done my best to do so. In response, I apologise to anyone who feels that their (or their relatives') views have been misrepresented. At all times I have endeavoured to treat all of the individuals concerned with respect and compassion. I hope that this is evident.

Of course I owe the greatest thanks and the greatest love to my immediate family: my partner, Dr Norry LaPorte and my daughter Danu and her partner Joe. All of them have been, and continue to be, quite magnificent all of the time. Thank you.

Introduction

We are all familiar with the mentally broken soldier of the First World War. The shell-shocked man – often the shell-shocked boy – who was too traumatized to fight embodies contemporary popular judgements about the First World War: it was too brutal, too cruel and too futile. Men were unable to deal with it. Yet in retrospect, the deeply traumatized First World War soldier is also a strangely comforting figure. It is thanks to this mistreated victim of the trenches that we began to learn the importance of 'managing' trauma. In response to traumatic events such as natural disaster or terrorist attack, we now routinely provide counselling, we recognize grief and we encourage the expression of anxieties. It was the shell-shocked soldier who first began to dismantle the Victorian 'stiff upper lip', and it was the shell-shocked soldier who refused to fight in this most bloody of wars – sometimes paying for this refusal by facing a hasty court martial and an unwarranted execution.

On a popular level there is still widespread agreement that the First World War was pointless in a way that other wars, notably the Second World War, were not. In Britain, the Great War plays a central role in academic and cultural life and in concepts of national identity. There is no antithetical relationship between history and memory; rather, there is a strong symbiotic relationship between popular perceptions of the war and academic history, and the popular understanding of the First World War is largely based upon a shared memory of that particular war as collective trauma.[1] This perception of the war is most visibly expressed in the Lost Generation thesis, an idea that was initially propagated by elite literature. Siegfried Sassoon and Wilfred Owen expressed it forcefully in their poetry: they were 'doomed youth led blindly to the slaughter by cruel age'.[2] Elite literature does not often impact upon populist political commentary, but in November 2008, the eightieth anniversary of the 1918 armistice agreement, the BBC website was awash with comments about the slaughter, the sacrifice and the senselessness of the Great War. It is unsurprising that the BBC chose to highlight the 'Have your say' section with the following comments from Suki Handal of Coventry, 'We should honour those who fought and died in all wars, but recognize that WW1 was utterly unnecessary.'[3] Handal's comments perfectly encapsulate much of British public opinion.

These and other popular myths about the First World War have recently been the subject of much academic debate. Historians such as Gary Sheffield, Brian Bond and Dan Todman have begun to debunk long-standing beliefs about 'lions led by donkeys' and the unremitting failures of the British armies in the field.[4] Reconsidering the whole futility thesis, Adrian Gregory has argued that the First World War was not at all meaningless to those who fought and that 'it qualifies as a necessary war'.[5] He also demonstrates that mistakes, miscalculations and sheer bungling cannot be confined to one dreadful, atypical war – the Second World War was similarly characterized by a 'litany of British catastrophes'.[6] It is not only historians who have begun to reconceptualize the First World War. In direct opposition to fiercely held popular beliefs, psychiatrist Simon Wessely has argued that 'military and medical authorities were not blind to the psychiatric consequences of war' in the years 1914–1918.[7]

The idea of the First World War as a futile war has been so pervasive for so long that it has framed the way in which the history of shell shock has developed. This has not always been productive, and Roger Cooter has complained that the Great War has been reduced to 'the war of shell shock'.[8] A publication celebrating the centenary of the Royal Army Medical Corps (RAMC) insists that the conflict of 1914–1918 was a 'very different war', which forced the RAMC to deal with a number of novel conditions such as gas gangrene and shell shock.[9] By reconfiguring the story of shell-shock treatment as the story of an institutional inadequacy conquered, the RAMC fosters a sense of its own progress narrative. In addition, it is not simply that the story of shell shock has now come to dominate First World War narratives, but that shell shock, that is, psychological collapse during warfare, is generally seen as a particular reaction to the unprecedented horrors of one unusual war. This highlights the supposedly unique nature of the First World War but obscures the longer and more complex history of men's responses to warfare and of mental collapse more generally.

It is important to stress two points in order to contextualize mental breakdown in warfare. First, most men did not become psychological casualties during the First World War; rather, most men dealt reasonably well with the stresses and strains of intense warfare.[10] Secondly, although British military psychiatry has its origins in the First World War, the history of war and mental breakdown is far older.[11] Of course the First World War was the first total war, the first mass industrial war. It was also the first war in which psychological casualties appeared to represent real problems of both morale and manpower. Yet although the First World War was undeniably horrific in many ways, it was certainly not the first time that men had been traumatized by warfare. The literature of war, both fictional and otherwise, is dominated by stories of men who have been disturbed by war, and by the various coping mechanisms they have employed to deal with their distress. War neurosis is not simply modern man's response to industrial war: as early as 1685 the Royal Hospital recognized the psychiatric disorders of warfare.[12] It is clear that men have long had complex responses to the stress of battle, and a few examples will suffice to illustrate this point.

In November 1794, Major Watkin Tench was a marine serving in the Royal Navy. Britain was at war with revolutionary France and Tench's ship was captured, leaving many men wounded.[13] In a letter to a friend, Tench explained how he tried to cross the part of the deck that was being used as a hospital, but he was overwhelmed and after two attempts 'to penetrate across this stage of woe', he gave up.[14] It is not just that Tench was unable to face the wounded and dying men; most crucially he lacked the words to describe his emotions and so he turned to Milton, writing that the sight of such suffering 'quelled my best of man'.[15] Was Tench unmanned by his war service? War is ostensibly, and historically, the most masculine of activities, yet men have often been represented as emasculated or feminized by war and – like Tench – of being unable to find the words to communicate their responses.

One of the most famous literary examples of the old soldier is surely Tristram Shandy's Uncle Toby. Captain Toby Shandy received a groin wound at the siege of Namur when a large stone fell from the parapet and crushed his pubic bone. In the course of his long and painful convalescence, Uncle Toby was plagued by visitors who were unable to understand his war stories. In response, Toby and his man Trim – his old corporal from the campaigning days – decided to recreate sieges in the grounds of the family estate. There is a stark contrast between Uncle Toby's inability to describe his campaigns and the extraordinary attention to detail that he and Trim display when constructing ravellins, bastions, curtins, hornworks and so forth. Uncle Toby is obsessed by his war, but he cannot talk about it; he re-enacts his war because of his inability to describe it.[16]

This sense of being dominated by war memories and by an inability to articulate them continues. In February 2009, Lance Corporal Johnson Beharry, a highly decorated Iraq war veteran, received much media coverage for his story of his own war neurosis and his comments on the poor treatment available to mentally wounded veterans via the National Health Service. On the *Today* programme, Beharry told listeners, 'I didn't know I would get worse.' [17] He went into more detail in the *Independent* where he described some of his very negative and aggressive symptoms and the difficulty of managing his anger in ordinary everyday situations.[18] Like Tench, Beharry struggled to find his own words. He turned not to Milton but to the words of a psychotherapist to explain his – literally – unspeakable anguish, 'I find it difficult to talk to normal civilians ... it is memory pain, the body catching up. My psychotherapist explained that the body could only deal with a certain amount of pain at a time so it comes out later.'[19] Unlike Uncle Toby, Beharry does not have a family estate on which to stage cathartic battle re-enactments and so he does so in inappropriate situations, 'You spend six months on the battlefield and you have to defend yourself every day and then you come back to normal life and go to Tesco and someone runs into your trolley. You have to stop and think – it is only a trolley, you are not on the battlefield.'[20]

All of these stories demonstrate the long-term characteristics that mark memories of war, in particular memories about the traumas of war. First, there is the inability to talk about war in a meaningful way. Well-worn clichés about the old soldier constantly repeating the same old war stories lie in the veteran's long-standing inability to construct meaningful dialogue, especially with those who have not experienced combat. This is why wartime comradeship, such as that between Uncle Toby and Corporal Trim, remains so important long after wars are over. Secondly, these stories demonstrate that war is potentially emasculating. War can unman in a variety of ways: Tench's loss of courage was expressed in unmanly behaviour whereas Uncle Toby's wound damaged his marriage prospects. Beharry's inability to control his emotional responses is similarly problematic because the idealized, socialized male must demonstrate controlled – not uncontrolled – aggression. As Beharry clearly recognizes, the truly masculine soldier does not horrify non-combatants needlessly; he does not run amok in Tesco. Yet a loss of masculinity is not necessarily permanent, and just as soldiers have long struggled with their war memories, they have also developed coping mechanisms and strategies to deal with emotional shock. It is this transition from the tests and traumas of the battlefield to the more normal conditions of civilian life that forms one of the primary subjects of this book.

Although scholars have written extensively about wartime shell shock, the life of the mentally wounded man after the armistice has been strangely neglected.[21] Peter Barham is the striking exception here, but his work *Forgotten Lunatics* is devoted to those men who came home and were incarcerated in lunatic asylums.[22] In contrast, this book is largely about those men who were shell shocked during the First World War but who were in a position to rebuild their lives afterwards. For shell-shocked men and their families, mental breakdown was not the end of the story. Far from being 'forgotten', many of them continued to be a real and very visible problem for their families and for the politicians and civil servants who had to organize veteran welfare in the 1920s. Sadly, Beharry was not the first soldier to find that his mental health problems grew worse after demobilization: research into pension claims during the 1920s indicates that many men found life increasingly difficult once they had returned home.

There is of course an overwhelming amount of material about the First World War: personal testimonies abound as do medical and military reports, newspaper articles and so on. Most notably, there is a wealth of combatant literature. Not only are old soldiers renowned for reminiscing and for constantly retelling their war stories, but veterans of this particular war are renowned for writing and publishing their war stories. In the words of Cyril Falls, a military historian and journalist, 'The Great War has resulted in the spilling of floods of ink as well as floods of blood.'[23] Yet among these 'floods of ink' there are relatively few direct accounts of personal mental breakdown; the voice of the ordinary shell-shocked soldier is largely silent.[24] There are of course good reasons for this. As Watkin Tench, Uncle Toby and Lieutenant Beharry have attested, it is hard for men to express their complex emotional reactions to war. Even in early twenty-first century Britain – a society dominated by public confessions – mental breakdown is a great taboo and is rarely discussed openly. The taboo was even greater at the beginning of the twentieth century, and the First World War soldier lived in a world in which it was unacceptable to broadcast nervous collapse. However, a reticence to discuss publicly the impact of mental breakdown does not mean that mental breakdown was routinely ignored or denied. On the contrary, this book reveals some of the many means employed to ensure that shell-shocked men managed to cope with their psychological wounds. Some of these tactics were, of course, more successful than others. The point is that although men were reluctant to discuss personal crises in a public forum, men did not break down alone.

In the relative absence of the shell-shocked voice from the trench, this book pays particular attention to the voices of those responsible for the care of the mentally broken man. It is these voices that provide us with a glimpse into the world of the shell-shocked. This world was primarily framed by pre-existing attitudes to madness and nervous debility: we cannot isolate mental breakdown in war from mental breakdown more generally. Moreover, warfare is a social activity and so a man usually started to show the signs of nervous breakdown when he was with his fellow soldiers. As a result, soldiers and officers on the fighting fronts grew accustomed to the signals of imminent mental collapse. More crucially, many soldiers wanted to avoid dispatching their comrades to the official treatment system and so they developed informal, ad hoc ways of managing shell shock. Medical officers and nursing orderlies also had close contact with shell-shocked men. Their responses indicate the way in which shell-shocked men were treated during the war; they also provide us with a sense of context. In retrospect it easy to see the Great War as the war of shell shock: medics' responses make it plain that shell shock was just one of a whole host of trying conditions that they had to manage.

Alongside the politicians and civil servants who were officially responsible for veteran welfare, there were also charity workers. The physical and emotional needs of veterans were acute in the 1920s, and so despite the government commitment to veteran welfare, there was also a very necessary and extensive network of voluntary care. As far as shell-shocked men were concerned, the primary charitable organization was the Ex-Services' Welfare Society (ESWS). The ESWS was established in 1919 to provide care for mentally wounded ex-service personnel and their families. It was, and remains, the only British charity specifically dedicated to the care of psychologically wounded veterans, and its papers have provided much of the material for this book.[25] It is through the actions of this charity that we can reconstruct the lives of mentally broken men after the war. In addition, it is through the ESWS that we can see how some men managed to recreate meaningful lives for themselves after their mental collapse. For the mentally broken men of the 1920s it was not always possible to recover fully from the psychological wounds of the war – minds cannot be mended easily. This goes some way to explaining why shell shock has become so symbolic that in some cases it now functions as a metaphor for the war itself.[26] However, as Peter Leese has acknowledged, too great a focus on the iconic or cultural nature of shell shock has obscured the very real sufferings of men and their families.[27] Furthermore, it has obscured the history of those who tried to manage shell shock and those who tried to recreate their lives afterwards. In response, this book aims to highlight the narratives of those who endeavoured to cope with shell shock: the mentally broken men and those who tried to mend them.

Shell Shock and Weak Nerves

*Rumour had it that the constant twitching and jerking and snorting was
caused by something called shell-shock, but we were not quite sure what
that was. We took it to mean that an explosive object had gone off very
close to him with such an enormous bang that it had made him jump
high in the air and he hadn't stopped jumping since.*

ROALD DAHL MEETS CAPTAIN HARDCASTLE[1]

'Is it strange that men's nerves broke under the strain?'[2] This is the question that
the *Optimist* asked in November 1929. To mark the commemoration of the 1918
armistice, the *Optimist*, 'the national organ of the cheerful giver', published an
issue dedicated to 'the awful tragedy of the nerve-wracked war hero'.[3] Underneath
a picture of men in a trench on the Western Front, the *Optimist* presented its
readers with the following challenge:

> In the hush of the Two-Minute Silence, while an Empire mourns its mighty dead,
> will you spare a thought for the men who also braved Armageddon, and came back
> broken in mind by the horrors they had witnessed, the terror that froze their souls?
> Not theirs to reason why; soldiers, sailors, airmen – theirs but to 'carry on' with every
> nerve shrieking for relief. In Flanders Fields, the poppies form a crimson pall on a
> hundred thousand corners of some foreign field that is forever England. But at home
> thousands of ex-servicemen remain mentally wrecked, penniless, workless, hopeless.
> Today you are paying tribute to the heroes who died . . . Dare you forget your debt
> to their comrades, the heroes who live?

On this Armistice Day, the ESWS was primarily concerned not with the war dead,
but with 'the heroes who live'.[4] The images used by the *Optimist* are ones with
which we are familiar: a packed communication trench, mud, wounded soldiers
lying on stretchers in the open air. This sort of image has long dominated the
visual discourse of the First World War. A later ESWS advertising poster is based
on a photograph of soldiers going 'over the top', arguably one of the most iconic
of Great War images, and superimposed over the photograph, are the words

'Do you Remember?'[5] Whether the observer actually remembered or not was irrelevant because the immediate message was so obvious: we must not forget those men who are still suffering from the war. Yet this immediate message was reinforced by a very particular demand: by the late 1920s, those caring for shell-shocked men were trying to create a special place for them in public memories of the war, and were arguing that shell-shocked men had an exceptional claim on the nation. This special place was due to them not just because of their painful neuroses, but because shell-shocked men were uniquely unable to forget the war and all its traumas. Post-war Britain was a society dominated by the war, and the urge to 'remember' was accompanied by a threat: Lest We Forget. Although no one could actually forget the war, it was shell-shocked veterans who lived most closely with their memories. In the words of the *Optimist:* 'nightmare memories such as this remain for ever with the war-shocked ex-serviceman.'[6] Shell-shocked men continued painfully to remember the war long after the armistice, and herein lay their special claim.[7]

Those who campaigned to ensure that the mentally wounded veteran occupied a privileged role were, in some senses, very successful. The mentally wounded soldier has now come to dominate the narrative of the First World War in Britain. Given that the First World War has come to be seen as a pointless struggle in which young soldiers were carelessly led to their deaths by incompetent generals, the shell-shocked soldier, the man apparently driven mad by war, is the perfect emblem for an insane conflict.[8] Shell shock is now 'the war's emblematic psychiatric disorder'.[9] Even those quite uninterested by history in general, or by the Great War in particular, will 'know' that men became shell-shocked in the trench warfare of 1914–1918.

How did this situation come about? Why has shell shock become such an effective, and enduring, metaphor for the Great War in Britain? The links between shell shock and the First World War seem so obvious to British commentators that it seems almost unnecessary to discuss them. During the war, shell shock was an apparently novel and highly traumatic condition and so it easily came to symbolize the distress of men in the trenches, and the war in general. This was a large-scale, industrial war, which dragged on for more than four years, and almost every family in the country suffered in some way.[10] Shell-shocked men with their physical tics and their tortured dreams were clearly illustrative of such unprecedented, widespread anguish. Yet these logical and apparently obvious links are not inevitable. Shell-shocked men were indeed piteous, as were the victims of gas attacks, as were the men with frozen feet, as were the men with severe facial injuries. Certainly in France, *les gueules cassées,* the men with smashed faces, have long been presented as the most grievous victims of the war.[11] Soldiers of all nations succumbed to war neurosis, so why has the shell-shocked soldier become such an enduring feature in specifically British narratives of the First World War?

REMEMBERING SHELL SHOCK

First World War shell shock, its treatment and the legal and medical ramifications are clearly important issues in themselves, and there is now much literature on the history of shell shock as a medical condition.[12] This is central to the medical and military history of the war. Yet to understand the long-term importance of shell shock in Britain, it is also essential to understand the cultural framework in which shell shock arose, and to describe the early responses that were generated by a growing awareness of war neurosis. There is now a common consensus that many shell-shocked men received inadequate treatment during the Great War, and this is largely true. However, this does not mean that there was a unified and dismissive response towards all psychological casualties at the time. Political, medical and military authorities reacted to the condition in a variety of ways, and more general viewpoints, as expressed in the press, were similarly diverse. These initial definitions and developments explain why shell shock as a condition became so crucial to later memories of the war itself. Shell shock became culturally significant in Britain because of pre-existing attitudes towards 'weak nerves'; because of the linguistic confusion that added layers of meaning to the illness; and because of the initial, often unwieldy, arrangements for shell-shocked patients.

Recent works on early cases of shell shock indicate the diversity and complexity of this subject. The shell-shock narrative can be examined through any number of prisms, from military discipline to eugenics.[13] Shell-shock treatment can be seen as fundamental to the development of psychology in Britain; it can also be used to illustrate masculinity in crisis, or more widespread attitudes to disability and the debased body.[14] On a political level, the treatment of shell-shocked soldiers can be used to discredit the military High Command, the political system it represented and the conduct of the war as a whole.[15] Alternatively, the history of shell shock can be used as a starting point for a history of war neurosis and treatment regimes. The relationship between shell shock in the Great War and later war neurosis is clearly crucial, as it was during this period that medical and military authorities began to develop systematic and comprehensive methods of dealing with psychological casualties. In addition, the experiences of the Great War ensured that military and medical elites distanced themselves from the term 'shell shock' so that it is now uniquely associated with the First World War. Later terms such as combat stress or Post-Traumatic Stress Disorder (PTSD) simply do not carry the same symbolic weight.[16] In short, the history of early responses to shell shock has focused mainly on the way in which initial approaches affected later military and medical procedures. In addition, there is now a wider social and cultural history of the war and the way it has been remembered.[17] Of course most people in Britain today do not 'remember' the war at all. When we talk of the collective memory of the war, we refer to a set of widespread assumptions and understandings compiled from a host of sites: family stories, war memorials, school history lessons, television documentaries, popular film and literature.[18]

The term 'shell shock' is part of our everyday language and it is used widely to describe any great emotional shock. It is now so embedded in national culture that it requires no further explanation even through the term is used in such a variety of different ways. On the morning of President Obama's election victory, the *Guardian* described the defeated Sarah Palin as looking 'shell-shocked'; in May 2009 a BBC reporter described Tamil refugees – homeless and distraught as a result of the long civil war in Sri Lanka – as 'shell-shocked'.[19] Shell shock now functions as a useful shorthand for a whole gamut of emotions ranging from unpleasant surprise to serious trauma. Yet during the First World War, shell shock was the name given to a series of complex medical conditions that afflicted servicemen, both during the war and afterwards. Some men had short episodes of mental breakdown; others remained mentally damaged for life. Extensive references to shell shock seem to indicate a widespread acceptance of the condition in the 1920s and the 1930s. One could easily assume that interwar Britain was populated with peculiar men, all still twitching from the war. Was Roald Dahl the only schoolboy to wonder if a teacher's eccentric behaviour was induced by shell shock? Certainly fans of Lord Peter Wimsey, Dorothy Sayers's fictional detective, were familiar with shell shock, and Wimsey's odd behaviour was presented as something one simply had to tolerate because it could not be cured.[20] On a more sinister note, Orwell describes the howls of shell-shocked men in the tramps' hostels; a decade after the armistice, some men still could not sleep at night.[21] It is obviously impossible to say how many shell-shocked men remained traumatized for the rest of their lives, or how many families had to deal with husbands or sons who could never fully recover from their ordeals.

It is not actually possible to say how many were shell-shocked at all. In 1918, 18,596 pensions were awarded for shell shock, neurasthenia and other nervous complaints. By 1921 the number of men pensioned for nervous complaints peaked at 65,000, but this was reduced to 50,000 by the beginning of 1922.[22] By 1929 official figures indicate that 47,669 men were receiving pensions for stabilized neurasthenia and 7,800 were still receiving pensions for unstabilized neurasthenia. This gives a total of 55,469, a figure slightly greater than that of 1922, although it does not include those categorized as suffering from psychoses.[23] Of course these figures exclude those who were suffering but were not awarded pensions, and those who may have been suffering from nervous disorders but were diagnosed with other complaints. Experts at the time were open about the difficulty of obtaining accurate statistics. Sir Frederick Mott, a pathologist to the

London County Council who pioneered much of the early research into shell shock, estimated that shell-shock cases could account for about one-third of all discharges; Dr Henry Waynard Kaye, a temporary captain in the RAMC, admitted that 'total numbers' of shell-shock cases were simply not available.[24] Yet the significance of shell shock lies not in the numbers of men affected. Rather, shell shock is significant because all aspects of the condition, from its very name to its causes, treatment and prognosis, were topics of serious debate at various points, both throughout the war and afterwards. It was not just the nature of shell shock itself, but individual responses, associations and assumptions, which resulted in shell shock becoming a way of criticizing those responsible for the conduct of the war, and later, a symbol of disenchantment. In addition, these responses were often marred by inconsistency, as public sympathy existed alongside personal misunderstandings and a more traditional – albeit highly misplaced – fear of madness. These complexities, and the contradictory nature of so many responses to shell shock, explain why the condition and its victims came to play such a large role in post-war memories.

NERVES, CLASS AND GENDER AT THE BEGINNING OF THE WAR

Psychological casualties first became apparent in September 1914 during the retreat from the battle of Mons. At this stage the war was one of mobility, and so shell shock is not exclusively a product of trench warfare, although for obvious reasons the associations are strong. Psychological casualties grew to unprecedented numbers while men were in the trenches, and the number of shell-shock cases noticeably decreased once the war became one of movement again in late 1918. However, the key point about all initial responses to shell shock is the way in which the condition was largely perceived as a wholly new problem. Viscount Knutsford, an established medical reformer and one of the first to fund-raise for 'Special Hospitals' for shell-shocked men insisted that: 'These hospitals are a product of this war. No other wars have made them necessary.'[25] Knutsford's emotive language is reflected in more nuanced medical discourse, such as that by Grafton Elliot Smith, Professor of Anatomy at Manchester University Medical School, and his colleague Tom Pear, lecturer in experimental psychology, who recognized that the symptoms of shell shock were not new, but argued that the conditions of the Great War were indeed unique, 'Never in the history of mankind have the stresses and strains laid upon body and mind been so great or so numerous as in the present war'.[26]

Shell shock was seen as one of the many new problems provoked by mass, industrial warfare, all of which produced widespread anxiety and a number of different professional and popular responses. Yet despite the apparent novelty of shell shock, war has always been brutal and men have always broken down in armed conflict. We have already mentioned some complex responses to warfare in the Nine Years' War and in the Napoleonic wars – Uncle Toby and Watkin Tench – but there are examples of war neurosis dating as far back as Herodotus.[27] Modern armies and modern doctors began to treat psychological breakdown as a serious medical complaint in the Napoleonic wars, and the American Civil War made plain the links between industrial warfare, heavy firepower and mental anguish. In the Russo–Japanese War of 1904–1905, the Russian Army established a separate forward clearing hospital for psychiatric casualties, and this development was later discussed in French and German medical journals.[28]

Despite these innovations, the British medical-military community showed little interest in the study of psychological casualties. There are various reasons for this. First, the nature of the British Army differed substantially from its continental counterparts. At the beginning of the war it was a volunteer army, whereas the other European powers relied upon conscription; consequently, the British authorities assumed that they would not have to deal with the problems of the inherently unfit to any great degree. Certainly proposals for conscription sparked a wide-ranging debate about the very different, and some would say inferior, qualities of a conscript army. Captain James Henry Dible, a young temporary officer in the RAMC, spoke for many of his peers when he argued that voluntary service encouraged 'the right sort of chap' as opposed to the 'heterogeneous hotch-potch produced by conscription'.[29] Secondly, RAMC officers were often ready to dismiss psychological casualties as hysterical, and were reluctant to engage seriously with the problem of hysteria. Certainly hysteria has long been seen as a particularly female malady, based upon 'the sympathetic connection between the brain and the uterus'.[30] In 1910 the Encyclopaedia Britannica noted that hysteria was primarily associated with women, Jews and Slavs; in short, not the sort of condition that could be easily attached to the nation's soldiers.[31] Furthermore, those who had written about hysteria were primarily gynaecologists, not a factor that encouraged RAMC officers to pay much attention to the subject.[32] So despite the presence of British observers in the Russo–Japanese war, the *RAMC Training Manual* of 1911 made only the most perfunctory of references to psychological casualties, and in a short section entitled 'Mental Cases in the Field' it stated that, 'A certain proportion of mental cases may occur requiring special arrangements.' What these 'special arrangements' might be remained obscure.[33]

Of course, one can simply dismiss the RAMC as being far from the cutting edge of medical innovation, and some contemporary commentators did exactly that: civilian medical officers were often frustrated by what they saw as hidebound RAMC medical practices.[34] More specifically, Knutsford was highly critical of early RAMC responses to shell shock.[35] However, the widespread denial of mental health problems was not peculiar to the medical-military authorities in Britain. On the contrary, it was part of a wider cultural tendency. The ridiculous British propensity for denying mental illness had been satirized by Samuel Butler in *Erewhon* as early as 1872. In Erewhon, a fictional land, the inhabitants considered physical illness to be shameful, and in some cases it was even punishable by imprisonment. Yet everybody discussed their mental problems publicly and frankly. As a result, the people of Erewhon went to great lengths to conceal all physical illnesses, whereas mental disorders were treated openly and with compassion. Butler's message was plain: marking mental illness with shame resulted in concealment, denial and the exacerbation of symptoms.

However, the shell-shock problem quickly grew out of control, forcing the British military authorities to acknowledge military mental health problems despite all pre-existing taboos. Between April 1915 and April 1916, 1,300 officers and 10,000 men from the other ranks had been admitted to special hospitals in Britain. Some British Army bases in France had their own neurosis wards too.[36] From an early date, the Great War was seen as peculiarly horrific, not just because of its scale, but because it was felt that the war was strange and unique. For many Britons in 1914, a large-scale continental war seemed 'abnormal' and the war was perceived as a series of 'psychological shocks'.[37] The apparent novelty of the Great War and its impact on a traumatized generation is now a matter of some debate, but it is certainly the case that many contemporaries expressed their anxieties about the war in this manner and that shell shock seemed to be one of many new and disturbing consequences of modern warfare.[38] Yet the current focus on the perceived novelty of the Great War in general and shell shock in particular should not obscure the fact that the concepts of mental illness, nervous breakdown and madness were not new at all. Elliot Smith and Pear, who at one level acknowledged the exceptional conditions of the war, also insisted that 'shell-shock involves no *new* symptoms or disorders. Every one was known beforehand in civil life.'[39] This was of course the case. Despite popular – and even medical – associations between women and hysteria, male hysteria had long been recognized. Micale traces the medical history of male hysteria from Charles Lepois's work in seventeenth-century France. These ideas were then largely ignored, but in the late nineteenth century Jean-Martin Charcot published extensive case studies on his work with hysterical male patients, and the concept of masculine hysteria was 'widely accepted within mainstream European medical communities' by the 1890s.[40]

Meanwhile, although there were fierce taboos about the expression of emotional distress, British doctors had grown used to 'railway spine', the name given to the nervous complaints arising from the 'spinal concussions' that could be sustained during train accidents.[41] In addition to this prior awareness of male hysteria, concepts of mental illness, nervous breakdown and madness were heavily circumscribed by attitudes towards class and gender. Shell shock is often seen as the exceptional product of the First World War but attitudes towards the condition were formulated by widespread attitudes towards hysteria, madness, masculinity and class at the beginning of the twentieth century.

WEAK NERVES AND SIMPLE REMEDIES

So shell shock may well have appeared like a new complaint at the beginning of the war – the term was not officially coined until 1915 – but the British public was clearly already familiar with the concept of weak nerves.[42] More specifically, since the late-nineteenth century, 'railway spine' came to be used for a wide variety of industrial accidents. So, in many ways, shell shock seemed like less of a new condition, and more of an old condition in a new form. In the first year of the war, *The Times* ran advertisements for numerous medical products, notably the Turvey Treatment and the Wincarnis remedy, both designed to tackle nervous debility. The Turvey treatment was aimed at those suffering from neurasthenia, nervous debility and neuritis, and the advertisement reassured readers that, 'These diseases are increasingly common in these days of strain and worry, amongst both men and women . . . the Turvey Treatment can be forwarded to all necessary directions to any part of the country or abroad.'[43] The Wincarnis remedy, which was explicitly aimed at soldiers, was less specific, promising to help 'when your nerves are "on edge"'.[44]

The text surrounding these adverts provides a clear picture of the cultural context in which shell shock emerged. The language implies that all men and women could be vulnerable to nervous collapse and this view prevailed throughout the war as much medical opinion grew to accept that shell shock was simply nervous breakdown in combat conditions. The Turvey Treatment was aimed at both men and women, but by stating that the product could easily be sent abroad the manufacturers were indicating that it could be helpful for the troops. Those offering the treatment promised total confidentiality, implying that there was something embarrassing about nervous debility despite the fact that all were vulnerable to it. There was an even stronger implication of shame in later advertisements, when neurasthenia was categorized alongside alcoholism and drug addiction. Both of these products were marketed as medically respectable: the Turvey Treatment boasted 'medical credentials' while the Wincarnis remedy was advertised alongside a lecture from 'Nurse Wincarnis'. The prevailing message was that the medical community could be trusted to cure neurasthenia in either civilians or soldiers.

The similarities between nervous debility among civilians and mental collapse on the front were equally visible in the more radical *Labour Leader*. The paper carried adverts for Dr Cassell's tablets, which offered 'a certain cure' for nervous breakdown as well as many other complaints.[45] The paper also promoted Vitaloids, a product that nourished exhausted nerve cells and so cured 'nervous exhaustion, brain fag, neuralgia, backache, irritability and all nerve weaknesses'.[46] The *Labour Leader* was the official newspaper of the Independent Labour Party and it maintained a highly critical approach to the war throughout the conflict. Nevertheless, it imbibed much of the prevalent military culture of wartime Britain. Military language and military images dominated much of its advertising and the advert for Vitaloids began with a caption headed 'Are you a shirker?'[47] Across divides of class and political persuasion, there existed a kind of popular consensus concerning both nervous breakdown and military values.

Shell shock developed in a culture that already stressed the importance of personal moral responsibility for both mental and physical health. As the war developed, medical and military responses to shell shock repeatedly stressed the importance of will power and of the man's personal commitment to his own recovery. This emphasis upon self-control was not simply the consequence of military discipline during a wartime crisis; it also reflected a pre-existing culture. Eugene Sandow, the bodybuilder and 'famous health specialist', ran a campaign for health, fitness and endurance at the beginning of the war, and stressed the way in which one could cultivate and develop nerve force and will power. He offered books on the subjects of neurasthenia and nervous disorders, and described the neurasthenic in pejorative terms as 'nervous, impulsive, erratic, unstable and a creature of moods'. However, neurasthenia was not simply unattractive. Mr Sandow insisted that 'weakness is a crime today', and made clear links between neurasthenia and lack of military success.[48]

> Will power can be developed through the nervous system just as the muscles of arms or legs are developed by the specific repetition of certain movements . . . Nervous strength is indeed, the distinctive characteristic of success in every sphere of life. All great military leaders from Napoleon to Kitchener have been men of great nerve force and a compelling personality . . . The neurasthenic on the other hand is literally foredoomed to failure.[49]

These popular representations of mental collapse and its cures produce a complex and contradictory picture of attitudes towards nervous breakdown at the beginning of the war. On one level they acknowledge that anyone can be vulnerable to weak nerves or nervous breakdown, yet they also suggest that nervous collapse is somehow shameful, especially during wartime. In addition, the insistence that individuals had a personal responsibility to address such problems was tempered by the belief that weak nerves could easily be cured by the application of both will power and medical expertise.

These mixed messages characterized popular perceptions of mental illness and also featured in the official discourse, which recognized the validity of nervous complaints while simultaneously making explicit associations between nervous debility, idleness and fraud. The initial official responses to shell shock stemmed from research into fraudulent compensation claims in the workplace, and it is no coincidence that Sir John Collie, the pre-war expert in malingering, eventually became responsible for managing Homes of Recovery for shell-shocked men and for the allocation of war pensions.[50] In an early article, significantly entitled 'Studies in Diseased Personality', Collie described neurasthenia as 'a bankruptcy of nervous force', and went on to outline some of the attitudes that later characterized responses towards psychological casualties of the war.[51]

Collie did accept the existence of genuine mental collapse and acknowledged the need for medical treatment. However, he also insisted on the responsibility of the patient to play an active role in his own recovery and was highly ambiguous about the relationship between neurasthenia, nervous breakdown and insanity. He recognized that neurasthenia and insanity were not necessarily connected, but admitted that it was 'sometimes almost insuperably difficult' to distinguish between the two conditions.[52] This awareness of medical inadequacy led him to suspect malingering, and he complained that: 'Too often crafty workmen encouraged an illness so that they might obtain their pension.'[53] Elliot Smith and Pear noticed the scepticism with which many physicians approached this sort of complaint and pointed out that 'it is not uncommon to meet the expression "*detecting*", instead of *diagnosing* hysteria'.[54] Consequently, the later well-remembered links between shell shock and malingering were not simply a product of military wartime culture but were part of the civilian political and medical mores, which pre-dated the onset of shell shock.

MENTAL ILLNESS, CLASS AND MASCULINITY

This overt suspicion of the workman raises the issue of mental illness and class. As a generalization, one can say that working-class soldiers were not treated as well as middle- or upper-class officers. This is hardly surprising. For all the propaganda about class unity and comradeship at the front, early twentieth-century Britain was a firmly hierarchical society and the exaggerated attention paid to social elites can seem bizarre to a modern reader. *The Times* ran a regular 'Condition of invalids' column, in many ways a forerunner of our celebrity and 'gossip' pages. At the beginning of March 1915 readers were told that, 'The Duchess of Rutland is confined to her room with a sharp attack of influenza . . . Lord Spencer is now able to go out.'[55] On the following day we learn that, 'The

Archdeacon of Westminster had a better night, and is progressing slowly.'[56] Of course, *The Times* was aimed at a middle- and upper-middle-class readership; nevertheless, these reports seem incongruous during a time of such extensive warfare – the battle of Neuve-Chapelle was just about to begin on the Western Front – but they provide real insight into the extent of class consciousness in First World War Britain. This was a world in which experiences and opportunities were largely dictated by class, as was access to health care. The 1911 National Insurance Act provided all working people with a state health insurance scheme for the first time, yet there was nothing approaching a comprehensive medical service. It is certainly true that military health-care regimes discriminated in favour of those from the social elites. Yet we also need to remember that civilian health-care regimes were equally, if not more, culpable, and that soldiers from the other ranks did sometimes have access to high quality, innovative mental health care: the Red Cross Hospital at Maghull being one example.

We will focus later on the language of shell shock in some detail but at this stage it is pertinent to make some comments about language, shell shock and class. This is an area fraught with complexity and contradiction, yet it is notable that language developed in such a way as to avoid labelling officers in a disreputable manner. In much of the literature of shell shock, there is a key categorical distinction between neurasthenic officers and hysterical men, and the subtext is clear: the man suffering from neurasthenia is more respectable and more refined than the man suffering from the more vulgar, and more physical, hysteria. Yet it is important to remember that neurasthenia had not always been solely associated with the mental complaints of the elite. Collie had originally identified neurasthenia with working-class men, and he argued that they were peculiarly vulnerable to this condition because of their limited intelligence and education.[57] Working-class neurasthenia was closely associated with fecklessness prior to 1914, yet as the war developed more and more young officers were labelled as neurasthenic and during the conflict the term was rarely used to describe men in the ranks. Young officers suffered from nervous collapse in disproportionate numbers yet this could not be blamed on a lack of intelligence or education, nor were young officers very likely to be accused of malingering. As a result, the term neurasthenia was borrowed from the vocabulary of medical compensation boards and attached to young middle- and upper-middle-class officers. The pervasiveness of the class system then ensured that 'neurasthenia' became a respectable term because of its association with a young, well-educated martial elite. When working men had been described as neurasthenic, the term hinted at malingering and duplicity; when officers were described in the same way, the word became shorn of those pejorative associations.

Certainly many doctors made it clear that they believed crucial class differences revealed themselves in cases of extreme mental distress. Sir Robert Armstrong-Jones (RAMC) worked with aphonic cases – with men who had lost their voices – and he noted the rarity of the condition among officers, due, he insisted, to 'the better education of the officers who are more able to reason and to understand, and who are thus less liable to emotional shock'.[58] Mott agreed that officers and men displayed different symptoms when mentally ill, and maintained that, 'Among officers a large proportion are pure shell shock cases, but among the men there are cases of hysterical paralysis and other signs of hysteria.'[59] What is most notable about these comments is that they date from 1917 and 1918, a period in which an increasing number of officers had risen from the ranks, yet medical commentary still referred to the distinctions between officers and men as though the categories were completely watertight.

Clearly class impacted upon diagnoses of shell shock; in addition, responses to shell shock were framed by perceptions of masculinity and war. From the beginning of the conflict, commentators indicated a recognition of the complexities of human psychology alongside a more simplistic understanding of martial values and heroic behaviour. In the first winter of the war, *The Times* medical correspondent produced an investigation into the complex feelings and reactions of men under fire for the first time. It was not a sophisticated article but it did recognize that it was important to understand the processes that made men either heroes or cowards, and it also implicitly recognized that this was a subject that men found difficult to discuss:

> The man who has not been under fire always desires eagerly to know what were the feelings of the man who has been during this ordeal. It is probable that he does not frequently find the information given by veterans either satisfying or enlightening.[60]

In contrast to the considered tone of this article, several weeks later *The Times* produced a letter from a young officer describing the war in high-spirited tones:

> The Germans, and we too of course, pepper the main roads pretty continuously during the day just to make it jolly for anyone coming along . . . I stumbled on hoping to come across somebody who could guide me to my battalion. My luck was in, for almost the first man I met was on the way to their headquarters was a delightful Irishman who was as merry as a sandboy, and who regaled me with long-winded yarns of their doings in the trenches, until we got near up and it was unwise to laugh too loud. It was a piece of luck because when I started out on this mission I was quite sure I was going to be in a devil of a funk, and when it was all over I was mighty surprised with myself to find I had been too much interested and

amused by the Irishman really to take in that there were bullets buzzing about . . . Of course there was a lot of noise of rattling rifle fire, but not nearly as much as at a public school field day.[61]

The soldier then finishes his day by having 'some most ripping sloe gin' with the other fellows in the trenches.[62] The letter displays schoolboy enthusiasm alongside English stereotypes of class, ethnicity and gender. Of greatest significance is the reference to the school playing field; an image that would have resonated with those brought up 'to play the game'. The boyish humour of the young officer was to become a site of attack for those who later criticized or mocked the English officer class. In this letter we see the seeds of the military caricatures in *Oh What a Lovely War!*, countless *Monty Python* colonels and Major Gowen, the bumbling ex-officer who lived in *Fawlty Towers*, oblivious to everything apart from the cricket scores and the opening of the bar. Closer to our own time, we have of course Lieutenant George, the upper-class twit whose gusto for the war stands in such contrast to the deadpan cynicism of Captain Edmund Blackadder, the middle-class professional soldier.

However, although these juvenile and somewhat flippant representations of the war did exist at the time, it is important to modify the prevailing view that the male, educated elite simply portrayed war as a game. In early 1915, the Vice Chancellor of Oxford University described the serious spirit in which undergraduates were volunteering, and commented that, 'There is hardly a sign of the light-hearted acceptance of war as a kind of sport.'[63] And although *The Times* can be accused of portraying war as a kind of schoolboy sport, it also wanted to note that it recognized the real gravity of the conflict. An article in 1915 made this position clear by commenting that 'when we speak of war being the "greatest game" it is with the silent implication that it really is something far more serious, which calls game players to prove themselves'.[64] The narrative of war as a great game did dominate many accounts of the war, both during the conflict and afterwards. Early in the war, Captain Bruce West, a temporary medical officer, kept a diary divided into two columns, one marked 'war' and one marked 'golf' – the day's martial and sporting records were recorded and maintained side by side.[65] Yet there is, in fact, no necessary contradiction between the representation of war as a game and the construction of honourable, serious masculinity. Philip Gibbs, the respected war journalist, described a French officer's reactions to a British soldier who went over the top with a football. '"He is not mad," said a French officer who had lived in England. "It is a *beau geste*. He is a sportsman, scornful of death. That is the British sport."'[66] By kicking a ball into No Man's Land, the British soldier was letting his enemy know that he was not afraid to die; this was the sign of a true warrior because the presence of the football was a symbol of the soldier's disdain for death. Consequently, the construct of war as a game is not as trivial as it might initially appear. In addition, although this representation stemmed from public school traditions, the idea of war as an exclusively masculine sport was particularly useful in a mass war because of the way in which it enabled commentators to present an image of frontline solidarity and mask the potential for class conflict in the trenches.

In *Mr. Britling Sees it Through*, the young Hugh Britling joined the war as a keen, middle-class private – the public schoolboy spirit was not the exclusive preserve of the officer class. During the war he developed a fierce hatred for a young cockney private, an ex-grocer's assistant who was uneducated and crude 'a little cad with a snub nose . . . he is conscientiously foul-mouthed'.[67] Yet life in the trenches forged a sense of solidarity. Hugh Britling came to appreciate the virtues of working-class men and was genuinely distraught by the private's death:

> For a time I kept trying to get him to drink . . . I couldn't believe he was dead . . .
>
> And suddenly it was all different. I began to cry. Like a baby. I kept on with the water-bottle long after I was convinced he was dead. I didn't want him to be *aut* of it! God knows how I didn't. I wanted my dear little cockney cad back. Oh! Most frightfully I wanted him back. I shook him. I was like a scared child. I blubbered and howled things . . . It's all different since he died.[68]

Cross-class relationships, primarily the relationship between a young officer and his men, feature strongly in the post-war literature too. This is particularly noticeable in *Sherston's Progress,* where Sherston, Siegfried Sassoon's fictional version of himself, is genuinely motivated by a concern and a compassion for his men.[69] It is even more evident in the Lord Peter Wimsey stories. Wimsey was rescued from his post-war shell shock by Bunter, his ex-sergeant; Bunter then became Wimsey's valet. The relationship remains hierarchical but is deeply symbiotic: Wimsey and Bunter are eternally united, almost wedded, by their shared war experiences. Bunter never marries, and when Wimsey eventually does find a bride, he chooses someone who will never threaten the Wimsey–Bunter union.[70]

These fictional or semi-fictional texts demonstrate the importance of a shared masculinity in the trenches. Similar values are evident in press commentary. Writing on the psychology of men in combat for the first time, *The Times* medical correspondent observed that, 'Under fire these men found a self hitherto unsuspected, that elusive quality which for want of a better title is called manhood'.[71] The idea that trench warfare produced a sense of universal harmonious manhood is clearly erroneous. These images were far from the lived reality of the trenches because many battalions recruited from specific social milieux – the London Rifle Brigades, for example, even maintained the 21-shilling joining fee until 1916.[72] Even where social classes did meet in the trenches, a modern-day commentator can easily object that this frontline solidarity was based on social paternalism rather than true fraternity. Yet a shared belief in the nature of appropriately masculine behaviour did provide a level of consensus among all troops, and shell-shock treatments were consistently based on the understanding that British soldiers, whether officers or men from the other ranks, should always act like men.

Psychological explanations for shell shock did develop throughout the war, but large sectors of the RAMC and many of the military elites remained largely hostile to such changes. In the main, the much more traditional military view prevailed: the idea expressed in *The Times* that coming under fire turns boys into men. An atmosphere of exclusive masculinity was also essential for those who had been wounded. In 'The Spoilt Soldier', an article discussing the care of the convalescent soldier, the author insisted that 'husbands were infinitely nicer before they had been converted into heroes and spoiled by the ministrations of "kind and beautiful ladies" in French and English military hospitals'.[73] This attitude was prevalent in medical texts too. Mott also disliked the interventions of 'well-meaning ladies' and insisted that they did more harm than good:

> Discipline is very essential; laxity of discipline, over-sympathy and attention by kind, well-meaning ladies giving social tea-parties, drives, joy-rides, with the frequent exclamation of 'poor dears', has done much to perpetuate functional neuroses in our soldiers.[74]

The wholly masculine environment was particularly characteristic of the shell-shock hospital, but the implication, which can be drawn from all of these commentators, is that the viable masculinity required to win the war needed a solely male atmosphere in which to flourish.

There has been a strong trend towards positing a gendered analysis of shell shock as a medical complaint. Elaine Showalter has argued that shell shock threatened the entire construction of madness as a female malady, and that shell shock can be seen as the body language of masculine complaint due to 'the heightened code of masculinity that dominated in wartime', which was 'intolerable to surprisingly large numbers of men'.[75] Responses to shell shock have also been subject to a gendered analysis because mental breakdown may well have undermined both male authority and traditional sex roles.[76] There were clearly cultural difficulties inherent in the very nature of a soldier suffering from a nervous breakdown because military values were linked with the masculine traits of bravery and self-control under adverse circumstances, and it was self-control that appeared to be so conspicuously lacking in cases of shell shock. Nevertheless, the situation was more complex than many gendered analyses allow. In the first place, from very early on in the war the authorities attempted to make a definite distinction between shell-shocked soldiers and lunatics. Neurosis and insanity are quite different conditions, but they can easily become confused in popular parlance. Military and political elites were aware that shell-shocked soldiers could be dismissed as 'mad', and aimed to combat any such confusion: Lord Newton, speaking for the War Office, insisted that the government had 'no intention of treating these unfortunate men as ordinary lunatics'.[77] In short, the afflicted men were not lunatics, they were soldiers, and this distinction was clearly designed to preserve the dignity of male combatants and to ensure that shell shock did not undermine male authority.

It is also important to state that fear of inadequacy was not necessarily gendered but may well have reflected wider concerns about the impact of modernity upon the health of the nation. The opposition to conscription was largely founded upon the fear that many men were in some way inadequate, especially those from the industrial towns.[78] These fears did seem to be borne out by contemporary research. The Ministry of National Service assessing the physical examinations of 2,425,184 men, calculated that 250,280 of them should be categorized as 'Grade IV'.[79] Grade IV men were described as being 'permanently unfit for military service' and ministers clearly blamed the unwholesome qualities of industrial life for these sobering statistics:

> The presence of such dwarfed and ill-developed creatures can be attributed only to the conditions of life created by our industrial development, and be reckoned without fear of contradiction as eminently calculated to cause racial deterioration and to give every opportunity to the ravages of disease.[80]

Much attention has already been focused on the way in which eugenicists expressed concern about the fitness of urban males, but there were worries about the quality of recruits from rural areas too, and Dr Fearnside of the Royal Society of Medicine commented that 'the village idiot and his kind have been drafted not infrequently'.[81] This general alarm at the apparent mental and physical weakness of some soldiers reflected eugenicist fears about racial degeneration, and contributed towards a medical climate which emphasized the importance of predisposition in cases of mental collapse. An emphasis upon predisposition did not necessarily lead to dismissive or unsympathetic treatment, but sometimes this was unfortunately the case. In 1916, Dr Cicely May Peake's research into the mental health history of a selection of shell-shocked men led Mott to conclude a large number of 'so-called shell shock' cases occurred in individuals with a nervous temperament or in those with an acquired or inherited neuropathy. Clearly Mott considered that these men were not suffering from 'real' shell shock – the Captain Hardcastle variety – they were merely displaying the symptoms of a degenerate constitution.[82]

This focus on the importance of predisposition was reinforced after the introduction of conscription in 1916, when it became easier to argue that shell-shocked men were cowards, otherwise they would have enlisted earlier. This argument was then strengthened when it became clear that a number of men began to suffer from the symptoms of war neurosis even before they left Britain. Research indicated a high level of neurasthenia or mental instability among newly recruited Home Forces, a factor that tended to reinforce conventional suspicions about the mentally ill. Burton-Fanning, a temporary RAMC officer conducting research in a Cambridge hospital, argued that the majority of neurasthenics in civil life remained in paid work: they had not become ill because they had joined the army; rather, they had only been diagnosed as ill because they had joined the army. He also, somewhat contrarily, asserted that in the majority of cases, his patients' mental conditions were linked to the unconcealed resentment they displayed on being called up.[83] Henderson, another temporary RAMC officer researching the same question, came to similar conclusions about the high rate of mental disorder in Home Troops, and he argued that recruitment policies had to be more selective so as to exclude mentally vulnerable men.[84] Clearly men in the Home Forces could not have suffered mental collapse as a result of combat conditions, and so this research reinforced the idea that predisposition was the single most important factor when assessing mental breakdown in soldiers.

POPULAR REACTIONS AND PUBLIC SYMPATHY

Mentally wounded soldiers were obviously affected by the way in which doctors understood the condition of shell shock, but they also needed support from society at large. Early in the war, when Knutsford launched his campaign to raise money for special war-neurosis hospitals, he wanted to generate sympathy and understanding for shell-shock victims at the same time. He was partially successful in that press reports about shell-shock casualties were generally compassionate in tone during the early war years. Nevertheless, shell-shocked men returned to a society that was uncertain in its response to this type of mental illness. There are contradictory accounts of the British public's initial response to shell shock. The Knutsford campaign indicated that there was a clear measure of support for men with war neurosis, but at the same time many sufferers felt that they were socially stigmatized by their illness. Esplin, a returning soldier, described the shame of arriving at the military hospital at Netley as one of a party of the mentally wounded. 'We were not the battle-stained heroes who had been expected. There was a silence which could be felt. "Let's get off home," a buxom loud-voiced dame counselled, "There's only some of the barmy ones here."'[85]

In this case it is clear that both the sufferer and the audience associated shell shock with madness and with a failure of masculinity, although it must be stressed that such explicit comments are rare. It is obviously difficult to make a generalization about something as complex as a social stigma. Post-war research indicated that many men disliked being labelled as shell shocked whereas others appreciated it because 'it savoured of the noise and din of battle, screeching shells and great explosions'.[86] However, it is possible to assert that widespread support for nerve-shocked men in the abstract did not necessarily translate into a genuine sense of understanding and sympathy in response to individual casualties. Also, attitudes towards 'ordinary lunatics' had not become more enlightened as a result of shell shock. The process merely resulted in the redrawing of categories in an attempt to ensure that military men and lunatics occupied very different spheres.

Shell shock was also a particularly suitable subject for stories about the horror of war, and, given its apparent novelty, the terrors of this war in particular. From early on, the trauma of war was expressed through the description of personal breakdown. A story entitled 'The ghastliness of war' was published in the *Labour Leader* in May 1915, and it contains hints of what would soon come to be widely described as shell shock. As the subject became more politicized, the paper came to focus more on the plight of young working-class men in the trenches. However, the first real 'shell-shock story' was about a gentleman from a good public school and a good family who broke down and had to be discharged after four months in the trenches:

> [he] began laughing, a queer laugh. He went on laughing and I knew it was because the horrors he had been through were so incongruous with his experience of life till then that it seemed a joke . . . the more imaginative you are, the better educated you are, the worse it is for you. The temperament you have got is what matters for you to be a good soldier. If you're imaginative you might as well not go.[87]

There has been little research into the way that the socialist press reported war neurosis. Yet these representations are significant because, despite its radicalism, the *Labour Leader* was displaying the image of shell shock, which later became representative of the somewhat elitist disillusionment school. This particular story provides what came to be a very typical picture of a shell-shock case: the officer was upper middle class or aristocratic, well-educated, highly imaginative or with an artistic temperament. On the whole, the *Labour Leader* made little comment about war neurosis itself, and commented more fully on the wider social and economic consequences of the condition. For example, the paper highlighted the penury faced by a woman whose husband was housed in a local asylum.[88] It also made veiled reference to the class conflict that was to develop in many later accounts of shell shock. The *Labour Leader* noted that Private Albert Osbaldeston, of the 6th Cheshire Territorials, wrote home to say that he was in

Boulogne 'guarding British soldiers who have gone mad from the noise of the guns on the battlefields'.[89] Yet the point about apparently insane soldiers and the attendant issues of discipline and class betrayal were not developed at all, and the paper then moved on to comment about the need to provide a living for disabled soldiers. As far as the *Labour Leader* was concerned, shell shock was not an initial focus for much political opposition, even from those opposed to the war, and when it was an issue, the paper used the image of a young officer that had aroused so much sympathy from readers of *The Times*. The early public responses to shell shock provide little indication as to its later status as a metaphor for war itself. However, the background of civilian attitudes towards mental health, and problems of definition and organization, indicate that shell shock was potentially a very awkward condition.

Shell shock has to be understood in the wider context of the war and of societal attitudes towards mental health, class and gendered behaviour. The condition quickly became problematic because attitudes towards nervous breakdown were already coloured by an atmosphere of stigma and by a popular culture that had promoted the miracle cure. Official systems, both military and civilian, had developed in such a way as to link nervous debility with malingering and with unmasculine behaviour. At the same time, doctors, officials and some elements of the general public clearly did appreciate the complex realities of nervous breakdown. These competing narratives of mental collapse endured throughout the war and, as a result, the memory of wartime trauma is dominated by a conflict between several highly differing approaches. Shell shock developed its post-war status not just because it represented a crisis in masculinity, although that may have been one element of the condition; shell shock was important because it also reflected and reinforced pre-existing class- and gender-based attitudes towards madness, as well as current fears about a weak or degenerate population. Also, the civilian population displayed highly contradictory attitudes towards shell shock throughout the war, demonstrating both deep sympathy and a real lack of understanding when faced with war neuroses. These initial responses to shell shock were crucial in laying the foundations for later memories of the war, and for enabling the subject of shell shock to become a suitable vehicle for criticism of the war long before it had ended.

LANGUAGE AND SHELL SHOCK: 'BEWARE OF LANGUAGE, FOR IT IS OFTEN A GREAT CHEAT'[90]

Medical conditions require a clear classification because otherwise communication within the medical profession and between physicians, patients and their families is impossible. Yet language is often far from transparent, and the language of shell shock indicates the way in which words can not only cheat but can also create confusion. Sir Charles Myers, a Cambridge academic who became consultant psychologist to the British Expeditionary Force in 1915, was the first to employ the term 'shell shock' in an official capacity, although the term was already in popular usage.[91] He outlined three case studies in which men displayed peculiar symptoms as a result of shell blasts. One corporal described being dug out of his trench after a shell had buried him, 'It was dark when they dug me out. After I got out a chap said "The fellow's mad" and I said "You're a liar".' Reports then confirmed that the corporal's doctors also thought that the man was "off his head".'[92]

Myers was clearly perplexed about these symptoms, as his concluding comments acknowledge:

> The shells in question appear to have burst with considerable noise, scattering much dust, but this was not attended by the production of odour. It is therefore difficult to understand why hearing should be (practically) unaffected and the dissociated 'complex' be confined to the sense of sight, smell and taste (and to memory). The close relation of these cases to those of 'hysteria' appears fairly certain.[93]

Myers went on to develop a sophisticated understanding of shell shock as a psychological condition, but the idea that shell blasts made men mad clearly endured. This conviction persisted for a number of reasons. First, it accorded with the long-standing belief that the 'wind of the bullet' or the 'wind of a shell' could cause nervous injuries.[94] Secondly, if shell shock was a purely physical as opposed to a psychological complaint, then it made the condition less problematic for the individual soldier. A straightforward physical wound, even if undetectable to the naked eye, was clearly more honourable than a mental collapse. Myers came to regret coining the term shell shock, but by then it was too late. Medical officers later complained that the condition became a 'parrot cry' at courts martial, yet, despite official censure, the phrase remained both popular and effective.[95]

Difficulties of terminology arose in 1915 and, arguably, were never resolved. The term shell shock was employed widely but without precision. In a discussion at the Royal Society of Medicine in 1916, Dr Henry Head complained that shell shock was being used for 'a collection of different nervous affections from concussion to sheer funk'.[96] The term shell shock was obviously a difficult one, and it is one indication of the unprecedented difficulties facing the medical profession during the war. Doctors wanted to control the language of war neurosis as part of the process of demonstrating that they could control and manage the condition itself. Yet Mott indicated that he did not have the language he needed to define or describe this war. Quoting Meynell's popular novel *Aunt Sarah and the War*, he struggled to find the right words: '. . . some men blind, some men dumb, and other men crazy, and these all of them MEN, with a newly-earned meaning in the word; for there's a new meaning now in many an old word. We shall want a brand new Dictionary . . .'[97]

Roy Porter has indicated the way in which the medical profession has been wont to indulge in jargon and to blind outsiders with science so as to maintain its own mystique and power. The process by which the language of disease moved from the vernacular to the professional ensured that by the turn of the nineteenth century medical jargon had become quite separate from the lay idiom.[98] By avoiding colloquial speech, doctors inflated their authority and created a protective smokescreen for themselves.[99] In short, medics have used language to bolster their own power at the expense of the lay community. Shell shock is a decided exception to this pattern. One of the medical elite ensured that the term became part of the medical vocabulary of the Great War, but Myers, and the majority of the medical profession, quickly acknowledged that the term was a singularly unhelpful misnomer. Consequently, the authorities tried to discourage the use of the term shell shock from 1916 until 1922. Yet they were quite unsuccessful, and the history of this expression raises questions about the extent to which elites have the power to construct language and to dictate meaning. Expressions like 'collateral damage' and 'friendly fire' indicate that ordinary people can be led to use certain terminologies, yet in the case of shell shock, people were not persuaded to change their language.[100] One can even argue that the persistence of the term shell shock, especially in the officer class, indicates that the diagnosis was a sign of patient-power.[101] The term has certainly endured, despite the wishes of the authorities at the time, and in many ways it grew more powerful by the end of the 1920s. The words may have been medically imprecise but they clearly did not lack meaning.

As has been said, those in the political and medical establishment tried to avoid the term shell shock. The *Journal of the RAMC* used the expression sparingly and with caution, *The Times* preferred to refer to 'shock' or 'nerves', David Eder of the Medico-Psychological Association referred to 'war shock' rather than shell shock, and the army tried to substitute shell shock with the category of Not Yet Diagnosed Nervous (NYDN). At the end of 1915 the Army Council issued a directive stating that 'shell-shock and shell-concussion cases' should have their casualty reports marked with the letter 'W' if their condition was due to enemy action. Those labelled NYDN (W) would then be categorized as wounded and entitled to a wound stripe and pension, whereas those diagnosed as NYDN (S) would be considered as sick and would not be so privileged.[102] That the Army Medical Service then outlawed the use of the term shell shock in 1917, two years after it had been officially replaced, indicates that all attempts at a new diagnostic procedure had been a failure.[103] This changing nosology was clearly designed to ensure that all diagnostic power lay with the military and medical authorities for fear that too many soldiers would otherwise diagnose themselves with shell shock.

However, neither 'war shock' nor NYDN entered everyday language, nor were they used consistently by medical professionals. It is certainly the case that most commentators were united in the opinion that shell shock was an inappropriate term, yet no one was able to provide a suitable alternative. As early as April 1916, Elliot Smith opened an article by referring to the inadequacy and inappropriateness of the expression 'shell shock'. It soon became commonplace for the medical professionals to refer to shell shock at the same time as apologizing for doing so.[104] In June 1916, Harold Wiltshire began his paper on the aetiology of shell shock by insisting that, 'The term shell shock is used unwillingly in this paper,' and complained that 'bad terminology' had confused the understanding of the condition.[105] This linguistic uncertainty persisted. Even the post-war Committee of Enquiry into Shell Shock, whose very title explicitly recognized the validity of the term, opened its report by insisting that 'shell shock is a grievous misnomer'.[106] Unlike trench foot and gas gangrene, shell shock was not just an apparently novel wartime condition, it was also one which seemed impossible to either describe or define.

According to Salman Rushdie, 'A culture is defined by its untranslatable words.'[107] Shell shock has no direct translation, although one can assume that fear is universal and it is certainly the case that soldiers of all nations demonstrated similar neurotic symptoms. As Winter has noted, the difference between the alliterative Anglo-Saxon shell shock and the French *hystérie de guerre* or the German *kriegneurosen* lies not in the condition but in the label and the meaning attributed to it.[108] Shell shock is not only particular to Britain, but to the British experience of the First World War; the term was not used in later wars, and its meaning is now historically and culturally specific.

All combatant countries experienced similar problems when trying to describe psychological casualties. The French generally referred to *hystérie de guerre*, but also used *commotion par obus,* a term implying a far more organic or physical wound.[109] The Australian experience was similar. They too adopted the label of shell shock but found it unsatisfactory as this report from the Australian Army Medical Services confirms, '[Shell shock] was loosely applied to all cases of physical and mental breakdown within the battle zone without apparent wound. It had become indeed a diagnostic shibboleth and an open sesame to the base.'[110] This comment plainly reflects British concern that shell shock had become a parrot cry at courts martial. Clear definitions of shell shock were required for medical reasons, but it was also important because a soldier's diagnosis determined his treatment, future pension rights, and possibly his promotion opportunities. This was later articulated by Colonel Butler of the Australian Army Medical Services, who wrote that, 'The sustaining by a soldier of a "battle-casualty" carried the right to a "wound stripe", and commonly a trip to "Blighty", and precise definitions therefore became necessary.'[111]

As has already been noted, the initial diagnosis of shell shock as the result of lesions in the brain became quickly discredited. Shell shock is now widely used as a term to describe the condition of men who had suffered from some kind of madness or nervous breakdown as a result of combat, or more particularly by the emotions of combat. Shell shock is not madness, but shell-shocked men were often described as such, and a small number of men were eventually confined to local lunatic asylums – the traditional home of 'the mad'. However, neither madness nor nervous breakdown are unproblematic terms in themselves, and the extent to which mental illness is partially or wholly an organic condition was, and still is, a highly debateable issue. As a result of this linguistic ambiguity, the medical-military profession was unable to assign one clear discrete meaning to the term shell shock, and this confusion was reflected in diagnostic and treatment regimes, as well as in later post-war recollections of shell-shock treatment.

SHELL-SHOCK TREATMENT AND WAR WEARINESS

Shell-shock treatment has to be seen in the wider context of medical treatment for all military personnel. When Britain entered the war, services for disabled soldiers and sailors were uneven and poorly organized. The Royal Hospital at Chelsea traditionally cared for a selection of army veterans, the War Office provided some services for army officers, and the Admiralty did much the same for naval personnel. A locally based patchwork of services existed to provide varying levels of care and advice for soldiers' and sailors' families. Quite simply, government ministries were unprepared for a long war involving several million enlisted and active servicemen. During the summer of 1915, the Ministry of Pensions instituted a more systematic system with the aim of providing disabled men with financial security, health care and re-education or training, if required.[112] There was even an official recognition that the state would provide long-term care for those whose disabilities were the secondary result of war service.[113]

This state-led care did not negate the need for the voluntary sector, but it did ensure that the state began to accept statutory responsibilities for disabled veterans. Servicemen realized this, and the citizen soldier of the First World War did not accept that the state had a right to use him as canon fodder and then abandon him. Yet an acceptance of obligation is easier than establishing a practical network of care, and when it came to creating treatment regimes for shell-shocked men, the British government and the military establishment were obviously handicapped by a real lack of hands-on experience. The first psychological casualties were sent to ordinary military hospitals, but it soon became clear that they required more specialized treatment and an official care system for nerve-shocked men was rapidly established in the United Kingdom.

Initially such men were treated in general wards and at D Block of the Royal
Victoria Hospital in Netley, the traditional institution for the treatment of army
mental patients. However, the large number of cases was accompanied by a
growing recognition of the need for categorization and for special institutions.
A programme of separation and categorization was implemented, and those
with functional paralysis and neurasthenia were separated from those with
severe mental disorders. In December 1914 the Red Cross Military Hospital at
Maghull was handed over to the War Office. It was to be used for 'borderline'
cases requiring more supervision than could be given in a hospital, and also for
those who had been transferred from Netley because it enabled them to avoid
the public asylum system.

As demand grew, further state-run institutions were developed. Those who
required only a short probationary course were sent to the 4th London Territorial
General Hospital, whereas Springfield War Hospital was created to deal with
severe and protracted neurasthenics, and borderline cases. Napsbury War
Hospital was to serve those suffering from acute mental disorder and Dykebar
also contained certifiable patients with severe forms of disorder – although, in
accordance with official policy, none of the patients were certified as persons
of unsound mind.[114] In May 1915, neurological sections were established in
all territorial general hospitals throughout England, Scotland and Wales. The
aim was to ensure that these hospitals would be 'officered where possible by
physicians specially versed in nervous diseases' although medical staff were free
to transfer serious cases elsewhere.[115] At all times, officers and men were treated
separately.

In April 1915 the Bill for the Mentally Sick made special provision for soldiers
who had suffered a nervous breakdown as a result of shock or exposure. At a
time of real crisis in the treatment of the mentally ill, the Bill was welcomed
as a highly reforming piece of legislation, the key point of which was to free
men from the stigma of certification. The bill was worded so as to create loose
and flexible categories: men would be treated, free of charge, if their nervous
breakdown had been caused by 'wounds, shock, disease, stress exhaustion, or
any other cause'.[116] This gave doctors the power to treat a wide variety of war-
shocked men. Moreover, during treatment, men were to reside in nursing homes
or other institutions not associated with the administrative care of lunacy. Men
certainly benefited from the way in which their treatment had been officially
separated from the asylum system. Local asylums contained a large number of
pauper lunatics, and the notion of inherited deficiency was widespread, casting
shame upon the victim's family as well as upon the individual sufferer. Images
of the incarcerated pauper lunatic clashed unsettlingly with that of the British
combatant who was engaged in the fight to save civilization. In this context,
shell shock served a useful function because it created a respectable, masculine

category for nervous breakdown. Medical and military elites may have abhorred the term but it nevertheless was one way in which the prestige of the combatant was preserved at a time when many individual combatants were falling victim to what might otherwise have been a highly stigmatized condition.

A similarly enlightened point of view characterized debates on the War Pensions Bill in 1915. Neurological cases were to be divided into four classes in an attempt to make treatment regimes more case-specific, and during this debate Knutsford acknowledged that War Office arrangements for dealing with 'nervous or organic shock were particularly good'.[117] He admitted that sometimes men were housed in buildings that had formerly been used as lunatic asylums, but insisted that the army medical services could be trusted to show kindness to soldiers who were mentally afflicted. So by mid-1915 it seemed as though the government was tackling the problems of psychological casualties with strength and a strong sense of compassion. However, from the beginning of the conflict and throughout the war, this compassion was matched by a more disciplinary and punitive approach, particularly from the higher echelons of the military. A General Order issued in July 1916 stated that any patient who was affected by nervous exhaustion 'arising from insufficient self-control' should be kept in France for treatment.[118] The development of treatment centres close to the Front was a positive move in itself, but the wording of this order has clear pejorative overtones. Advanced Neurological Centres near the Front did begin to deal with shell-shock casualties. These centres were a combination of hospital and disciplinary training camp, where treatment was supplemented by army drill and route marches. Non-commissioned officers remained in charge of the ranks, and patients had to report sick if they wanted to see a medical officer. The German High Command and German Army doctors shared a similar approach. They tended to look upon war neurosis as a weakness which could be cured by the 'hardening' effects of military life. In addition, war-neurosis stations were designed to be exclusively male environments, far from the 'softening and disturbing influences of the *Heimat* [homeland]'.[119] Among all combatant nations, medical treatment was tempered by military discipline.

In Britain, the state treatment system had been complemented by private charity from the very beginning. When Knutsford launched his first appeal in November 1914, he called for the public to help soldiers suffering from nervous collapse. The term shell shock was not in widespread use at the time and public understanding was obviously limited. Consequently, Knutsford felt responsible for explaining the situation of these particular casualties. He described them as 'gallant soldiers . . . suffering from very severe mental and nervous shock, due to exposure, excessive strain and tension'.[120] Knutsford was careful to stress the honourable masculinity of those afflicted and to insist that their inadequate treatment was due to a problem of resource management rather than medical inability in the face of an apparently novel condition. Aware of the importance of maintaining morale, he insisted that, 'These men can be cured if only they can receive proper attention.'[121] Furthermore, a number of doctors had already offered their services for free, and so Knutsford's message was that only premises were wanting before the problem could be solved.

The campaign was a success: by January 1915 the appeal had raised £7,700. As a result Knutsford opened his first Special Hospital, at Palace Green, Kensington. £7,700 was a significant sum: Knutsford had calculated that for £10,000 he could fully equip and run the hospital for two years.[122] Palace Green was referred to as a 'Special Hospital', a term which was not associated with the asylum, yet the public must have been aware of its nature because it had been openly described as a hospital for men who were in a state of nervous shock. Nevertheless, people demonstrated sympathy for the project, and it was also given royal support. Queen Alexandra visited the hospital in January 1915, and there was another royal visit a month later.[123]

Knutsford's work continued to attract support and in May 1915 Robert Leicester Harmsworth MP (Liberal, Caithness and Sutherland) donated another large house, Moray Lodge in Campden Hill.[124] Eventually Knutsford raised enough money to institute four voluntary hospitals. The first provided almost monastic seclusion for three to four weeks. The second, opened in April 1915, acted as a convalescent home for those who had passed through the first hospital; patients usually stayed there for about six weeks. Hospital number three was designed for men who had developed shell shock as a result of being wounded, and hospital number four was created for definite cases of mental disorder.[125] Knutsford had not initially specified that his homes were only for officers, but by 1915 the War Office had become alarmed at the number of officers who had fallen victim to nervous complaints. This was the point at which the authorities had to recognize that mental health problems could not be dismissed as a condition exclusive to the lower orders. In response, they insisted that Palace Green hospital be restricted to officers.[126]

As a result of the Knutsford campaign, shell shock had developed a relatively high public profile by 1915. Obviously campaign literature is designed to be appealing and optimistic rather than purely informative, but given the limited amount of information available in the British media at the time, Knutsford's appeal may well have provided many people with their first understanding of war neurosis. Consequently, non-medical members of the public were able to access information about shell shock for the first time. In an attempt to explain this new phenomenon to its readers, *The Times* presented an article on 'The Wounded Mind and Its Cure', which stressed that 'wounds of consciousness' should receive the same serious attention as wounds of flesh or bone.[127] Although many men clearly did feel ashamed of their nervous collapse, the early publicity surrounding shell shock was largely sympathetic, and it generally attempted to emphasize that nerve-damaged soldiers were wounded, rather than weak, incapable or mad. By 1916 public understanding had clearly changed, and people were far more familiar with concepts such as shell shock or nervous damage. *The Times* no longer felt the need to provide comment or explanation when discussing psychological casualties, and articles were presented with the strong implication that readers were familiar with the condition.[128]

The extent to which Knutsford's campaign increased the general acceptance of war neurosis as a legitimate medical complaint is debateable. What is less debateable is the extent to which these homes for officers reinforced existing class boundaries. Psychologically wounded officers were housed in single rooms in secluded residences because medical opinion was strongly influenced by the rest cure, which had long been the conventional treatment for nervous debility among the wealthy. Elite casualties required special treatment, and descriptions of Palace Green indicate that young officers were treated in a very pleasant environment:

> It would not be easy to find a more sequestered and restful spot in the midst of a great city. Within sight are lofty trees, green spaces and the time mellowed brick of Kensington Palace – as much tranquil old world charm, perhaps as survives anywhere in London.[129]

This was in stark contrast to the treatment meted out to the men in the other ranks. Just as the hospital at Palace Green was becoming established, Lord Beauchamp, President of the National Hospital for the Paralyzed and Epileptic, Queen Square, announced that the War Office was arranging to send him soldiers suffering from shock, who were to be treated in hospital wards specially set apart for the purpose.[130] The Red Cross Hospital at Maghull may have been staffed by excellent and committed physicians, but the food was scarce, wards were dirty and the temporary huts that accommodated many men were 'a disgrace'.[131] So, a single room was vital for recovering officers – but not for their men. Nervous casualties from the other ranks could be dispatched to filthy asylum-like conditions, but gentlemen-soldiers went to something more like a country house.

While the Knutsford hospitals were enjoying some success and recognition in 1915 and 1916, the official network of care for shell-shocked men was quickly becoming inadequate. Systems that had initially seemed so enlightened and far-reaching faced collapse in barely more than a year. For the first time, respectable commentators began to criticize systems of care, not just for inefficiency or inadequacy, but also for being inhumane. In a furious letter to *The Times*, Sir Frederick Milner, a former Conservative MP who later devoted much energy to the post-war care of shell-shocked soldiers, complained about the 'cruel treatment of some of our gallant men'.[132] It is hard to assess accurately the degree of war weariness by this time, but it is certainly the case that desertion rates peaked in 1915 and were far higher that year than they were to be in any other year of the war.[133] In the following year, conscription was introduced; the Battle of the Somme resulted in an unprecedented number of both physical and mental casualties, and military disaster loomed. At this point, restrictions on the home front also began to appear particularly onerous. The war, which many hoped would be over by Christmas 1914, was far from over, and 1916 was the point at which it began to seem 'endless'.[134] According to Private Leonard Hewitt, a young volunteer from Leicester, after the initial burst of enthusiasm, soldiers started to feel that 'there wasn't any idea of any war ending whatsoever'.[135] This decline in public and military morale must be seen alongside the development of pre-war idealism. The notion of the pre-war golden Edwardian summer, such a staple of post-war mythology, was already visible by early 1916. A article in *The Times* describing pre-war journalism, commented that before the war, 'Town and season rioted joyously ... The morning paper of those days was for the most part a very joyous companion of coffee and rolls.'[136]

This was clearly not the case. Pre-war Britain was characterized by a high level of social and political strife: the Irish Question was on the verge of turning into civil war; there was serious labour unrest; suffragettes were continually – and sometimes violently – agitating for the vote. The point, however, is that the collapse of the initial system of care for shell-shocked men coincided with a serious decline in morale and a deep nostalgia for an imagined pre-war world. As a result, the treatment of shell shock, although medically innovative in places, continued to be associated with military, medical and political failure. In particular, the inability to maintain a coherent system of care led to intense grievances among many shell-shock victims and their families. In this context, sending shell-shocked officers to splendid houses redolent of 'old world charm' was more than simply a statement of class privilege: by returning the men to a peaceful, pastoral, comfortable world, the War Office was, in essence, temporarily returning shell-shocked officers to an idealized pre-war England, and so was unwittingly helping to construct the later myth of the pre-war idyll, which had been destroyed by the outbreak of war.

DIAGNOSTIC DIFFICULTIES AND MEDICAL PROGRESS

Psychiatry's performance during the war could not be relied upon as a source of comfort. Shell shock exposed an area of mental medicine about which many asylum doctors knew little.[137]

It is certainly the case that even doctors with asylum experience were bewildered when first faced with shell-shocked men, and doctors without such experience were at an even greater loss. Obviously doctors developed more techniques as they grew accustomed to psychological casualties, and as a result historians have tended to focus on the changes in medical attitudes that took place throughout the war. Shell shock did have a profound effect on psychological medicine and the condition may well have provoked changes in popular perceptions of mental illness.[138] Yet this is no simple progress narrative, and psychoanalysts in particular were frustrated by their wartime experiences. There was a greater understanding of Freudian ideas after the war but these did not necessarily benefit the mentally ill. On the contrary, many people still associated mental breakdown with sexual deviance and moral degradation.[139] Some medical attitudes did shift during the war but there was definitely no linear progression in terms of the medical or psychological understanding of either shell shock in particular or mental illness more generally.

This uneven development is best indicated by looking at the way in which doctors were able to conduct research into mental trauma during the war. Shell shock did provide new opportunities for research in this field, which is why the war can be associated with progress in psychological medicine. By 1916 it became clear that war neurosis was a real problem and that it would produce a serious manpower shortage if not dealt with effectively. Consequently, the condition was being taken more seriously, even by those who were not directly involved in the war, and the American Medical Service sent doctors to Britain and France to conduct research into war neurosis. Yet in many ways, research into mental health problems was impeded by the war. The international medical community had been seriously disrupted since August 1914, and the British medical community was in a similar state of upheaval. The Medico-Psychological Association had difficulty in finding speakers or even contributors to its journal during the war, and as early as October 1915, the *Journal of Mental Science* indicated some concern about the number of staff who had left local asylums to serve at the front.[140] Mental health issues may have become more of a priority within the armed services, but all medical energies were focused firmly on the immediate war effort and little wider research was possible. In addition, medical progress was hampered as a result of physicians having to treat the complexities of mental neurosis within a rigid military system. In terms of psychology, the war provided opportunities for much observation but did not provide many chances for practical psychological innovation. As Myers complained, 'From a military standpoint, a deserter was either "insane" and destined for the "mad house", or responsible and should be shot.'[141]

Wartime research was obviously very closely linked to military needs, but at the same time, wartime psychology also drew heavily on traditional domestic values. The Special Hospital for Officers was thus primarily an:

experiment in psychological medicine. It has proved very successful. The house is home-like, large, and comfortable, above all it is cheerful. Each officer has a bedroom to himself, and there are public rooms where convalescents can meet one another; there is also a large garden. New cases are kept in bed and at rest until the acute stage has passed. Friends are admitted to see them, and they are allowed to get up and go for walks and drives. Meanwhile specialists see them frequently and special treatments are administered. These special treatments include electricity, massage, and dieting. In a few instances psycho-therapy is resorted to. Always the larger psycho-therapy of cheerfulness and encouragement is practised.[142]

To a great extent shell shock was recognized as a psychological complaint but the scientific practice of psychology itself was often dismissed in favour of commonsense and cheerfulness. Despite some pioneering medical practices, there was a continued emphasis upon traditional values such as 'character', and this social conservatism marked the treatment of shell shock from the very beginning of the war. This did not just affect army discipline and propaganda but also impacted upon clinical regimes. Collie, for example, stressed the primary importance of character and personality when staffing institutions for shell-shocked men.[143] These were factors that he clearly prized above medical training. The importance of 'character' is even prevalent at relatively high levels of academic debate. Charles Mercier, a renowned physician with a long-standing interest in mental health, argued that the education system should have three main aims. First, it should foster 'character', the most important attribute; secondly, it should promote clear thinking; and thirdly, it should deal with facts. Within this scheme, an understanding of science was given a low priority. In Mercier's words, 'In the subject of medium importance, clear-thinking, science is superior but much less so; and in the vital element of education, formation of character, science is of little or no value.'[144] Given such an intellectual environment, it is unsurprising that traditional medical values prevailed. As a result, establishment figures generally did not welcome any input from the relatively new discipline of psychology, and in terms of shell shock, medical progress was impeded despite a significant amount of good will at a high political level.

At this point it is pertinent to ask why shell shock was such a difficult condition to diagnose even after it had been made quite clear that war neurosis was a psychological response to the obvious strains of trench warfare, just as nervous breakdown was often a psychological response to the strains of civilian life. As has already been noted, cases of shell shock were roughly divided into categories defined as either hysteric or neurasthenic, a medical division that broadly reflected the class-based military hierarchy. However, the persistence of such a distinction does not imply a uniform precision in the diagnostic procedure. The confusion of a casualty clearing station, or even a base hospital, did not make for clarity or consistency of diagnosis. As a result, there was a great difference between theory and practice in the treatment of shell shock, and the debates in medical journals were often far removed from practice in military hospitals or local asylums. Also, clinical objectivity was influenced by military requirements, pension demands, and by assumptions of class, gender and even ethnicity.[145] Furthermore, the medical profession itself was unclear about the boundaries defining psychological problems. An article on malingering in the *Lancet* referred to 'hysteria, neurasthenia [and] hybrid hystero-neurasthenia' while being unable to provide clear definitions of the differences between each state. There were also numerous references to 'nerve-shaken men', 'traumatic hysteria', 'concussion of the brain', 'hysterical lesions', 'nervous manifestations' and 'emotional shock' – all terms used to describe men suffering from mental breakdown as a result of war. Consequently, it is safe to assume a high degree of subjectivity in the diagnosis of mental breakdown in war. This was openly acknowledged by Arthur Hurst, physician and neurologist to a number of military hospitals, then Consulting Physician to the British Forces during the War. He introduced the subject of functional nervous disorders by stating that, 'It is difficult to classify them satisfactorily . . . No scientific classification will therefore be attempted.'[146]

This diagnostic confusion was accompanied by a similar confusion within treatment regimes. During the war, physicians were generally united by two clear aims. Initially, they wanted to treat their patients and return them to the trenches. If that proved to be impossible, then they had a secondary aim which was to avoid creating any unnecessary burdens on the post-war pension system. However, there agreement ended and the medical treatment of shell shock was often characterized by uncertainty, best described by R. H. Steen of the City of London Mental Hospital who commented that, 'War shock or shell shock appears to vary from time to time, and different hospitals seem to admit differing cases.'[147] This comment was reinforced by Major-General Sir William Macpherson, who reflected upon wartime medical practice in the early post-war years and concluded, 'It was difficult at the outset to decide on the most effective form of treatment. Indeed treatment had often to be largely empirical.'[148] This ad hoc approach was largely due to the lack of psychiatric or psychological training within the profession, which meant that doctors learned from their own particular experiences. There was little opportunity for wider consultation, and this led to 'chaos of opinion, thought and practice'.[149] A lack of professional unity was exacerbated by the conditions of warfare. Hospitals were overcrowded, communication systems broke down, and doctors in England found it hard to obtain reliable medical histories of the men who had just arrived from France. Temporary RAMC doctors McDowall and Mott were not alone in complaining that it was almost impossible to find their patients' case notes because the notes so often became lost in the system.[150]

Like McDowall and Mott, many doctors were vocal about their grievances throughout the war, and their comments framed a large part of the cultural context in which responses to shell shock were formulated. The difficulties faced by doctors during the Great War are central to an understanding of the impact of the war in general, and of shell shock in particular. This is not simply because doctors treated shell-shocked men, but also because doctors were in a unique position during the war. They were influential non-combatants and were highly aware of the physical consequences of the war in a way that other non-combatant groups were not. They did not take part in the killing but they were far closer to it than, for example, politicians or financiers. As articles in the *Lancet* reveal, doctors were also self-conscious representatives of civilization and humanitarian progress, the very values for which the war was allegedly being fought.[151] On the whole, doctors were supportive of the war effort and committed to their role in what had come to be known as the Great War for Civilization.

Yet the role of the doctor in warfare was a complex and sometimes troubling one. Personal diaries reveal that although doctors were prepared to commit themselves to military medicine, they often strongly objected to having to participate in other military roles, for example in a disciplinary manner.[152] However, doctors were also aware that they were part of the modern scientific community that had made such a war possible in the first place. As a result, the medical community had its beliefs and practices severely challenged during the war. The evidence indicates that most men coped adequately with the strains of warfare, but the war also provoked shock and unmanageable distress, and not just among combatants.[153] The wide variety of medical responses, at times bordering on confusion, indicated that, in many ways, the medical profession was unable to manage effectively the mental traumas of the war.

This inadequacy calls into question the extent to which wartime practice prompted modernity among medical professionals. In some senses there is an obvious correlation between the war and modernity: the war prompted more efficient organization, and as the war progressed there was certainly more precise categorization and a higher degree of state input into the management of mental health. Another clear indicator of modernity was the way in which the new disciplines of psychology and psychiatry were becoming more respectable in Britain, as well as a in a number of other countries, such as Canada.[154] However, the association between the war and the 'birth of the modern' is not a straightforward one.[155] During the conflict, pre-modern traditions and belief systems persisted, and even grew. As Winter has observed, 'The Great War, the most "modern" of wars, triggered an avalanche of the "unmodern".'[156] The use of electricity or 'faradism' is a prime example of the coexistence of the modern and the traditional in this sphere. Electrical treatment can be perceived as a progressive method employing pioneering technology. It can also be viewed as straightforward punishment, which is the most reactionary and irrational of all approaches to nervous breakdown. However, although the use of electrical treatment can appear to be highly modernistic in that it employed an impressive array of equipment, it was actually a far more traditional device in which science and technology were used as mere aids to suggestion. This is certainly the view presented by Mott when commenting on Dr Yealland's success in using electricity to cure an apparently intractable case:

> I think the imposing array of electrical machines, coloured lights and other strong suggestive influences were partly instrumental in accomplishing what I had failed to do, but also I think the knowledge of success in other difficult cases, attending to Dr Yealland's effort, played a very important part in curing by strong suggestion this apparently hopeless case.[157]

Here we can see some juxtaposition between a primarily organic diagnosis and a treatment regime based very much upon faith, discipline and will power. More tellingly, in Yealland's theatrical performances we can see the remnants of early modern medicine in which the doctor was a showman – or even a conman.[158] There is another reason for the persistence of apparently 'unmodern' medical practices: quite simply, doctors were at a loss; they often did not know what to do and so were relieved when a cure materialized. In September 1915, Francesco Ummarino, a young Italian lieutenant, was admitted to hospital after having been struck dumb by a violent explosion at his feet. He remained mute for several days and made no response at all until the King visited the ward, at which point he leapt up and cried, '*Il re, sua maestà!*' [The King, his majesty!], burst into tears and was fit for duty. Both the King and the medical staff were visibly moved by the event.[159] This story is very redolent of the old European tradition of divine healing by the royal touch. That it was worthy of an approving report in the *Lancet* indicates, at the very least, a crisis of confidence in the medical profession, and a willingness to applaud anything that might work, no matter how unscientific it may have appeared.

Doctors' responses to shell-shocked patients had long-term effects on the way in which those patients were treated, and also on the way in which the war was remembered. Some individual physicians worked hard to ensure that shell shock was recognized as a largely psychological complaint; doctors were also responsible for determining whether or not a man was eligible for a pension. In the longer term, the shell-shock debate ensured that the political authorities recognized the need to plan for psychological casualties in all future wars. On a more negative note, the medical confusion surrounding the diagnosis and treatment of shell shock often resulted in practices that appeared to be cold and unfeeling, and this lack of official concern for the ordinary soldier subsequently became incorporated into the way in which the war was remembered and retold.

Pre-existing cultural attitudes towards 'nerves' played a crucial role in early assessments of shell-shocked men and the treatment they required. Moreover, attitudes towards 'nerves' and nervous complaints were broadly similar across the boundaries of both class and political commitment. These early responses to shell shock were clouded with contradiction and confusion. There was an official desire to protect the masculinity of war-neurotic soldiers; yet, at the same time, the shell-shock problem prompted deep concerns about both the state of masculinity and racial degeneration in Britain. The language of the shell-shock debate, and the controversies over the term itself, highlight these contradictions well. Moreover, the early faith in the possibility of a simple and straightforward cure for war neurosis explains the growing frustration with a medical profession that could not always provide that cure. Given the public interest in shell shock, and doctors' own perceptions of their wartime roles, it was important that the medical and military authorities were seen to be dealing with shell shock effectively. One can argue that the condition of shell shock was quickly incorporated into public notions of honourable suffering. This reinforced the importance of finding a fair and compassionate way of treating such soldiers and their families. However, as the following chapter indicates, the internal structures of the medical and military hierarchies ensured that shell shock as a condition was marginalized, and the treatment of shell shock later became associated with all that was unjust, inefficient and uncaring in the British establishment.

2

Encountering Shell-Shocked Men

*Hullo! Smith, you have had a lucky escape my lad. What? A bit shaky?
That's the way it takes a lot of fellows, but you will be alright in a day or
two. There is really nothing wrong with you except that injury to your
finger, which I shall soon fix up for you.*[1]

SIR JOHN COLLIE, 1917

The shell-shocked Smith has had a lucky escape in more ways than one. He has survived the battle with barely more than a scratch, and, thanks to the cheery commonsense of his doctor, he is going to avoid long-term psychological damage too. Collie was a firm advocate of the 'cheery chap' school of medicine. He did recognize that some men became seriously traumatized as a result of war but was convinced that it was possible to divert men's attention away from their neuroses and so facilitate a speedy recovery, or even avoid breakdown altogether. In this case, Smith's attention is drawn away from his nervous shakes and he is encouraged to think about his wounded finger – a simple injury that can be treated immediately. Collie created this fictional encounter between the 'lucky' Smith and the jovial doctor to illustrate an important medical-military point: this type of approach was exactly what was required to prevent the potential neurasthenic from developing a full-blown mental breakdown. Unfortunately, not all encounters between medical officers and wounded soldiers were quite so straightforward. First, shell shock was a complex problem, which often could not be managed in such a breezy manner. Secondly, medical officers were not always in a position to make clear judgments about a man's condition. Finally, the army medical services were often overwhelmed by the sheer number of casualties, by extraordinary wounds and by a variety of new medical conditions. Quite bluntly, the RAMC was unprepared, not just for shell shock, but for four years of prolonged industrial warfare.

So how did the wartime medical profession treat mentally broken men? Accounts range from the triumphant to the condemnatory, but today most commentators agree that the official treatment of shell shock was often remiss. A number of reasons have already been put forward to explain this weakness. One can argue that RAMC doctors were punitive, and that therapeutic regimes were simply tools for military discipline.[2] Or that the fault lay with successive wartime and post-war governments, all of whom were motivated by a desire for financial stringency and a return to pre-war values.[3] Yet to understand the encounters between shell-shocked men, whether officers or men from the other ranks, and their medical officers, we first need to understand the culture of the medical-military profession at the beginning of the twentieth century, and the specific factors affecting the RAMC during the war.

MEDICS AT WAR: A BRIEF HISTORY OF MILITARY MEDICINE

I was in the midst of it all – saw war where war is worst – not on the battlefield, no – in the hospitals.[4]

British Army Medical Services had improved during the late nineteenth century. Armies have always needed doctors but military-medical care has not always been exemplary. On the contrary, the traditional medical hospital was gruesome – it was a fetid place in which men who were not yet dead were sent to die of disease. There was no magic transformation during this period – the casualty clearing stations and the military hospitals of the First World War could still be bloody and ghastly – but significant changes had taken place in the Victorian era. These can largely be attributed to the increased professionalization of medicine and to attendant changes in popular and political expectations.

In an age dominated by science, reason and a widespread belief in progress, the medical profession as a whole became much more respectable. Medical journals became important for the dissemination of ideas and practices: the *Lancet* was established in 1828 and the *British Medical Journal* in 1840. The profession also became subject to more formal regulation. The Medical Act of 1858 established the General Medical Council, which was responsible for the Medical Register. All legally authorized practitioners were listed on this register, and so were publicly recognized. The quacks, charlatans and showmen of an earlier age were thus dismissed from the official world of medicine, and doctors became polite, educated gentlemen – only later, and more rarely, were they women.[5] The educated gentleman-doctor was a man of state-sanctioned science, but he also prided himself on being progressive and enlightened. When Thomas Wakely established the *Lancet* his agenda was explicitly reformist, as he explained in the first edition: 'A lancet can be an arched window to let in the light or it can be a sharp surgical instrument to cut out the dross and I intend to use it in both senses.'[6]

Victorian and Edwardian doctors may well have been socially conservative but they also saw themselves as pioneers of social progress. Public attitudes towards health care began to change too, and slowly the wider population came to believe not only that doctors could provide dependable medicine, but also that there should be a widespread entitlement to medical care. Social elites had long had access to private doctors and throughout the nineteenth century the growing middle class had become increasingly more able and willing to pay for medicine and surgery. As more workers became insured and trade unions began to organize medical services for their members, more of the working class grew to expect that they too should be able to call on a doctor in times of need. These workers had the same, or possibly even greater, expectations when they became soldiers. In response, politicians, mindful of the outrage caused by the disastrous medical arrangements during the Crimean and Boer wars, knew that it was no longer acceptable to send men off to fight with only a handful of doctors and stretcher-bearers. By the early twentieth century it was inhumane, inefficient and not modern to send men to war without proper medical backing.

Changes in the wider medical profession obviously had an impact upon army medical services, although arguably the medical-military profession reacted to change more slowly than its civilian counterpart. Until the end of the nineteenth century medical officers were attached to particular regiments, but were not incorporated within the rank structure of the British Army. This changed with the formal establishment of the RAMC in June 1898, and after this date medical officers held both rank and responsibility. Shortly after this, the RAMC was sent into active service in South Africa. Yet the RAMC was not fully equipped for the Second Anglo–Boer War. The RAMC insistence upon NBR – 'no bloody research' – ensured that, just as in previous wars, soldiers were more likely to die of disease than of wounds.[7] Six thousand British soldiers died as a result of enemy fire and 16,000 died from diseases such as typhoid and dysentery.[8] Consequently, the Advisory Board for the Army Medical Service complained that military hospitals were held to be in 'a very unsatisfactory state of affairs' and it became clear that more reform was urgently required.[9] In response to an obviously inadequate performance, the RAMC went through a period of reorganization in the years 1902–1914: there was greater clinical and scientific teaching, an increased focus on training and research, and the *Journal of the Royal Army Medical Corps* was established to keep members abreast of military-medical problems and developments.[10] When the First World War broke out in August 1914, the RAMC was staffed by about 1,000 officers, all of whom were scattered about the world in response to the demands of Empire. In this new European war, the RAMC had to make good the failures of the African campaign and demonstrate that the reforms had worked.

DOCTORS IN THE FIRST WORLD WAR: SUCCESS ON THE WESTERN FRONT?

The blankets on our beds are soaking wet and we can wring the water out of them
... cigarettes have to be dried before we can smoke them ... yet we are quite a happy
little family.[11]

During the war many press reports presented the wartime medical services in a
resolutely cheerful manner: overcoming all the odds and smiling in the face of
adversity, doctors fulfilled their duties and kept spirits high at the same time. This
type of account may well have been good for morale, and it was clearly designed
to comfort friends and relatives on the home front. The highly optimistic tone
is also present in much of the literature produced immediately after the war. For
many commentators, the medical profession had definitely triumphed during
the Great War and its achievements were to be celebrated. Writing immediately
after the armistice, Brereton insisted that, 'To the general public, then, it has been
clear from the very commencement of the war that the RAMC was ready for the
work expected of it ... Those results have been phenomenal.'[12]

For Woods Hutchinson, an American who was writing about Allied medical
services as a whole, the greatest medical achievements lay in the way in which
doctors dealt with disease and infection:

The Doctor has made this world struggle probably one of the least deadly ever fought
in proportion to the numbers engaged ... of the wounded who survive six hours,
90% recover, and of those who arrive at the base hospital, 98% get well.[13]

It is certainly the case that the medical profession in general and the RAMC
in particular had much to be proud of during the First World War. Successes
include the widespread vaccination policies, the more effective use of X-rays,
the improvements in sanitation and infection control and, most notably, the
tremendous progress in maxillo-facial surgery and orthopaedics. These were
all significant developments, and they were important for two reasons. First, as
has already been said, the RAMC wanted to create a respectable reputation after
the difficulties of the South African campaigns. Secondly, many doctors saw
themselves as men of both science and progress, and they were consequently
troubled by the development of scientific warfare. Since the eighteenth century
the development of science and the growing respect for scientific learning had led
to progress in medicine. Readers of the *Lancet* certainly assumed that scientific
work was fundamentally humanitarian and that, moreover, men of science were
essentially men of civilization and generally had 'leanings either to music, or art,
or poetry'.[14]

Yet in this war scientific development could be seen as far from civilized – the use of poison gas in particular was widely held to be barbaric. For those who believed that science was an essentially civilizing discipline, the war was a disappointment, and the left wing *Labour Leader* was not alone in bemoaning the 'sorry spectacle of the scientific fraternity split by the successful designs of Junkers, chauvinists and jingoes'.[15] H. G. Wells adopted the more simplistic line of decrying Germans as 'apes with all science in their hands'.[16] Of course, one could just blame the beastly Hun for being innately resistant to all civilizing influences, and racist attacks upon individual Germans and German *Kultur* had been commonplace since the atrocity rumours of 1914–1915.[17] Yet not everyone responded in this way, and some asked themselves: could it really be the case that the scientific revolution had led straight to industrial carnage? During the war many doctors were clearly troubled about the way in which scientific developments were being used for the detriment, rather than for the betterment, of mankind, and the *Lancet* produced a number of articles that questioned the relationship between science and civilization. William Osler, Regius Professor of Medicine at Oxford University, acknowledged that modern science had increased the scale of destruction and had made war dirtier and more savage. On the other hand, modern medical services were nothing short of 'miraculous'. When trying to answer the question, 'Is science for or against humanity?', Osler insisted that mankind ultimately benefited from the advances of science, 'The wounded soldier would throw his sword into the scale for science – and he is right.'[18]

Would the mentally wounded soldier throw his sword into the scale for science? Historians have disagreed about the extent to which the treatment of wartime shell shock advanced the treatment of mental illness more generally, and contemporary commentators were similarly divided. However, for many wartime medics, shell shock appeared to be a peripheral issue. It is perhaps unsurprising that pre-war military-medical texts ignored war neuroses, but the position was not tremendously different by the end of the war. *Hints for RAMC Officers* was produced in 1918 to help civilian officers accommodate themselves to army life and the conditions of warfare, yet it contains no mention of war neurosis at all. An official manual for *Training in First Aid and Nursing* was much the same. The book was produced in 1918 by an RAMC officer and was aimed at medical military personnel but it mentioned neither shell shock, neurasthenia, hystera nor war shock.[19] Psychological casualties were simply not included, despite the large numbers of mentally broken men by this stage.

An apparent lack of interest in shell shock is evident in post-war celebratory literature too. Hutchinson argued that those who broke down in war were inherently unstable, and that their nervous breakdowns had been hastened rather than caused by the shock of the war.[20] 'What has been the net result of four years of continuous war upon the nerves of the soldiers?' he asked; he then answered

his own question in unequivocal terms, 'Astonishingly little on the whole.
Indeed, far the heaviest nerve-strain of this War has fallen upon the anxiously
waiting or bitterly weeping wives and mothers and sisters at home.'[21] This type
of thinking was echoed by R. H. Norgate, Medical Superintendent of the Poor
Law Infirmaries in Bristol:

> We sometimes ask who has had to suffer most, men or women. There has been a
> greater strain thrown on women. I often wonder if we men really appreciate what
> many of these poor women went through during the War in their own homes – the
> strain, the anxiety, and the suffering, the racket of children, the crying of babies, the
> perpetual worries about food, and the quiet hours of suffering and thinking.[22]

At the root of this apparently dismissive attitude was the belief that most men
were able to deal effectively with the strains of warfare. Wounded men, especially
mentally wounded men, were in danger of looking vulnerable. By denying that
men had been shattered by war, commentators like Hutchinson and Norgate were
reminding readers that it was really women who were the weaker sex. War was
certainly hard, but as far as men were concerned, it was a natural and therefore
manageable task.

It is also the case that accounts of war neuroses were marginalized because the
military authorities actively discouraged debate. In 1916 the Director General of
the Army Medical Services (DGAMS) made it quite clear that he was 'strongly
opposed to the publication of articles on "shell shock".'[23] Of course a number
of prestigious practitioners did write about the treatment of war neurosis, and
did prioritize the care of mentally wounded men. Articles appeared in elite and
scholarly journals such as the *Lancet,* the *British Medical Journal,* and the *Journal
of Mental Science.* Even the *Journal of the Royal Army Medical Corps* published
articles about nervous and mental shock in 1916 and 1917.[24] Physicians, even
those firmly within the RAMC, were not always minded to listen to the DGAMS.
These analyses are important in that they demonstrate that wartime shell shock
was sometimes treated seriously and with compassion. Nevertheless, elite debates
in the *Lancet* were far removed from the day-to-day realities facing shell-shocked
soldiers and their medical officers. The lives of shell-shocked soldiers were largely
governed by the attitudes and practices of RAMC medical officers. These were
the officers who determined whether or not a man was sent home, what sort
of treatment he received and whether or not he was eligible for a pension or
a retraining grant. Many medical officers were sympathetic towards mentally
wounded men, but it is certainly the case that the RAMC did not always serve its
psychological casualties well. Criticisms of the RAMC's performance have long
been evident. On the left of British politics, the *Labour Leader* provided a voice
for those who were afraid that shell-shocked men were being wrongly executed

for cowardice. On the conservative wing, Lord Southborough went as far as to concede that 'dreadful things may have happened to unfortunate men who had in fact become irresponsible for their actions'.[25] These are not direct criticisms of the RAMC, but they do indicate that there was widespread concern about the treatment of shell-shocked men, and the RAMC was the institution that was ultimately responsible for this care.

Clearly war neurosis presented the Army Medical Services with a tremendous and unprecedented challenge. Yet many of the RAMC weaknesses were not simply the result of unparalleled strain – although that clearly played a part – but were also due to the institution's own culture and organizational practices. Many regular RAMC officers found it hard to cope with the influx of new, civilian personnel throughout the war. Some of these new members were hostile to, or critical of, army medical practices. Furthermore, the low status of mental medicine ensured that conflicts were at their most potent when dealing with shell shock. It is also important to note the practical problems of dealing with psychological casualties at the front line. Our current preoccupation with shell shock as the war's emblematic disorder has resulted in a tendency to look at shell shock treatment in isolation. Yet shell shock was just one of a vast number of military-medical complaints, all of which had to be treated quickly and effectively.

CIVILIAN DOCTORS AND THE RAMC

> I think the civilian medical profession has good reason to be rather proud of its own little bit.
>
> Kaye, 12 February 1916[26]

It soon became clear that the RAMC would need to expand to deal properly with the European war, which quickly developed in the summer and autumn of 1914. Just as the army needed more fighting troops, the RAMC suffered extreme shortages of personnel. In August 1914, the British Expeditionary Force (BEF) required 800 army medical officers immediately. Fifty per cent were supplied from the RAMC and 50 per cent from civilian volunteers, so very quickly the corps of established RAMC officers was diluted with newcomers.[27] After the Battle of the Marne, new plans were implemented rapidly. Under the direction of Sir Arthur Sloggett (DGAMS), distinguished members of staff from civilian hospitals were appointed as consulting physicians and surgeons within the army in France. This scheme was then extended to armies across the world.[28] There were also calls for volunteers, as in the following advert, which appeared in *The Times* in January 1915:

It is notified by the War Office that there are several vacancies for temporarily commissioned officers in the RAMC. Candidates should be British subjects of pure European parentage, fully qualified medical men under 40 years of age, and physically fit for military service.[29]

The RAMC did expand rapidly: in January 1914 there were 3,012 medical officers but the figure had risen to 9,626 by November 1915.[30] Yet the shortages were still grave, and at the beginning of 1916, Alexander Ogsten, President of the British Medical Association, insisted that:

It is a matter of national importance that those medical men who are over the age limit of the Army Medical Department should at once combine to offer their services to the nation, provided that their health and circumstances warrant their doing so. It seems certain that the supply, from civilian sources, of medical officers for the Army is nearly exhausted, and, if not at present inadequate, will shortly be so.[31]

Senior RAMC officers were unwilling to accept help from other organizations, believing that civilian medics had no understanding of military-medical practice. Yet in the context of mass warfare, the institution had little choice.[32] The BEF was supplemented by doctors from the United States and the Dominions, and from private organizations such as the British Red Cross, the Order of St John of Jerusalem, and St Andrew's Ambulance Association.[33] The process was not an easy one, and in a private letter to Kitchener, Colonel Arthur Lee made it plain that there had been a great deal of hostility between the Red Cross and the RAMC at the beginning of the war.[34] RAMC officers were resentful because they believed that civilians did not understand military customs and practices.

Civilian doctors joined the RAMC as temporary officers and they were committed to the army for the duration of the conflict. Despite RAMC concerns, this expansion was clearly necessary – there were simply not enough doctors in the army. Moreover, in the conditions of mass warfare, the RAMC required different types of medical expertise. RAMC officers had previously assumed that they would only have to deal with fit men and so specialists were not required to the same extent as in civilian medicine.[35] The presence of wartime psychologists created particular problems, but in addition, the RAMC had to expand to include a large number of masseurs, pharmacists, opticians and so forth.[36] These changes were not without their difficulties. The presence not only of new men, but of new, previously unnecessary specialists was bound to cause problems in the rigidly hierarchical RAMC. Furthermore, the influx of new civilian doctors was problematic because there were crucial cultural differences between civilian and military-medical practitioners. Civilian doctors complained about army red tape, the poor research culture, boredom and loss of professional autonomy. In response, regular RAMC officers were often irritated by the new volunteers who were not properly trained, had no prior experience of work in the field, and who showed little respect for military traditions. Temporary officers, whether medical or otherwise, were often dismissed as mere 'civvies'.[37]

The RAMC clearly needed to prove its worth in the First World War. This was a potentially difficult task given that much of the work was being carried out by temporary, rather than regular, officers. As early as 1915, Captain Henry Maynard Kaye, a civilian surgeon who had been commissioned in 1915, noted that, in his own casualty clearing station, six out of eight officers were 'civilians by trade' and the unit had become 'practically a civilian hospital in its routine and administration'.[38] By the following year, Kaye was insisting that civilians were responsible for the 'far greater part' of all medical and surgical work in the army.[39] Moreover, temporary officers were not just playing a supporting role but were assuming positions of responsibility too. Kaye acted as Officer-in-Charge of the casualty clearing station after less than a year in service and declared that, 'I should not mind running my own show.'[40] Kaye's experiences in the RAMC convinced him that military medics were substandard. At this point in time RAMC officers were the subject of layers of prejudice. The British Army had not traditionally been held in high esteem, and well-educated elites had always tended to look for employment in the civil service or in business rather than the army.[41] Just as the army as a whole received little elite support, the Army Medical Services tended to recruit from the less privileged medical schools. It was not easy to make a comfortable living as a doctor in the late-Victorian and Edwardian years, and medical graduates required independent wealth, family connections or good social contacts to establish a private practice. Many without such advantages chose salaried public health appointments or joined the armed services. Given the links between class and ethnicity in Britain, the RAMC was consequently staffed by the less influential sectors of the profession, namely doctors from Scotland and Ireland. In 1911, Scottish and Irish doctors formed as much as one-half of the Army Medical Department although Scotland and Ireland accounted for only one-fifth of the population of the United Kingdom.[42] There were two crucial consequences of this demographic. First, combatant officers tended to be English whereas medical officers were more likely to be Scots or Irish; given the social hierarchy within the United Kingdom, medical officers were, therefore, at a disadvantage. Secondly, the situation reinforced the belief within the wider medical profession that an army medical career was less prestigious than a civilian one, and the following comment by a distinguished surgeon indicates the attitude of many civilian doctors to their military counterparts:

> any decent young man who wants to live in different parts of the world, who is fond of hunting, riding, and shooting, and who is prepared to do a fair day's work, may be

recommended to join the RAMC. Those who mean to make medicine and surgery
the preoccupation of their lives had better stay out of it.[43]

Finally, regular troops were often hostile to the RAMC too, and soldiers made
bitter jokes about the initials 'RAMC' signifying 'Rob All My Comrades'.[44]
Prejudices aside, it is also possible to argue that RAMC structures encouraged,
or even rewarded, a lack of interest in medicine. Experienced army medical
officers were promoted away from medicine and became increasingly occupied
with administrative work. Kaye believed that this preference for bureaucracy was
endemic, and that 'it is quite the exception to find a regular RAMC officer doing
anything in this line – for the most part you will find him doing administrative
work, which as a rule I think he much prefers'.[45] Kaye was particularly irritated
by what he saw as the complacency of senior RAMC officers. Apparently his
major barely moved from his office, unless it was to visit the mess, and in the
winter of 1915–1916 he only left the building three times: once to take a walk,
once to watch a football match and once to have a meal out.[46] According to
Kaye, this senior officer was stirred into activity on only one occasion. A high
level of air activity and a number of bomb casualties 'so rattled the major that
he fled out of his office, tore off his coat, and did three or four dressings – the
first attempt at anything of the kind he has made anyhow since mid-October'.[47]
Kaye's description reinforces our stereotypes about high-ranking First World War
officers: the major was idle, far from the action and easily panicked.

   Kaye was not alone is making caustic comments about regular army officers.
James Dible, a demonstrator in pathology at the University of Sheffield, enlisted
in the RAMC at the outbreak of the war and was highly critical about officers
in general and medical officers in particular. He considered that army officers
were 'usually drawn from the less intelligent public school boys', although he
did concede that the officer was generally 'quite a delightful fellow and usually
a thorough gentleman'.[48] He was even more scathing of his own senior medical
officer whom he simply dismissed as a 'fool', and the young Captain Dible also
complained bitterly of RAMC hostility to the new officers who had joined to help
the war effort.[49] One reason for this irritation was that many new RAMC officers
were bored and unsure about their responsibilities, especially at the beginning of
the war. This reinforced their already low opinions of medical-military officers,
and encouraged criticism. The boredom was especially galling for those who
had left thriving practices or for those who had abandoned promising career
opportunities. In addition, many doctors had joined the army in a spirit of
genuine idealism. Captain Maberly Esler, a doctor at a Norwich hospital before
the war, was not untypical in his sentiments on joining up, and he confided to
his diary that:

What I wanted to learn was the conditions of warfare in the field, the comradeship in arms, what fear really was and how to overcome it, and whether I was man enough to take it, in fact to learn about myself.[50]

Esler was disappointed at the contrast between his initial motivations and daily life on the Western Front, particularly given that he perceived his skills were being wasted. Kaye also complained about the lack of real medical work, and in 1915 he noted that 'field ambulances appeared to be tumbling over each other' and that many doctors spent their time engaged in non-medical work such as administration, transport, marches and kit inspection. He went on to comment:

Certainly I have done less medical and surgical work during the five months I have been in the army than I do in one week or 10 days in my ordinary life, and several of our officers who have been nearly ten months in the army have done next door to none at all.[51]

These grievances may well have been compounded by a sense of frustration at being away from the line of fire. Both Esler and Kaye worked in casualty clearing stations, and so were at some distance from front-line trenches. To provide efficient medical care in war doctors have to be protected from enemy fire, but the behaviour of many regimental medical officers indicates that the doctors often disliked this protection. The regimental medical officer was supposed to wait at the Aid Post for incoming casualties, but throughout the war many of them insisted on going into the front-line trenches with the men, even if they could do very little real medical work there.[52] The articles of the Geneva Convention prohibited medical officers from taking part in actual combat, but it is possible that many doctors simply felt that war service was not war service without being exposed to the dangers of front-line fighting.[53] A doctor in the trench may well have boosted morale, but many of them took unnecessary risks. It is certainly the case that there was a high casualty rate among doctors. By October 1916, 53 medical officers had been killed, 208 were wounded and 4 were missing.[54] Total losses rose to 1,000 by the end of the war – a number of about the same size as the entire pre-war RAMC.[55] These losses exacerbated public concerns about the sheer numbers of doctors serving in the army as medical officers. Eventually, half of the United Kingdom's 22,000 doctors were mobilized, and this had a real impact upon the civilian population.[56] For many at home, it seemed as though doctors were being wasted at the Front: medical officers were acting as stretcher-bearers and being needlessly killed while the home front was being denied its doctors.

John Lynn-Thomas, a respected surgeon at the Cardiff Infirmary who became

consulting surgeon to the Western Command during the Great War, insisted
that complaints about boredom were unfounded and that 'the statement as to
the over-staffing of the medical units of the army in France seems to be quite
unsupported by facts'.[57] So how do we assess the position of new doctors in the
RAMC? The horrific casualty rates of the First World War seem to imply that
it would have been virtually impossible to employ too many doctors, yet some
medical officers clearly believed that there was widespread underemployment.
It is possibly the case that new doctors were simply unprepared for war work. It
is an old cliché that war is 99 per cent boredom and 1 per cent terror, and so for
medical men, as well as for combatants, the war often consisted of extraordinary
levels of activity followed by long tiresome lulls. Private George Harding's war
began in a way that was very different to Esler's. Facing rapid German advances in
the autumn of 1914, Hardy's diary describes a period of almost continual activity
from 17 to 29 October. Far from field ambulances 'tumbling over one another', his
field ambulance had to continually move and recreate itself under intense enemy
bombardment.[58] It is not just that doctors were unfamiliar with the pattern
of medical warfare; they were also unsure about their day-to-day roles. The
regimental medical officer's main task was to maintain the health and fitness of
his men. In practice, this meant ensuring that the troops had adequate supplies of
clean water and food, effective latrines and acceptable levels of personal hygiene.[59]
Senior medical officers were largely responsible for matters of administration
and organization. The diary of Dr Alistair Robertson Grant, previously House
Surgeon at Aberdeen Royal Infirmary, indicates that as the officer in charge of
a casualty clearing station, he was almost totally preoccupied with arranging
transport.[60] These were not the sort of tasks normally carried out by a civilian
doctor, and the daily emphasis upon hygiene and administration contributed to
the already prevalent belief that RAMC officers were neither proper doctors nor
proper soldiers. In Dible's words, 'The traditions of the RAMC are not those of
medicine. They ape the soldier, and are laughed at for their pretensions by the
fighting troops.'[61] Yet as far as many established RAMC officers were concerned,
civilians like Dible simply did not understand their new job.

Despite these difficulties and misunderstandings, there was no widespread
acceptance of the idea that civilian doctors had to be trained to work within
the army. Unlike the vast majority of men who either volunteered or were
conscripted into the war, doctors were nominally employed in their peacetime
professions. Other men had to be trained anew but doctors remained doctors.
This attitude was reflected in the *Lancet* as late as 1917:

> the medical man has the privilege of being called upon by the State to serve his
> country by the exercise of the science and art in which he has been brought up; and,
> speaking generally he can do this without further special education.[62]

Regular RAMC personnel thought otherwise. Men from the 2/4 London Field Ambulance complained that the majority of civilian medical men had no idea that there was any difference between being a doctor to the civil population in peacetime and being a medical officer in war and, moreover, that some of them never learned the difference however much they tried to do so.[63] They also complained that civilian doctors were not in the habit of taking orders, and so seldom read them. If they did read them, they often did not grasp their importance.[64] These complaints were more than just retrospective grumbles. A government report of 1922 admitted that many medical officers went directly to the front from civilian hospitals and knew little of the duties they had to undertake.[65] Field-ambulance personnel did not always have a medical background, and it was rumoured that the RAMC had attracted many artists at the beginning of the war.[66] Certainly 17-year-old Leonard Stagg had no prior first-aid experience when he joined the RAMC as a nursing orderly in 1914. He was not alone: 'several fellows' fainted during the preliminary lectures'. [67] On a more subjective note, some RAMC officers insisted that the new medical officers were not of a particularly high quality; on the contrary, they were 'selected from certain low medical categories and had to be trained from scratch'.[68] Of course, this is exactly the complaint that the civilians made about established military doctors. One can argue that the problems lay as much with the RAMC training and induction process as with civilian inability to appreciate military-medical culture. Also, the sheer numbers of new medical officers ensured that the quality of the intake was inevitably variable.

The primary RAMC complaint, namely that the new civilian doctors simply did not understand their military duties, was particularly acute in the management of war neurosis. Dr Charles Myers is an example of a physician who constantly struggled with military procedures, believing that the military approach to war neurosis was completely at odds with effective medical practice. Despite, or perhaps because of, his prestigious position, Myers seemed to ignore or to reject very basic military principles. On several occasions Myers examined patients accused of desertion – and his methods were very different to accepted RAMC practices. On examining a young soldier 'so deficient in intelligence that he did not in the least realise the seriousness of his position', Myers labelled him 'insane' and sent him home. However, the soldier was clearly not insane and so was returned to France with a report stating that there was no sign of insanity.[69] On examining a further, very similar, case of desertion, Myers recommended that the lad be punished and returned to base duty. His recommendation was ignored and the young soldier was returned to the front; a few weeks later he was sent down after having tried to bomb his officer. Shortly afterwards, Myers made the same recommendation in the case of 'an intellectually feeble, stuttering young French Canadian'. Yet again the advice was rejected, and the soldier quickly deserted a further three times.[70] The military authorities simply did not understand why Myers would not follow the accepted procedure when it came to cases of desertion. Equally Myers did not understand why the military insisted on treating young men in ways guaranteed to ensure recidivism. Like his military counterparts, Myers wanted to safeguard the fighting strength of the army – there are no differences of aim or principle in these stories – it is simply that many civilian methods were radically different to those of the army.

ARMY MEDICAL OFFICERS AND 'POOR TOMMY'

Myers of course was a very high-profile case, and he was not a typical medical recruit. Nevertheless, his difficulties were reflected in the experiences of the more ordinary doctors who joined the RAMC. One of Dible's greatest concerns was that army discipline resulted in the neglect, or even the mistreatment, of the ordinary soldier. On his first posting he was told that 'most supposedly sick soldiers are "scrimshankers"' and he went on to complain that scrimshanking 'is the RAMC's second most frequent disease'.[71] Stagg, a nursing orderly with the 2/3 South Midland Field Ambulance, agreed, saying that 'we were always on the look out for malingerers'.[72] Dible was worried that RAMC officers were labelling too many ill men as 'scrimshankers' and so were dismissing illnesses rather than treating them. However, Dible was not overly sympathetic. Like his military colleagues, he was infuriated by 'difficult' patients, such as neurasthenics, and commented that:

> They exasperate me beyond endurance, but I rather prefer to kick them out of my presence with a few well-rubbed in words of worldly wisdom [sic] than to hand them over to their NCOs as 'scrimshankers' . . . I loathe this out-patient kind of work, with the debasing idea pervading everyone that the men 'go sick' to escape duty. I absolutely refuse to co-operate in schemes for catching scrimshankers, because in the event of a mistake such shocking miscarriages of justice would occur . . . This shows the innate suspicion of poor Tommy which pervades the RAMC.[73]

Dible was writing early in the war, long before there were any widespread concerns about the execution of shell-shocked men. Yet his words indicate a realization that, in some circumstances, sick soldiers could easily be misdiagnosed and punished. Unlike regular RAMC officers, Dible was very reluctant to involve himself in any disciplinary actions. As James Barrett, the assistant director of the Australian forces' medical services, explained, this is exactly why the civilian doctor was 'a source of trouble' to the RAMC.[74] In the army, everything had to be done for the good of the service, but the civilian doctor tended to focus exclusively on the sick man and so was 'almost certain to desoldierize him'.[75] Civilian doctors believed that army discipline could conflict with their professional autonomy, but the RAMC officer perceived army discipline to be an integral part of his work.

The differences between military and civilian medical approaches were often crucial but, as has already been noted, civilian and military doctors shared the same overall aims: they both wanted to maintain the fitness of the fighting troops. Consequently, many ordinary civilian doctors made compromises and changes as they grew more accustomed to military life. Medical officers have been presented as either triumphant heroes or as hard-hearted brutes dispensing 'medicine and duty' to men worn down by fighting and disease.[76] These representations can appear even starker in cases where medical officers had to make decisions about possible malingerers: in such cases they can be seen as either champions of justice or as military martinets, guilty of sending mentally wounded men to their deaths. However, the reality of military-medical encounters was complex, and new doctors had to learn how to recognize the boundaries between grousing, malingering, insubordination and mental collapse.

Esler was an example of a civilian doctor who adapted well to military traditions. At his first sick parade, Esler excused from duty all men suffering from lumbago, and as a result the numbers complaining of lumbago grew. Esler quickly became aware that he was being 'taken for a ride' and subsequently returned all men to duty, whether they claimed to be ill or not:

> Strange to say the epidemic disappeared like magic! Later, in France, when we might be having a tough time in the trenches, I would turn to a group of men and say "any of you fellows feel lumbago coming on?" That always got a good laugh for they remembered my first few days with them when I had been taken for a sucker.[77]

Esler the new recruit may well have been taken for a sucker, but this was not an accusation that could be levelled at him by the end of the war. In 1918 Esler had to attend the execution of a man sentenced to death for desertion, and as the presiding medical officer it was his job to pin a piece of coloured flannel to the man's heart. Although recognizing that the man had 'a superior sort of courage' when facing death, Esler insisted that the sentence was just:

> It was absolutely essential. It was setting a bad example to the men. They were beginning to feel that you only had to walk off during a battle and come back afterwards and you escaped any penalty of death or mutilation.[78]

Esler was no longer a naive and inexperienced young medical officer. It is possible that he had simply imbibed military values and that, like his more-established colleagues, he had grown to see the RAMC as 'as an extra branch of the provost corps, intent on securing the extreme penalty for such offenders wherever possible'.[79] However, there are alternative explanations. The understandable concerns of newly recruited doctors did not transform the army medical service into one that was ready to excuse unmilitary behaviour on the grounds of mental collapse. In the first place, both civilian and military doctors were unsure about mental illness, mental breakdown and neurosis in general. Very few doctors, whether civilian or military, could claim an expertise in mental health care. Secondly, and perhaps somewhat paradoxically, RAMC staff seemed confident about recognizing a clear borderline between shell shock and malingering. Stagg, who had claimed that he was always on the lookout for malingerers, insisted that 'you couldn't simulate shell shock. You could heart disease, or one or two other things. Not shell shock'.[80] Civilian experts may have disagreed but ordinary medical staff on the ground seemed assured: they may not have been able to define shell shock, but they were sure they could spot someone shamming it. Finally, much treatment of shell shock was ad hoc and informal. When medical officers or nursing orderlies encountered shell shock at the front they did not always react in accordance with officially sanctioned procedures. These encounters were far from uniform but they do indicate that medical officers, and others, tried to keep what they saw as 'genuine' shell-shock cases away from the arena of army discipline.

MENTAL MEDICINE IN THE RAMC

The majority of RAMC officers, temporary or otherwise, were reluctant to engage fully with the concept of shell shock as a medical condition. There were a number of reasons for this apparent neglect of an important subject. In the first place, psychology was not scientifically respectable, and neither psychiatry nor psychology had yet been established as secure disciplines.[81] Secondly, the RAMC had no regular medical officers with specialist training and experience in mental or nervous diseases or disorders.[82] Moreover, mental specialists were treated with utter disdain by the vast majority of the military. As a result, individual officers could not hope for career advancement by specializing in psychology, and the RAMC as a whole could not win more respect from the military hierarchy by investing in psychology. Furthermore, men like Myers, who were truly innovative in their approach to shell shock, were not only prestigious in their civilian field, but also were somewhat at odds with the official culture of the army. When Myers began to implement shell-shock receiving centres in each Army Area – a policy which was ultimately successful – Sloggett initially insisted that it was impossible to treat 'mental cases' in Army Areas.[83] Temporary officers were often unsupported when they did try to implement changes, and so many psychiatrists and psychologically minded physicians found it hard to gain acceptance within the RAMC. This lack of recognition was so serious that many of the individuals concerned were either deterred from continuing their careers after the war, or were seriously disillusioned as a result.[84] Myers was particularly disgruntled about the way in which those dealing with shell shock had been treated. Myers himself was awarded a CBE but he felt that many of his colleagues had been slighted. On his demobilization, Myers asked for recognition on behalf of certain junior medical officers in the neurological section, but this was not forthcoming and he complained that, 'Neither in France nor in the UK, so far as I was aware, had a single "mention" or other distinction been up to that time conferred on any medical officer in the British Army for this work.'[85]

Civilian doctors were uninformed about mental health issues because the mentally ill were normally treated in public asylums, but entering the asylum service was widely perceived to be an 'intellectual death'.[86] Psychiatry was the Cinderella of medicine: conditions of service were poor, there were few opportunities for research and asylums were physically remote, generally being situated far from towns or research institutions.[87] At the beginning of the twentieth century 'mad doctors' were not derided in the way that they had been in the past, yet they were still of very low status within the medical hierarchy, and many doctors paid little attention to questions of madness or mental breakdown. From 1893 to 1932 the medical curriculum remained essentially unchanged, and although the study of mental disease was compulsory it was also highly limited. A medical student had to attend 4 out of 5 of a series of 12 lectures on mental disease, and attend 12 clinical demonstrations at a recognized institute for the insane. At the end of this training a doctor would have been expected to do no more than 'recognize an insane person when he saw one'.[88] Even a temporary medical officer with asylum experience may well have had very little opportunity to develop specialist knowledge. Junior doctors worked almost exclusively with chronic cases and so had little opportunity to develop research specialisms; in any case, asylum doctors were often in charge of at least 400 and sometimes 600 patients.[89] This was clearly not the sort of doctor-patient ratio that encouraged the development of research programmes. As a result, both temporary and regular RAMC officers were largely unwilling to engage with psychological medicine, and this lack of enthusiasm had an obvious impact on the research and treatment of shell shock, which had largely, although not completely, been established as a primarily psychological problem by about 1916. We should also note that we cannot simply condemn doctors for their reluctance to engage with psychology. The mistrust of psychology was endemic and there is evidence to suggest that ordinary soldiers also disliked mental specialists. Recollecting his experiences at the Red Cross Hospital at Maghull, near Liverpool, W. H. Rivers, a pre-war anthropologist who had joined the RAMC to serve as a military doctor, noted that patients were reluctant to discuss their dreams. Their reluctance lay in the belief that 'dreams were being used by medical officers as a means of testing whether their patients were to be sent back to France'.[90] This level of suspicion was perfectly understandable – doctors did want to send men back to the front; nevertheless, it did mean that there was little effective dream-interpretation work at Maghull.

The consensus of RAMC doctors reporting to the post-war government enquiry into shell shock was that special training in nervous and mental disorders was not desirable in a regimental medical officer. The following comments are typical:

> I would rather have an experienced man about 35 years of age, a man of the world rather than a youthful medical officer with some special bee in his bonnet.
>
> Dr Wilson

> He should get to know the soldier and to live with him. He need not know much medicine – a smattering of neurology would be useful. He should not be a peacetime psychologist, this would be a great disadvantage.
>
> Major Adie[91]

SHELL SHOCK, SELF-INDUCED INJURY AND MALINGERING

Myers's frustration at the RAMC suspicion of psychology was not unfounded. Medical officers openly acknowledged that they had neither the time, the interest nor the experience to treat shell-shocked or neurasthenic patients.[92] The lack of time may well have been a valid complaint, especially during periods of intense bombardment. The lack of training was also a real problem, but there may have been more to the lack of inclination than Myers was prepared to recognize. As Dible's words imply, when treating 'difficult' patients it was easy to stray into accusations of malingering. Malingering and self-inflicted injury are two separate conditions, but they are linked in that they can both be attributed to a loss of nerve. The malingering soldier deliberately exaggerated or prolonged his wounds or illnesses, and further along the same spectrum one encounters the self-induced injury or illness. In both cases, the military-medical response inevitably required a disciplinary response too.

On an intellectual or academic level, an exploration of the links between mental health, malingering and self-induced injury can be fruitful. Sir Frederick Parkes Weber, an established civilian expert in self-mutilation, noted that soldiers were inducing grave cardiac disorders by swallowing tobacco. Men were also swallowing cordite and injecting themselves with petroleum.[93] These were seriously grave practices, and most medical officers were ill-equipped to deal with them. In the world of civilian medicine, many experts had long regarded self-mutilation as a serious psychological complaint. Townsend, who served as a Temporary Surgeon in the Royal Navy during the war, considered that such extreme self-mutilation 'could justifiably have originated from the stress and strain of active service'.[94] Parkes Weber argued in a similar vein. Unlike Stagg, Parkes Weber believed that malingerers sometimes did successfully simulate some of the symptoms of shell shock, yet he also recognized a clear and medically established link between malingering, shell shock and mental illness.

In essence, Parkes Weber and Townsend were arguing that self-mutilating behaviour could be interpreted as the symptom of a mental illness caused by combat conditions. This argument was a clear challenge to army discipline. To imply that one could officially exonerate self-mutilation on active service indicated a complete lack of understanding of military culture. The military elites were committed to maintaining the discipline required to win a war. Senior officers had neither the time nor the inclination for any debate about the nature of the boundary between illness and criminality. As Parkes Weber noted, the official position was clear and 'men who disable themselves in this way are liable to be court-martialled'.[95] During active service, the needs of the man who deliberately wounded himself were superseded by the needs of the army as a whole. In the words of Lieutenant-Colonel Grevet of the Grenadier Guards, 'If you once allowed people to go away you felt you were not playing the game to the army.'[96]

The regular army was already accustomed to dealing with cases of malingering and self-induced injury but procedures had to be modified during the war. Mass mobilization meant that there were more cases than ever before and the British Army also had to deal with conscripts for the first time. Men who really did not want to be in the army may have been more prone to such coping mechanisms, and even regular soldiers may have attempted self-induced injury after a significant and demoralizing period in the trenches. As a result, self-inflicted injury was included as an offence under the Defence of the Realm Act in 1916. The standard military response to self-inflicted wounds was made plain in a confidential memo from Headquarters to the Director of Medical Services (Second Army) in December 1917:

> Instances have been recently brought to notice of patients admitted to medical units suffering from a [sic] inflammatory condition of the skin and subcutaneous tissues about the knee joint, the cause of which was not readily explicable.
>
> As medical officers who saw these cases were of the opinion that the condition was not due to accident or disease, enquiry was made and it has been ascertained

that the condition was caused by the hypodermic injection of petrol into the limb near the knee cap.

The object was undoubtedly to evade service in the front line.

The attention of medical officers should be drawn to this practice with a view to the detection of any cases which may occur in the future.[97]

In this memo, medical officers are being told in no uncertain term that their duty lay in 'playing the game to the army'. Yet there was a discrepancy between the official army position and actual practice: not all medical officers were prepared to act as military policemen.

While working in a military hospital after the battle of Mons, Esler noticed many cases in which newly healed, or almost-healed, wounds became open and inflamed. This happened to such an extent that it could not have been coincidence and Esler came to the conclusion that the men were doing it themselves: they did not want their wounds to heal because they did not want to go back to the front. Esler did not report any of these incidents to the relevant authorities. Instead, he covered all the wounds with plastic dressings so that the men could not interfere with them, and they had little choice but to allow themselves to get better. Esler had a similar attitude towards a number of Sikh troops he encountered in 1915. They all had wounds in the palms of their hands and it was clear that they had been self-inflicted. Once again Esler chose not to report anyone, and he went on with the business of treating the wounds as best he could.

The first comment to make about Esler's experiences is that his actions cannot be attributed simply to him being 'a sucker'. He was not working alone and his colleagues must have colluded with him because none of the staff reported these self-induced injuries and Esler does not seem to have encountered any opposition from anybody. Esler, and presumably his colleagues, understood the self-mutilation to be the result of what we would now term 'battle stress'. He insisted that the men were not cowards, rather that they were shocked because the Battle of Mons had been 'terrible'.[98] In such circumstances one could overlook a military crime. Yet Esler also recognized the boundary between overlooking a crime and supporting gross dereliction of duty. He did not report the men, but he did all that he could to treat them so that they could be sent back into the line again. An army doctor's role is somewhat ambiguous: he or she has to cure someone who has been wounded in battle so that they can be sent back to the battlefield as soon as possible. Even the military triage system seems counter-intuitive. The army doctor has to neglect the most seriously injured so as to prioritize the least wounded. In this way the fighting strength of the unit is maintained. Given the importance of collective strength, Esler's actions can be seen as pragmatic as well as compassionate. It made little sense to waste time accusing and punishing the men; it made a great deal of sense to heal them and send them back to the front so that they would carry on fighting. The soldiers also recognized a boundary. The plastic dressings were more than just a physical barrier: they were also a signal that alerted the men to Esler's suspicions. Esler was sympathetic, but he would not brook outright insubordination. If a man had removed the plastic dressing to inflame the wound he would have been making an overtly defiant gesture and would have lost Esler's sympathy. Stagg's responses to self-inflicted injury were similar. Insisting that 'it was not done wholesale but it was done', Stagg went on to describe how men would take the bullet from a cartridge and chew the cordite. This produced a temporary heart flutter or palpitations. The response of the medical staff appeared to be phlegmatic: 'it would be found out and they would be back up the line again'. Yet if a man persistently induced injury, then the situation was different and Stagg acknowledged that the crime was regarded very seriously 'if it happened more than once'.[99]

Medical-military staff recognized that malingering and self-inflicted injuries were military offences. However, they did not always recognize that these offences had to be treated in a formal disciplinary manner. Sometimes it seemed kinder, or possibly even more sensible, simply to ensure that the man returned to duty in a reasonable period of time. For their part, soldiers seemed to realize that the law was not always strictly implemented. Hewitt, for example, knew that sleeping on duty was theoretically punishable by death, but was not completely sure whether this actually happened or not 'whether that [the death penalty] was ever coming, that was another point but that was what you was told'.[100] Stretcher-bearers saw all manner of injuries and realized that some men would simply respond badly to the stress of battle. Frank Dunham adopted a very matter-of-fact approach when describing a man who had shot himself through the hand: he commented that the man's nerves were in a bad state and that he really had 'done his bit, having served in the trenches for two years'.[101] Dunham was similarly non-judgemental when describing a battalion suicide who had 'lost his nerve'.[102] This kind of approach is also reflected in more elite attitudes. John Fortescue, historian to the British Army, told the Government Enquiry into Shell Shock that 'numbers of men went out of their minds in the old campaigns, as they still do'.[103] One can therefore argue that the implementation of military law was nuanced and finely balanced. Senior officers considered the context, the man and the possible repercussions, and then tailored punishments to fit, or even ignored the crime altogether if that served the collective interest better. On the other hand, one can equally argue that military law was arbitrary and that it was executed in an inconsistent and therefore unjust manner.

MANAGING MENTALLY BROKEN MEN: UNOFFICIAL
RESPONSES TO SHELL SHOCK

I've known a huge guardsman run for a rabbit hole at the drop of a pin almost.[104]

During the First World War some soldiers were treated as malingerers when they were suffering from nervous collapse, and some men were accused of self-inflicted injury when they were really suffering from war-induced neurosis or mental strain. Yet shell shock was not always associated with malingering or self-inflicted injury, and an overemphasis upon these associations has obscured other ways of understanding or responding to wartime shell shock. The search for the typical patient-doctor encounter is of course elusive. There are gaps in the text books, contradictory responses, and a wide range of ad hoc or informal treatments. Moreover, the incidence of shell shock was not uniform because men were liable to break down more in some sectors than in others. This means that individual recollections of shell shock attribute different levels of importance to the condition. Stagg, remembering his time on the Somme in 1916, recalls that 'one was always seeing cases of shell shock', whereas Oxley, remembering Ypres in 1918, concludes that shell shock 'was not common in my particular time'.[105]

For many medical men, shell shock was common and it did provoke sympathy. A man's loss of courage and control – the most essential of masculine attributes – may have provoked official censure in some circumstances, but a mentally broken man also provoked compassion. This was particularly the case when the man in question had previously been renowned for great strength or bravery. Esler's comments on a soldier's eccentric behaviour are commonplace:

> I remember a fellow joining us who had been very heavily shot over Mons. He joined us in the later stages of war. The first time we went out on a route march we had to move from one place to another, every time we heard a shell we took no notice of it, we were so used to them not coming near us or hitting us, he threw himself on the floor you know, lay down until it had all passed. That was a case of shock that he's seen so much of that, that he'd seen so many killed by it that he expected every shell that came to kill him. He threw himself down on the ground at once.[106]

Esler was describing someone who had lost the ability to keep his nerve under shell fire, but there is no hint of condemnation in his words. The man had suffered heavy firing at Mons and was clearly no coward; his actions were understandable and so were accepted.

Yet shell shock did not always induce men to run away or to hide themselves. Contemporary commentators make it clear that shell shock was often associated with unnecessary risk-taking: dealing with shell shock sometimes meant holding a man back. Hewitt tells just such a story about a shell-shocked officer. Hewitt was in a dugout during some shelling when an officer appeared shouting, 'Let me get at the bastards.' He wanted to climb out of the trenches to attack the Germans, and seemed prepared to kill his own comrades in the process. Hewitt and another man had to pull him in and sit on him to restrain him.[107] Was this man really suffering from war neurosis? Would an experienced psychologist have attributed his actions to battle-strain? It is of course impossible to say, yet it is significant that the soldiers perceived his behaviour as that of a shell-shocked man. The term shell shock clearly provided an explanation for reckless behaviour.

Sometimes such reckless behaviour was too difficult to be managed on an informal basis. In a military hospital in Aire (Pas-de-Calais), Stagg was confronted by a shell-shocked patient who was fully armed and ready for combat:

> I heard a scuffle behind me, and there was this shell-shocked man, tin hat on and his pack, rifle and bayonet, and his bayonet was about thirteen inches from my tummy. I said
>
> – Good morning
>
> – I want to go back to my unit
>
> I said
>
> – I beg your pardon
>
> – I want to go back to my unit.[108]

The soldier's desperation was so extreme that he was a danger to others. Eventually he was restrained and the colonel ordered the ambulance staff to 'send him down' – military code for sending a man to the base for shell-shock treatment.

'Sending a man down' was not taken lightly and was often expressed in a tone of finality. Charles Moran was a distinguished medical officer in the First World War and he went on to become Winston Churchill's physician in the war of 1939–1945. He writes about men reporting their shell-shocked sergeant 'as if we had already lost the war' and goes on to note that as far as the man himself was concerned, 'the game was up'.[109] Officers and men from the ranks, both medics and combatants, tried to protect the shell-shocked by attempting informal treatments or concealment. Oxley, a non-commissioned officer with the 23rd Battalion Middlesex Regiment, described how some men had refused to go to the front lines and in response the officers were 'very considerate' giving the men 'jobs behind the lines'.[110] Oxley himself simply left a man behind when he thought that he was not well enough to be part of a wiring party.[111]

Leaving a man behind seems like unmilitary behaviour, but these officers and non-commissioned officers were motivated by two key considerations. First, that nervousness or hysteria could quickly become contagious, and so allowing the men the opportunity for some unofficial rest was a pragmatic approach. Secondly, many medical officers shared Moran's belief that 'men wear out in war like clothes'.[112] By saving the men's strength for more important battles, such officers were wisely maximizing the strength of the fighting unit. There is also evidence to indicate that some physicians thought that just leaving a man to recover naturally might be as efficacious a remedy for nervous shock as anything else. In the spring of 1915 Moran encountered a mentally damaged stretcher-bearer whose party had been caught by a shell. The man was physically unhurt but his three companions had been killed and he had been spattered with their blood. In Moran's words:

> Now he seemed done. I sent the corporal away and resolved to keep the bearer until things were quieter. I got him to lie down on the stretcher on which I slept. Almost at once to my great wonder he fell asleep. It occurred to me that there might be an outside chance of saving this fellow the mishap of going to the base with shell shock. I dropped a blanket down so that he was hidden and made him some hot stuff to drink. He slept for nearly twenty-four hours. When he awoke he seemed all right. He went out with me next day and never looked back again.[113]

In Moran's story, concealing the nervous collapse appeared to be successful. In other cases, the tendency to avoid medical treatment can appear as highly dubious behaviour. Esler's account of a shell-shocked officer is more disturbing:

> A well-known shell-shocker, he'd done it before, an officer came in, threw himself upon the floor and said "oh I'm shell shocked, I'm shell shocked" and went into sort of spasms. He was just a frightened man . . . I never reported that to anybody of course, just sent him back.[114]

Esler's comments imply that this man was not really suffering from war neurosis at all. His dismissive approach seems callous because, to a modern mind, the 'well-known shell-shocker' should be sent away for immediate treatment. After all, constant breakdown at the front is the sign of a genuine psychological problem. Yet understandings of mental breakdown were somewhat different during the First World War. While it was widely accepted that men could break down under the strain of battle, it was also accepted that such a breakdown would be short-lived. If a man did not respond well to treatment, or if a man suffered from repeated bouts of mental collapse, it was widely assumed that his mental state was not the result of war strain but of some constitutional weakness.[115] In such a context, Esler's response seems more compassionate. According to the logic of the day, this repeat 'shell-shocker' was either shamming or suffering from some pre-war character defect, and Esler's actions served to save him from the ignominy of making either situation public.

Even when a medical officer recognized that a man was genuinely traumatized by war-induced neurosis, he might be unwilling to send the man down straight away. This could produce responses that appear almost barbaric to the modern reader, yet it is important to bear in mind that sympathy could coexist alongside harsh treatment.

When Stagg was asked to consider whether or not people understood or sympathized with shell shock, he answered 'Oh yes, yes', and then went on to say that:

> They were apt to be rather stern. I remember one man came in, a big chap, six footer, and he was shaking with the shell shock and I was amazed, the colonel lifted his heavy stick and hit him across the head on his – he had his tin hat on – hit him across the head to give him another shock and he used the words "You're a bloody fool, pull yourself together." But that couldn't put the man right and he could see he really had gone beyond, so of course he was taken care of and he went down. But they did try sometimes to give them a type of reverse shock you see, to try and reverse the process but it rarely worked.[116]

It is important to stress that this colonel was a doctor. The idea of the 'reverse shock' had some kind of internal logic, but was certainly not based on any thorough understanding of mental injury. Nevertheless, reports from the trenches indicate that ordinary soldiers responded to psychological casualties in a similarly ferocious manner. One soldier attempted to rescue a friend who was then blown to pieces in front of him. The would-be-rescuer then became unconscious and when he came round he was both deaf and dumb. As a way of 'treating' him, his fellow soldiers beat him with a leather slipper and then nearly throttled him until he shouted 'Stop it!' There are also reports of soldiers tickling a shell-shock victim's feet or pouring boiling tea on to him.[117] These activities should not be seen as punishments but as rather crude attempts to shock a man back into normality. This culture of accepted violence indicates the appropriate context in which to evaluate shell-shock treatment. A harsh physical response to a mental condition was generally acceptable if it was ultimately successful. Of course it was usually not successful – Stagg notes that this type of treatment 'rarely worked' – yet as far as many men were concerned, any treatment, however painful, was better than being 'hurried away to the base to a shell shock hospital with a rabble of misshapen creatures from the towns'.[118]

PRACTICAL AND ORGANIZATIONAL PROBLEMS

Divisions within the medical community partially explain the way in which the RAMC responded to shell shock. RAMC culture and its accepted practices are also relevant, in particular the RAMC attitude towards research, towards psychology as a discipline, and to the problems of malingering and self-mutilation. Yet responses to shell shock cannot be attributed solely to the military's disdain for psychology: the tremendous number of practical and organizational problems facing the RAMC at the time must be taken into consideration. The medical officer's first priority was to assess men for front-line duty, but these assessments were almost exclusively based on physical criteria. Men were examined for contagious diseases, joint deformities and hernia. Doctors also inspected the recruit's heart, chest, eyes, ears and teeth. This procedure was in some contrast with the process in the US Army, which did include a level of psychological assessment in an attempt to filter out mentally vulnerable men.[119] British men could be rejected for 'mental deficiency', although guidelines were unclear and policy was not always implemented thoroughly.[120] Moreover, physicians were divided on the issue. Whereas there was a consensus that the most seriously deficient men should not be sent to the front, Dr G. Shuttleworth of the Medico-Psychological Association, insisted that the South African wars had demonstrated the way in which 'some reputably feeble-minded boys made, when they grew up, very good soldiers'.[121] Not all were convinced that the mentally vulnerable should be excluded from military service.

The conditions of trench warfare ensured that front-line medics were similarly focused on physical injuries: their immediate aims were the rapid evacuation of casualties and early surgery.[122] The First World War may now be seen as 'the war of shell shock', but at the time, shell shock was just one of many complex and urgent medical conditions.[123] There was a whole host of new or unexpected conditions to deal with: the wounds caused by high explosives and gas attacks, trench foot, trench fever, trench nephritis and gas gangrene, to name just a few. Much of the literature and many personal recollections focus on foot care. This may seem banal in comparison with the traumas suffered by the mentally wounded, but many men were permanently disabled by trench foot or frostbite on the feet. Myers, later famous for his pioneering work into shell shock, did not initially specialize in mental wounds, and his first piece of wartime research was on the problem of trench foot.[124]

Myers had insisted – quite rightly – that mentally wounded men needed immediate treatment. Today, all military medics accept the principle of forward treatment of psychological casualties; it is now the most basic tenet of military psychiatry.[125] Yet how possible was forward treatment on the Western Front during the First World War? Certainly orderlies and stretcher-bearers aimed to 'get rid' of shell-shocked men, and send them off to the base as soon as possible.[126] There were good reasons for this: first-aid posts were often very primitive, and they were situated as near to the fighting line as possible, sometimes they were in ruined buildings or even out in the open air.[127] In the 'unholy conditions' of a regimental aid post, it was often difficult to administer any aid at all.[128] T. H. Lewis of the 2/4 London Field Ambulances described how it took three of them nearly three hours to carry a wounded man for barely a mile.[129] In addition, there were few trained medical staff and equipment was limited: normally one could expect only to find dressings and morphia.[130]

The next point of care was the advanced dressing station, about two miles behind the lines. In many cases this meant that men would still have felt very close to the battlefield. As late as February 1918 an order was issued stating that guns should not be placed within a quarter of a mile of an advanced dressing station. Grant clearly thought that this decision was long overdue and grumbled that, 'This has been agitated for during the last 3 years.'[131] The first place for any real surgery or treatment of any intensity was the casualty clearing station. By the end of the war these stations could provide beds for about a thousand patients and they were equipped to carry out operative surgery.[132] In principle, these were situated just beyond the range of artillery, although they could be as far as 20 miles behind the lines.[133] The casualty clearing station at Bailleul was only ten miles behind the lines but soldiers usually arrived there between three and four hours after having been wounded, and it was not uncommon for a man to arrive eight hours after having been injured.[134] Men wounded in the trenches could be only be safely evacuated at night and this obviously had an impact on transportation times.[135] Motor ambulances moved slowly because the roads were in such poor condition, and in some areas there were no roads at all and men had to travel in horse ambulances. As a result, the journey from the trenches to the casualty clearing station was arduous in the extreme. However, even on arrival a shell-shocked man could not automatically expect to receive the right sort of treatment. Until front-line psychiatry was established at the end of 1916, most psychiatric patients were sent back to England for treatment.[136] Even after this date, treatment at the front was often poor. It was not until June 1917 that casualty clearing centres were each staffed with a medical officer experienced in the treatment of nervous or mental cases.[137] Furthermore, this medical officer may well have been seriously overworked: some clearing stations could hold over 2,000 patients at any one time.

There is also evidence that much of the medical practice rarely worked according to plan. Kaye was intensely frustrated by the way in which cases were improperly labelled and notes were lost. He was also convinced that Field Medical Cards were routinely destroyed when the soldiers arrived at hospitals in England. As late as 1917 he was petitioning Sir Alfred Keogh in an attempt to ensure that soldiers' records contained 'a continuous diary of movement' so that progress could be monitored and treatment properly assessed.[138] In the previous two years, many men may well have received inappropriate care because of this lack of communication within the RAMC. Treatment was also hampered by the issue of training for stretcher-bearers. Stretcher-bearers were not part of the RAMC: they were initially bandsmen with special training, and required no medical background at all. The men had received very little training prior to their appointments, and any further training was purely at the discretion of the local medical officer.[139] For the most part, neither stretcher-bearers nor medical officers close to the line were in any position to make the complex medical judgements required by shell-shocked men. In addition, mentally wounded men were not the only ones displaying unpredictable or eccentric behaviour. Kaye's diary is replete with descriptions of men going 'dotty' with pneumonia, epileptics, assorted 'mental cases', attempted suicides and 'the almost usual idiot' who became injured while playing with a live shell.[140] Kaye's diary displays a sort of everyday acceptance of irregular behaviour. He complains about 'various weird works' but seems to accept that life in a casualty clearing station involved having to manage the occasional 'obstreperous maniac'.[141] Retrospective criticism has tended to produce a polarized image in which the psychologically and the physically damaged were clearly differentiated from each other. Yet this image is too simplistic, and doctors in field ambulances, casualty clearing stations and base hospitals continually had to deal with a whole range of men who demonstrated a bewildering mixture of both psychological and physical complaints. Moreover, experimental treatment was not confined to the mentally wounded. Stagg recollected treating a man with rheumatism by giving him tablets daily: 'When his ears buzzed we had to stop it. What that had to do with it I don't know'.[142] It was not only shell-shocked men who were receiving inadequate or untried medical attention.

Physicians at the front were generally unable to identify mentally wounded casualties, and even if they could it was hard to ensure that a mentally afflicted man would be treated swiftly. A medical officer at the Ypres salient observed that he was beginning to display the symptoms of shell shock during April, May and June of 1915. Then, during an attack, he had an experience that convinced him that he was really ill. He looked at his watch and noted that it was 3.30. After what he perceived to be many hours, and believing that it was time for the twilight lull, he looked at his watch again and found to his horror that only a few seconds had elapsed. He continued:

> This added to my alarm. I repeated the experience; each time I told myself: 'surely it is evening now' but the intervals between looking only shortened.
> The watch showed only one second, yet I had lived in my mind a whole day.

The dugout was then blown up and the officer was rescued after three or four hours. He then drank a great deal of whisky and stayed with his battalion for another 24 hours. During this time he was reported as having displayed bad language, but he did not completely break down until the action was over.[143] The way in which this anonymous officer 'carried on' was not unusual. Military culture was such that men tried to manage their fear by refusing to acknowledge it, and according to Captain Webster of the RAMC 'what most of us dreaded was any demonstration of our own frightendness [sic]'.[144] Consequently, many of those with shell shock tried to avoid drawing attention to themselves and so were rarely prioritized. The focus remained on the physically wounded despite a growing awareness of the importance of war neuroses.

Army culture was an incongruous and ambivalent mixture. Charles Carrington, as a 19-year-old subaltern, had to deal with a 17-year-old private who was too afraid to go over the top. He noted that, 'The other men standing round looked rather sympathetic than disgusted,' yet Carrington used hearty schoolboy banter to encourage the young private and make him do his bit.[145] Neither Carrington nor the older and more experienced men would allow the boy to succumb to his fear, and this seems to be typical of the way in which front-line troops attempted to manage temporary losses in self-control. In cases where a previously courageous man did suffer a nervous collapse, there was a widespread acceptance that any man could suffer a genuine mental collapse and that such a man deserved sympathy: if he had already 'done his bit' he had earned his breakdown. Yet RAMC officers were not in the same position as the fighting troops. They had to decide what to do with those men who could not be cajoled – or bullied – into normal military behaviour. In the main they recognized that a mentally broken man needed treatment, but established officers were initially reluctant to accept civilian medical practices, and many temporary officers with an interest in psychology or psychiatry were often at odds with military-medical practice. Consequently, medical responses were inconsistent, treatment was often informal, and physicians were often overwhelmed. Most crucially, official RAMC efforts to play down shell shock appeared as attempts to dismiss or deny the condition: the 'shaky Smith' was not always 'alright in a day or two'.

In the immediate post-war years the RAMC was feted for the way in which it had provided medical support for the victorious army, and the wartime conflicts and divisions were largely silenced. Yet men continued to suffer from war neurosis throughout the 1920s and they continued to receive inadequate treatment. The rhetoric of victory and of medical success sat uneasily alongside large numbers of mentally damaged veterans, and so the wartime marginalization of shell shock began to be interpreted as either neglect or cruelty. If men had lost faith in established institutions by the end of the war, this was in no small part due to the way in which one particular institution, namely the RAMC, mismanaged the problems of psychologically wounded men.[146] This mismanagement continued after the war as governments, despite being nervous of veteran radicalism, failed to deal effectively with the problems faced by shell-shocked men in the 1920s.

3

Lest We Forget

The subject of shell shock can not be referred to with any pleasure. All
would desire to forget it.[1]

LORD SOUTHBOROUGH, 1920

Lord Southborough's comments aptly reflect the government's attitude to
shell shock after the First World War: it was a distasteful subject that would be
preferable to forget. Consequently, in the early post-war period, government
activity was designed to ensure that most people could comfortably put shell
shock out of their minds. An official commission of enquiry was established
in 1920 to reassure the public that all issues connected with the diagnosis
and treatment of shell shock had been managed effectively. Since 1915 the
government had also developed a limited state welfare system to support men
where necessary, and to encourage the majority of veterans to find work and to
recreate their civilian lives. Yet despite these efforts, shell shock remained both
important and controversial throughout the 1920s. The issues surrounding shell-
shocked men were continually being entwined with other issues such as courts
martial, eugenics, the commemoration of the war and the inefficient bureaucracy,
which was responsible for health and welfare. Neither Lord Southborough's
Commission of Enquiry nor the newly developed pension system could dissipate
the popular association between the war, shell shock and injustice. Quite simply,
it was impossible to 'forget it'. On the contrary, the shell-shocked veteran began
to attain a particular cultural status during the early 1920s. We will begin to chart
this development by looking at representations of war and madness in literary
accounts of the war. We will then go on to look at the Government Commission
of Enquiry into Shell Shock, into the construction of early post-war memories
and into the workings of the post-war welfare system.

LITERATURE AND THE WAR

For a twenty-first-century observer, the importance of shell shock is most
immediately apparent in post-war literature and poetry. First World War

commemorations are always dominated by the poetry of Siegfried Sassoon and Wilfred Owen, and images from *All Quiet on the Western Front*. Yet veterans did not start to produce war novels until the later 1920s, and the now well-recognized canon of disenchantment literature did not emerge until at least ten years after the end of the war.[2] This is, in part, because many combatants did not know how to frame their responses. It is also because there was little public appetite for this kind of writing immediately after the war – while Owen's war poetry was published in 1920, for example, it was not widely read. It is only with hindsight that the literature of disenchantment has come to be seen as exemplifying the genuine First World War experience.

Much wartime, and early post-war, literature was produced by non-combatants. These writers were the first to make explicit links between the war, violence and insanity. As early as 1916, in a work intended to persuade the United States to enter the conflict, one of H. G. Wells's central characters forcefully expounds the connections between war and lunacy. In a letter from the Western Front, Hugh Britling complains to his father:

> This going to and fro and to and fro and to and fro; this monotony which breaks ever and again into violence – violence that never gets anywhere – is exactly the life that a lunatic leads. Melancholia and mania . . . it's just a collective obsession – by war.[3]

This tradition continued into the 1920s when many artists were starting to present the war as grotesque or mad. Count Psanek, D. H. Lawrence's wounded Austrian officer in *The Ladybird* (1923), spoke for many when he insisted that, 'The world I was sane about has gone raving.'[4]

In the post-war world, key female novelists also began to make shell shock central to their work.[5] In Virginia Woolf's *Mrs Dalloway* (1925), Septimus Smith, a young shell-shocked soldier, completely lost his identity as a result of war neurosis. In his wife's words, he was 'not Septimus now'.[6] In the novel, Septimus's mental state was widely misunderstood and the medical treatment he received was so poor that it led him to take his own life. Septimus is a memorable figure in this account of life in post-war London, and his death provides a backdrop that indicates the traumatic and irresolvable legacy of the Great War. In contrast, Rebecca West's *The Return of the Soldier* (1918) is a poignant account of an officer's war neurosis. In this novel, Christopher Baldry returns home having completely forgotten the previous 15 years of his life; as a result he reveals a hidden past that has a profound effect on his immediate family. After a cathartic experience he is 'returned' to the modern reality of his personal relationships, and his masculinity – albeit intrinsically flawed – reappears intact.[7] Medical professionals and family members appear largely ineffective in both accounts, but Baldry does have access to an environment that enables him to reclaim his adult self.

Female literary commentary on the war was not always welcomed. Falls argued that 'it is not the place of women to talk of mud; they may leave that to men who know more about it'.[8] It is certainly the case that characters such as Septimus Smith and Christopher Baldry do not provide us with the authentic voice of the war-shocked veteran: this is shell shock as perceived and interpreted by the outsider. In a significant contrast, *The Secret Battle* (1919), a soldier's tale of shell shock, is measured and restrained: the focus is on breakdown, not lunacy, and the tale of Harry Penrose, who remains largely composed throughout, compares starkly with the tortured insanity of Septimus Smith and Christopher Baldry.[9] Nevertheless, the female commentary has been particularly influential and it reflects two significant and enduring post-war motifs, namely the neglected shell-shocked soldier and the more privileged officer. These images have endured in both popular memory and academic debate, and one reason for this is that they contain some truth. Sick and wounded officers were treated better than men. This was, of course, the usual practice within the military hierarchy, and one can argue that it had been somewhat democratized as a result of the expansion of the officer ranks during the war. Nevertheless, much bitterness developed after the war when it became known that shell-shocked men were trying to live on inadequate pensions or were struggling to find state-assisted medical help. The wartime confusion over shell shock remained in both medical and lay circles. Philip Gibbs, a frontline reporter during the war, wrote as late as 1920 that doctors and generals were unsure about the origins of shell shock. They did not know whether the causes were physical or mental, or whether nervy or stolid men were most likely to be affected. Gibbs was left to conclude that as far as war neurosis was concerned, 'there is no law. Imagination, apprehension, are the Devil too, and they go with "nerves".[10]

SHELL-SHOCKED MEN: 'THE CHEERY CHAP' AND THE RURAL DREAM

By the mid-1920s shell shock was a culturally significant condition, as these enduring narratives attest. The continuing confusion about the origins of shell shock served only to enhance its significance: it became an ideal symbol for the incomprehensible madness of the First World War. Yet for shell-shocked men and their families, shell shock was not a cultural symbol; for them it was a potentially controversial illness that raised awkward questions and which was difficult to treat. The subject of shell shock achieved a very high political profile during the final years of the war and in the years immediately following the armistice. This was partly due to the association between shell shock and courts martial, but

there were also more general concerns about the way in which shell-shocked
soldiers were being treated.

An incident in 1918 indicates the extent to which shell shock could easily
provoke public interest. John Hodge (Coalition Labour, Manchester Gorton),
the Minister of Pensions, proposed to move mentally wounded men from a
dedicated Home of Recovery in Golders Green to a general hospital in the
country. He argued that this would be beneficial as 'the cheery chap might shed
some of the sunshine of his presence over those suffering from neurasthenia'.[11]
As we know, Collie supported the 'cheery chap' school of medicine, but many
others rejected it out of hand and Hodge's words provoked opposition from the
medical and lay communities alike. In particular, Elliot Smith was highly scornful
about the 'cheery chap' approach and publicly described Hodge's policy as 'one
of reaction and disaster'.[12] The men themselves also opposed the move, and sent
the following statement to the *Times*:

1 That we, the undersigned patients at 'The Home of Recovery', Golders Green,
   having benefited, and in many cases recovered, desire to express our contentment
   and our satisfaction with remaining in this institution, having the utmost
   confidence in the secretary, the medical officers, and the conditions generally of
   the hospital. Our past experiences in general hospitals have taught us to appreciate
   being separated from other cases, especially the so-called 'cheery man'.

2 That all patients are agreed that after their experience of other hospitals and the
   company of the so-called 'cheery chap' they prefer to risk the air raid results before
   that of going to another hospital.[13]

Clearly medical professionals were willing to challenge government policy on
this issue, as were mentally wounded men. Their complaints indicate that they
had firm ideas about the sort of treatment they required, and that they were
not afraid to articulate their grievances. The fact that *The Times* published their
letter is indicative of contemporary public sympathy: shell-shocked men could
feel confident about receiving public support, as did men who had entered the
services with a history of insanity. Milner had already called for these men to be
treated as generously as those who had joined the army with no such history, and
insisted that, 'I am sure I will have the public with me in this protest.'[14] There was
still a stigma attached to madness and to nervous breakdown but it is clear that
shell-shocked men were not completely dishonoured by their condition. In some
circumstances shell shock carried the same status as a physical wound.

The extent to which the medical profession had refined its understanding of
psychological casualties as a result of four years of industrial warfare is highly
debateable. On the home front, Maghull Red Cross hospital was staffed by a
'brilliant band of workers who at that time made [it] the centre for the study

of abnormal psychology'.[15] Elliot Smith and Pear were keen to disseminate the findings of their work at Maghull, and produced *Shell Shock and its Lessons* to promote a wider understanding throughout the medical community. Yet, as far as many ordinary soldiers were concerned, there had been little obvious change in approaches towards shell shock. A soldiers' magazine published as late as Christmas 1919 parodied advertisements for the 'miracle cures', which promised a solution for neurasthenia.

Silver, Balfour and Coy
Cash Chemists

All victims of NEURASTHENIA should try our MENIN REST CURE, and supplement it, when necessary, by a voyage in our luxurious STEAM YACHTS. FREE TICKETS are provided to the HOME and to the DOCTORS by MOTOR and RAIL.[16]

This soldiers' parody suggests a continuity: the same sort of advertisements, offering miracle cures to shell shock sufferers, had been published since the beginning of the war. It is significant that the author of this piece makes reference to the rest cure, a pre-war treatment for neurasthenia, which was obviously still being seen as part of the response to war neurosis after the armistice. Such advertisements in the press imply that little had changed in terms of a popular understanding of mental breakdown. Dr Cassell's remedies were still promising a cure for nervous breakdown while Dr William's pink pills were recommended for 'starved nerves'.[17] So although many historians stress changes in medical practice throughout the war, most soldiers and their families did not believe that the medical, political or military authorities had learnt anything significant from treating psychological casualties during wartime.

The most obvious and consistent characteristic of government plans for the post-war care of shell-shocked men lay in its commitment to a rural system of treatment. A sense of rural idealism dominated the home treatment system both during the war and afterwards. Since 1916 the 'Country Hosts Scheme' had provided shell-shocked men (primarily officers) with the opportunity to recuperate in a country house, and an underlying anti-urbanism pervaded many treatment regimes because the antidote to a brutal industrial war appeared to lie in the creation of a rural idyll. Collie, whose main commitment was to ensure that men moved back into the workplace as swiftly as possible, was convinced that work in the open air was particularly therapeutic for shell-shocked men. Men at his Homes of Recovery were encouraged to take part in light horticultural work, and representatives from the Ministry of Agriculture were engaged to give patients advice on agricultural matters. In this way Collie hoped both to assist the men's recovery and to provide them with the skills they would require in the workplace.[18] He also believed that many shell-shocked men were unable to return to their pre-war indoor occupations. Referring to men at his Homes of Recovery, Collie insisted that 'they will be required to change their occupation, and that change must be from an indoor to an outdoor employment'.[19]

Warwick Draper proposed an even more ambitious scheme in 1918. He wanted to set up village centres for the recuperation of recovering shell-shocked veterans. These centres would regenerate rural life and 'the quiet healthy environment of the country' would restore the men back to full health.[20] Draper's centres received full endorsement from the government who provided patients with treatment allowances for the duration of their visit.[21] Referring specifically to the conditions in and around Bristol, Norgate made it very clear that life in the countryside would provide a much needed moral purity as well as a material one. He advocated treating shell-shocked men in specially built homes in the country where they could 'turn their mind to better thoughts'.[22] The belief that shell-shocked men fared far better in a rural environment characterized American responses to post-war treatment too. An article in the American journal *Medical World* stressed the importance of treating shell-shock casualties in quiet places, away from big cities.[23] Fenton's work is of even greater significance. From 1918–1925, Fenton, a US Army doctor, conducted extensive research into a group of shell-shocked US veterans and came to the conclusion that agricultural work suited such men far more than any other kind of occupation.[24] Nevertheless, these findings were not universally accepted, and in Germany neurosis stations were sometimes placed near factories so that recovering patients could participate in useful industrial work.[25]

British medical and political authorities perceived the countryside in general to be healthier and more morally wholesome than the urban environment. Britain was an urban society by the early twentieth century, even though recruiting posters largely depicted a rural Britain, as if the values men were fighting to defend were better represented by pastoral symbols than by industrial images.[26] There were practical reasons for this entrenched anti-urbanism. Throughout the war many doctors had been concerned about the quality of recruits from the industrial towns, and so the rural treatment of shell shock can be set in a wider eugenic context. Mott, who pioneered much of the early research into shell shock, was a committed eugenicist and one of the earliest and most consistent contributors to the shell-shock debate. Like many others at the time, he was convinced that war neurosis was the result of an inborn predisposition and that 'military service did not produce true insanity, but only excited, revealed or exaggerated it'.[27] Milner may have called for equal sympathy for such men, but from the eugenicist perspective shell shock was not just another troublesome war wound; rather, it was symptomatic of far deeper problems within Britain, namely the numbers of young men who were so inherently weak that they had developed strong neurotic tendencies. The links between the pastoral nature of shell-shock treatment and the propagation of a belief in the pre-war idyll have already been mentioned. In addition, the provision of a rural system of care and treatment for mentally wounded men was all part of regenerating a Britain that had been damaged not just by the war but by the degeneracy of pre-war society.

THE GOVERNMENT COMMISSION OF ENQUIRY INTO SHELL SHOCK

The widespread public sensitivity to the issue of shell shock, and political concerns about possible miscarriages of justice in early wartime courts martial, forced the government to act.[28] An official inquiry into the treatment of shell shock was instituted in 1920. Lord Southborough chaired the commission and it sat from 1920–1922, a period in which a large number of men were seeking pensions for mental health problems, which they claimed were attributable to their war service. In response these men were met with a combination of official concern and administrative neglect. Shell shock as an issue was a high-profile condition, but shell-shocked patients themselves were often poorly treated – a situation that created some bitterness among the patients and their families. Of course, many men were facing serious welfare and financial problems as a result of the war, but shell-shocked soldiers became a highly distinctive group among them, partly because of the disparity between official displays of concern and their lived experience.

The records of Southborough's commission are crucial to any understanding of the shell-shock debate in the 1920s.[29] My aim here is to highlight the internal workings of the commission to indicate the primary purpose behind the investigation, which was to reassure the British public that all was well and to silence debate. Those men who had agreed to sit on the committee were generally cautious and certainly conscious that they were working in a politically sensitive environment. Thus Major Stirling questioned the advisability of publishing details about a non-commissioned officer who had been shot for desertion 'on the grounds that it might give rise to unfair criticism by extremists'.[30] An example of the sort of criticism that concerned him had been published in the *Daily Herald* in the previous year. It was about men who had been accused of cowardice, and who were still being held in British military prisons after the armistice. The author argued that they ought to be set free because the strains of modern warfare were such that some men's nerves were simply unable to withstand it, no matter how hard they tried. This article contains no criticism, implicit or otherwise, of the soldier who had 'tried and failed', but it did condemn those establishment figures who had willingly sent young men into war and then condemned them for being unable to deal with it. Particular censure was reserved for:

> the red-tabbed martinets of Whitehall, the armchair critics of Fleet Street, all that legion who shrieked jingoism in safety while their countrymen agonised on the battlefields who insist on their punitive pound of flesh, and who say in callous chorus, 'No pardon for cowards!'[31]

Committee members were aware that the treatment of shell shock could easily become entangled with wartime disciplinary issues and could then become a very obvious and effective focus for popular anger. They were also aware that many ex-soldiers felt unjustly treated and so the committee was keen to dilute any resentment. At the same time, members had to bear in mind that they were dealing with a victorious army. The political and military elites were ready formally to acknowledge that there were lessons to be learnt from the war, but this was not the moment for serious criticism of the army as an institution, nor of its practices on the field. In short, the army had to be treated with respect.

In some ways, soldiers benefited from this approach. Southborough's report did consider links between shell shock, cowardice and malingering but a successful army simply cannot be accused of endemic weaknesses. The committee was in a paradoxical position: its remit was to investigate a serious flaw in a victorious army. Consequently, the initial emphasis was on the number of men who did not succumb to shell shock, and Southborough insisted that, 'The ever present and glorious wonder is that the vast majority of them stood firm and sound in mind and body to the end.'[32] This paradoxical situation also produced a conceptual difficulty given that the treatment of shell shock was often perceived as a conflict between the individual soldier and the army. Shell-shocked soldiers could not be condemned outright, they had to be treated with some respect and understanding, yet at the same time official army policies could not be too roundly criticized either. The committee faced the task of explaining and advising without allocating blame, and the social and political context of their investigation ensured that its members endeavoured to explain shell shock within a socially conservative agenda.

The anti-militaristic *Labour Leader* had used shell shock as an issue with which to criticize Britain's role in the war. It was a radical and marginal voice, but by the early 1920s the Labour party in parliament had made public the link between shell shock and the unjustified executions at the front. Southborough acknowledged the legitimacy of this subject by his comment about Labour's 'special interest' in the question.[33] However, the committee knew that the army did not routinely execute all shell-shocked men. An article in *The Times* stressed that special medical boards had been constituted to discharge men from the army on account of shell shock, neurasthenia or related conditions, and insisted that, 'No soldier suffering from the above disabilities will be discharged by a medical board unless one member of the board is a neurologist and concurs in the finding.'[34] Similarly, the *Labour Leader's* critical attitude towards the court-martial system was not accepted by the committee. Viscount Haldane referred to courts martial as 'merciful tribunals' and claimed that the number of wartime executions had been 'improperly and wrongfully exaggerated', noting that although 3,076 death sentences were passed during the war, only 343 were actually carried out.[35] So while the committee adopted Labour's demand to question the army, it did not accede to the more radical demand of criticizing the army. It aimed instead to divorce the question of shell shock from the wider question of condemnation of the war.

There was a level of genuine governmental concern about the way in which shell-shocked patients had been and were being treated, but committee members were also motivated by other aims. They wanted to identify the most appropriate treatment regimes so as to be better prepared in future wars. They wanted to establish pension entitlement, and they also wanted to investigate the more delicate question of courts martial and the possible miscarriages of justice that may have taken place.

The officially stated aims of the committee were unequivocal and far reaching:

> To consider the different types of hysteria and traumatic neurosis, commonly called 'shell shock', to collate the expert knowledge derived by the service medical authorities and the medical profession from the experience of the war, with a view to recording for future use the ascertained facts as to its origin, nature and remedial treatment, and to advise whether by military training or education, some scientific method of guarding against its occurrence can be devised.[36]

This aim recognized that 'shell shock' was complex and presented itself in a variety of guises. Yet it was also an essentially optimistic approach, as it worked on the assumption that it was possible to collate the expert knowledge and arrange it in such a way as to prevent the condition occurring in great numbers in the future.

The processes behind creating the committee's report indicate the difficulties of defining and discussing shell shock, as well as its importance in terms of the memory and understanding of the Great War. On an official level, there was a genuine desire to explain, to understand and to learn from the experience. This was accompanied by a determination to remove the popular association between war, shell shock and injustice. When Lord Horne spoke in the House of Lords to support Southborough's call for a committee of enquiry into shell shock, he also suggested that 'the term "shell-shock" should not occupy people's minds too much'.[37] Horne's words exemplify the dilemma of this committee: it had been established to conduct a thorough investigation into what Southborough referred to as a 'horrible disorder',[38] yet, at the same time, the committee aimed to reassure people that soldiers had been treated well and that all related issues had been effectively managed. In short, the committee was to provide the final word on shell shock so as to allow the matter to become 'forgotten'. The ultimate failure to do so led to shell shock becoming the primary symbol of all that was traumatic, unjust and brutal about the 1914–1918 war.

The fear that shell-shocked men had been inappropriately treated was, in essence, a fear that shell-shocked men had been treated like mad men. As has already been mentioned, the War Office insisted as early as 1915 that shell-shocked men were not to be treated like ordinary lunatics. This sentiment endured, and was reiterated by Southborough in 1920:

> There was an impression abroad that men were sent to asylums who should not have been there, not because they were not insane, but because as their advocates stated, they had suffered from shell shock with or without wounds and were therefore the class of patient who should receive special treatment from the state and not be treated as ordinary insane persons.[39]

The objection to the lunatic asylum was rooted in the belief that it was ethically wrong to send soldiers to such a place. In addition, men were sometimes sent to asylums that were far from their own homes. Consequently, many such men felt extremely isolated. Mrs Clarke, one of the founders of the ESWS, spoke for many families when she complained about the practice, stating that 'under existing conditions the authorities can detain the man in any Asylum in any part of England and their relatives may only visit them by permission'.[40]

There was also a great deal of public and medical opposition towards treating shell-shocked men in general hospitals. In the main the opposition was based on medical grounds, but these men, like their fellows in the asylum, could also suffer from extreme isolation. The case of Private William Connett illustrates these difficulties well. Connett was a married man with four young children. He enlisted in June 1916, and was diagnosed as suffering from neurasthenia after a gunshot wound in March 1917. The family home was in Camberwell, London, but between May and October 1917 he was treated at general hospitals in Scotland.[41] Even if his wife had been able to afford the journey, it would clearly have been difficult, and contact with his family must have been severely limited during that time. Under these circumstances, the Connett family were unlikely 'to forget' shell shock or to ensure that it did not occupy their minds 'too much'.

The committee's broad conceptual approach to shell shock encouraged it to gather evidence from a variety of witnesses, including medical experts, officers, and men from the other ranks. Nor did Southborough want to limit the committee to British expertise. He sought help from Dr Roussy, a French expert, and the committee considered representatives from Serbia, Germany and the United States. There was also a limited recognition that men were not the only ones who could contribute, and Lady Astor suggested that the committee seek opinions from 'the women who have engaged in looking after shell-shock patients'.[42] In the event, although the report acknowledged that nursing sisters 'were of the greatest value', there was very little opportunity for women to voice their thoughts or to describe their experiences of wartime shell shock. Only one female witness was called: Miss Cockrell, late Matron of the Maudsley Neurological Hospital, gave a very short report that simply described the pitiful condition of the men in her care.[43]

The committee's laudable and ambitious aims were hindered by two problems. First, the work was not as straightforward as the initial definition implies. As was indicated in the previous chapter, in terms of both diagnosis and treatment there was a real lack of consensus among medical and military authorities. Thus combatants, army doctors and their civilian counterparts could recount a wide variety of different forms of shell shock. There were many shell-shock experts, but with such a diversity of opinion and knowledge, there was no consensus on analysis. In Viscount Haldane's words, 'A great many people think they know, but very few people do know.'[44] In addition, hospitals did not always categorize 'nervous' cases in the same way and there were also difficulties of terminology in that diagnoses were far from consistent. Pension records indicate men seeking medical care and pensions for a wide number of complaints such as neurasthenia, nervous debility, shell shock, mental weakness and anxiety neuroses. All of these could have been described as shell shock, and shell shock could always have been categorized as some other condition.

Secondly, the amorphous nature of the term 'shell shock' meant that it had become a useful category for a wide number of war-related complaints. Consequently, Southborough was determined to limit the aims of his committee so as not to become involved in controversy. The committee excited much public interest and Southborough received many letters that show how the question of shell shock as a medical-military matter prompted highly contentious questions. In response, Southborough made it clear that the committee would make no comment on the reform of lunacy laws, no comment on the decisions of the Army Medical Services, and would most certainly not reopen individual court-martial cases. Indeed, Southborough was so concerned about the political sensitivity of this issue that he wanted to examine the court-martial evidence in secret. He even suggested that the War Office withhold the men's names from committee members.[45] Although entitled to make recommendations suggesting modifications of military law, Southborough was sufficiently cautious in this respect as to insist that Sir John Goodwin, Director General of the Army Medical Services, should only answer questions in a personal, rather than an official capacity. He did not want Goodwin to be in the position of having to answer questions in a way that might compromise the Army Council.[46]

These openly expressed limitations were important, but possibly of greater importance were committee members' privately expressed aims. Members were constantly aware of the public interest in their report and wanted to ensure that the end result was accessible. In particular, Major Waring urged the committee to avoid too technical a terminology because it would be of no use to the general public.[47] From the start committee members aimed to create an educational document, 'so that the public may understand from the evidence received how far astray they have been.'[48] This avowedly educational aim was clearly designed to reassure the general public, particularly with regards to those soldiers who had been executed as a result of courts martial. Southborough wanted to examine the relevant cases 'with a view to satisfying the public mind and imagination regarding them . . . [this will] probably do a great deal to relieve public misapprehension'.[49] Southborough initially wrote 'quieting the public mind', and then crossed out 'quieting' and replaced it with the more robust 'satisfying'– clearly he was very concerned about the state of the public mind. The use of the word 'imagination' is also significant here because it implies that qualms about injustice were at least partially connected with flights of fancy. Moreover, concerns about 'imagination' reflected fears of urban degeneracy and a belief in the supposed solid good sense of the country man. Colonel Soltau, an officer who had worked as a consulting physician in France during the war and who advised the Ministry of Pensions afterwards, insisted that 'imaginative city dwellers were more liable to nervous manifestations than the agricultural type'.[50]

The committee's approach was diametrically opposed to the highly critical tone adopted by the *Labour Leader*. In a press release announcing the creation of the forthcoming committee, *The Times* medical correspondent wrote that 'the fact is likely to emerge' that those who were unfit before they joined the service were 'more likely to mental upset than men in full enjoyment of health'.[51] Such an attitude exonerated governmental and military authorities, and implied that there were innate weaknesses in those men who fell victim to nervous collapse. One gathers that it was an aim of the report to reassure people that shell-shocked men had been treated well and that the British Army could be trusted to administer martial law effectively and justly. Yet the committee faced a number of procedural difficulties throughout its existence. Members were initially perplexed by difficulties of definition. They were all agreed that the term shell shock was 'too vague' and 'vulgar', but unfortunately there was no readily available alternative. Thus they set out to investigate the phenomenon known as shell shock, but were unsure about the condition themselves. There were even those who wanted to avoid providing a definition at first because they might well need to change it later.[52]

Given the level of general uncertainty surrounding shell shock, many witnesses were disinclined to come forward, and on more than one occasion Southborough had to intervene personally to persuade someone to participate. Sir Hugh Sandham Jeudwine, General Officer Commanding, the 5th division, Curragh, was initially loath to participate, claiming that he had 'no practical experience whatever of even one case of shell shock'.[53] Jeudwine had been a divisional commander in France throughout the war and it is unlikely that he had failed to encounter shell shock at all. Southborough responded vigorously. He insisted that Jeudwine's experience would be invaluable, and at the same time he informed the reluctant witness that his own superior, the General Officer, Commanding-in-Chief of the forces in Ireland, could see no objections to his participation. Faced with such pressure, Jeudwine had little choice but to participate. Nevertheless, Jeudwine really did have little to contribute. He simply agreed with the widely held view that shell-shock victims were innately flawed in some way, and in a letter to Southborough he stated that, 'Breakdown was purely a matter of "nerves" and that the nervous state might be temperamental and pre-existent or induced by worry, hardship, danger or bad health, though in all these cases a temperamental predisposition probably existed in a dormant state.'[54] His final report was noticeably short. Southborough's personal intervention was even less successful with Charles Myers. When Myers was first invited to attend, he politely requested the committee to excuse him. When Southborough then approached him personally, he produced a transparent excuse that made plain his unwillingness to participate.[55] By this stage Myers was seriously disheartened with the whole medical-military organization because he felt that his own wartime work had received so little support. The committee had access to an old memorandum which Myers had produced during the war, but he answered none of their questions and provided no post-war reflections on the subject.

Many witnesses, whether individually sympathetic to victims of shell shock or not, accepted the notion articulated by Jeudwine, namely that there must have been some kind of predisposition towards nervous shock. This was the conventional medical wisdom of the day and it did not necessarily lead to a dismissive or unfeeling approach. Nevertheless, an unquestioning acceptance of the importance of predisposition, combined with a general suspicion of psychology, ensured that potential witnesses were reluctant to participate fully and many were worried that the questions were too technical. Certainly the committee was forced to note that some witnesses were 'frightened' by the questions.[56] There were 38 questions in all, some of which were in several parts.

In response to witnesses' concerns, the committee decided that they did not all have to respond to every question. Rather, they were directed towards those questions that were appropriate to their expertise. Nevertheless, there were many questions, such as the one following, which required detailed knowledge and a high level of experience.

> Q6. What instructions did you receive with regard to estimating the nervous and mental stability of recruits? How far was such estimation practicable? On what observations did you base the conclusions you reached? Were you able to give effect to these conclusions with a view to recruits being suitably drafted?[57]

Witnesses were also worried about the way in which enquiries could potentially lead them into criticizing military procedure. Men who had established respectable military careers for themselves were certainly deterred by the fear of appearing unorthodox or critical of the establishment. Dr Wilson, an army doctor, initially did not want to participate, claiming that he was 'too heratical [sic] on some questions'.[58] Similarly, Major Adie was reluctant to have his evidence made public.[59] The responses of these men indicate the extent to which shell shock remained a serious and contentious political issue in the early 1920s.

Several witnesses were also discouraged by the questions which demanded a high level of abstraction. Question 13, for example, simply asks, 'What do you understand by the term "shell shock"?'[60] Many army doctors felt simply unqualified to provide an adequate answer to such a question. There were also procedural difficulties because a number of individuals and organizations felt that they did not have the time to commit themselves to a long-running committee of enquiry. Some military commanders were certainly unwilling to let their officers spend long in considering the committee's questions.[61] Perhaps this was because the question of shell shock seemed unimportant, or perhaps they believed that the subject of shell shock was so controversial that they did not want their officers to be involved with it.

Southborough wanted the opinion of experts to be complemented by the opinion of men who had suffered, and so thought it wise to include some personal testimony in the report. However, there was one critical difference between these cases and those who were physically wounded. The committee agreed that no patient under treatment could act as a witness, possibly as a result of government pressure: the Minister of Pensions, Sir James Ian Stewart MacPherson (Coalition Liberal, Ross and Cromarty) had informed them that it was 'not desirable that pensioners actually under treatment in hospital should be called as witnesses'.[62] Shell-shocked men were therefore excluded despite the fact that neurosis does not necessarily render a man either unintelligible or unreliable, as the men from Golders Green had so ably demonstrated in the spring of 1918.

Furthermore, those men who had been apparently quite cured of shell shock were often reluctant to talk about their experiences and the committee initially found it difficult to find appropriate witnesses. In November 1921, of six ex-patients who had been identified as willing participants, five were either unable to attend or had declined the invitation for some reason. As a result, the meeting scheduled for 24 November 1921 was cancelled.[63] In the final report, the committee heard evidence from 59 witnesses, only 4 of whom were pensioners who had suffered from war neurosis in the past; all the other witnesses were largely drawn from the medical and military elites.

REMEMBERING THE WAR AND MANAGING THE VETERAN: COMMEMORATION AND WELFARE

The immediate post-war treatment of shell-shocked men raises two issues to consider: the wider attempt at rehabilitation (to be discussed later), and the creation of popular First World War memories and commemorations. Throughout the early 1920s, people in cities, towns and villages throughout Britain raised funds for war memorials, and the first remembrance service was instituted on Armistice Day 1919. This tradition lapsed during the Second World War but was reinvigorated in the 1990s and is now an important annual event. Current British remembrance symbols were also created during the immediate post-war period, most notably the Flanders Poppy, which is now worn to commemorate all British war dead. Public remembrance ceremonies were designed to preserve individual memories of loved ones who had died, but they also had a more general and collective injunction: remembering the war also involved remembering the main lesson of the war, namely to 'never allow such a catastrophe again'.[64] The way in which the war was publicly remembered could easily conflict with private memories. There were, of course, wide varieties of war experiences and there were many diverse war memories; nevertheless, publicly expressed memories of the war tended to be homogenous.[65] In addition, inscriptions on British war memorials usually make reference to the 'honoured', the 'proud' and the 'glorious'. This language is neither angry nor regretful.[66] In stark contrast, the memories of shell-shocked men were fearful, and their nightmares, traumas and physical tics portrayed a different, darker memory of the war.

Many British war memorials depict soldiers as boys rather than as men. The images commemorate the giving of life, and the importance of remembering sacrifice.[67] This sort of memorial does not celebrate martial vigour; rather, it commemorates the sacrifice of youthful innocence. From this perspective the soldiers are all victims of the war, rather than grown men who have been trained to kill as effectively as the enemy.[68] Unwittingly these images resembled the representations of shell-shocked soldiers during the war. Popular accounts usually presented the shell-shocked soldier as a wounded boy – the shell-shocked young officer was likely to attract public sympathy whereas an old soldier who had lost his mind was a more threatening figure. Yet not all shell-shocked soldiers were officers and the average age of the shell-shocked man was 26 years, hardly a 'boy' by any definition.[69] Furthermore, all shell-shock victims grew older. As we will see, this was to create some representational problems later on in the decade when war-neurotic veterans clearly needed help but they could no longer be presented as nerve-wracked boys.

The most important post-war inscription was undoubtedly 'Lest we forget'. All of the campaigns, the monuments and the memorials were created so as to ensure that no one forgot either the war or its lessons. Yet at the same time, governments, business men and other sections of the community were calling for a return to 'normalcy', a situation which implies that the horrors of war had to be forgotten, at least to an extent. In some senses, forgetting the war was not remiss, it was vital for psychological survival. As Winter has observed, 'those who couldn't obliterate the nightmares were locked in mental asylums throughout Europe'.[70] Most veterans and their families therefore faced deep contradictions as they attempted to create some kind of psychological balance: they tried to remember the war at the same time as repressing those thoughts that were too painful to manage. In Sassoon's words, 'Remembering, we forget much that was monstrous.'[71]

The shell-shocked veteran occupied an important and paradoxical position in initial post-war memories. For some medical and military commentators shell-shocked men were symbols of degeneracy, especially of the urban decay which had depleted Britain's fighting stock. For others, shell-shocked men symbolized the youth and innocence of the British troops who had seen action. The memory of a killed or wounded boy is more poignant than that of a killed or wounded soldier. On another level, shell-shocked men were the ones who really did remember the war. They physically embodied the slogan 'Lest we forget', although their attendant sufferings made it plain that some memories really were too painful to remember. The conflict between remembering and forgetting was reflected in different approaches to treatment. Collie's 'common sense' attitude was based upon men forgetting their troubles whereas Rivers believed that it was impossible to banish some memories, and that patients had to learn how to make them into 'tolerable, if not even pleasant, companions instead of evil influences'.[72] This process by which individually traumatized veterans had to learn how to manage their war memories was reflected in society at large as all who had been affected by the war struggled to remember the war's primary lesson while forgetting those memories that were too painful to become 'pleasant companions'.

After the Great War many wounded soldiers returned home to an uncertain future, but shell-shocked soldiers occupied a particularly difficult position. The atmosphere was one of respect for the victorious army as well as concern about the problem of psychological casualties at the highest governmental level. Yet concern was compounded by economic uncertainty. Many ex-soldiers, both officers and men, had to be retrained. This was an expensive process and one that occupied a great deal of government attention because the alternative, namely large numbers of unemployable men, would have created an even more serious drain on public finances. However, the issues with retraining men with mental health problems were generally more complex than those associated with the retraining of physically wounded men. Moreover, as Table 1 illustrates, the government was still unclear about the process of defining and categorizing men with war neurosis.

Table 1 Officers and men pensioned for disability, 4 August 1914–31 January 1918[73]

	Officers		Men			
	Army	Navy	Army	Navy	**Total**	%
Nervous diseases, shell shock	258	9				
Neurasthenia	1,649	259	29,696	2,136	**34,471**	6.2
Miscellaneous	372	92				
Insanity	150	31	4,462	826	**5,469**	0.9

The government had always insisted that shell-shocked soldiers were not insane, and official categories reflect this distinction. However, the categories of nervous diseases, shell shock and neurasthenia were collapsed for the other ranks of both services, and some casualties were unhelpfully described as 'miscellaneous'. Clearly doctors attempted to apply more precise definitions when officers were concerned. According to these figures, men with nervous complaints accounted for 6.2 per cent of all pensionable veterans, a significant minority and one that warranted government attention.[74] Yet diagnostic confusion endured at all levels of the pensions and welfare system throughout the 1920s. After the war, the vast majority of nervous cases were categorized as 'neurasthenia', but there were also a variety of other terms, such as 'anxiety neurosis', 'debility', and 'nervous debility'. This was clearly a continuation of the lack of clarity, which had bedevilled the system during the war years, and there is clear evidence of diagnostic slippage within individual patient records. Walter John Collins, a motor mechanic from

Chiswick, joined the army in 1917, and was classified as B2, suffering from
Disorderly Action of the Heart (DAH) in December 1918. His pension award
sheet describes his condition as 'DAH' in October 1919. When he was re-boarded
in April 1920 he was described as suffering from neurasthenia, but in October
1920 he was again referred to as 'DAH'.[75] Collin's symptoms remained the same
throughout this process, and there is no indication that the medical diagnosis
changed during this time, simply that the terms 'neurasthenia' and 'DAH' were
being used interchangeably and without comment. This is one of the reasons
for the popular and professional retention of the term 'shell shock': no singular
term, phrase or description was able to replace it. The diagnosis of 'neurasthenia'
proliferated. As has already been shown, before the war the term neurasthenia
was routinely applied to working-class men – and associated with fecklessness –
but during the war it was almost exclusively reserved for officers. However, after
the war, the term was then widely applied to men from the other ranks too. The
label of neurasthenia denoted status during the war – certainly neurasthenic
officers were given more privileged treatment than were shell-shocked or
'nervous' men – yet by the early 1920s, the category of neurasthenia had ceased
to confer much advantage.

It is important to reiterate that even as Southborough's highly prestigious
enquiry was taking place, many soldiers and their families were suffering as
a result of scanty treatment regimes and inadequate pension provision. Long
before the end of the war, it had been clear that the treatment of all disabled and
discharged veterans was a potentially volatile issue, and this tension remained vital
throughout the interwar period. In March 1918 there had been a demonstration
of discharged sailors and soldiers at the Albert Hall, and later in the same month
there was a mass rally of wounded ex-soldiers.[76] On an even more contentious
note, the 1921 Armistice Day celebrations were disturbed by demonstrations
of disaffected ex-servicemen, and the 'savage and satirical' wreaths that they
left at the cenotaph were deemed to be so provocative that the police removed
them.[77] In the 1920s, unemployed ex-servicemen would sometimes demonstrate
at Armistice Day events. By this stage the destitute shell-shocked soldier had
become a familiar and visible figure, and shell shock could form part of the
repartee of the post-war soldier-beggar. An ex-soldier, begging from theatregoers
in London's West End, prefaced his act by announcing that, 'I served through the
whole of the war till I was shell-shocked at Delville Wood. Now I have a small
pension and I also have a wife and child.'[78] Such public presentations of the figure
of the shell-shocked beggar indicates yet again that mentally wounded men
were not completely stigmatized: clearly this man believed that he would attract
sympathy – and even money – by describing himself as shell shocked. Certainly
this short speech signifies that the term 'shell shock' was publicly recognizable,
that the condition was at least partly understood by the general public, and

that it was quite feasible to claim that a government pension was inadequate in such circumstances. Walter Cook, who served as a stretcher-bearer and a medical orderly on the Western Front, depicted a bleak picture of men defined by their limitations long after the war was over. Still using the term 'shell shock', he described the condition in terms of what its sufferers could not do: they had an 'inability to speak coherently and inability to keep still'.[79] He then went on to say that, 'Years afterwards I worked in an institution in the north of England and there were three shell shock cases there, and that was well after the war.'[80] It sounds very much as though the men in this particular institution were not recovering and were not being treated.

This public awareness of poor treatment worried the government. The authorities were well aware of the potential political power of the disgruntled veteran because the ending of the Great War had been accompanied by post-war revolutions in the defeated countries, as well as an increase in popular radicalism among the victor nations. As a result, even victorious governments were fearful of worker agitation. In Britain a large number of men had either volunteered or been conscripted for war service. The subsequent widening of the franchise meant that all of these men were entitled to vote in the post-war world, and it was not unreasonable to assume that many ex-soldiers felt entitled to make a real political impact. Also, a number of commentators were aware that pre-war Britain had been a place of great social conflict. Many of these conflicts had been postponed during the war, but they had not been resolved and so calls for a return to 'normalcy' were tempered by an awareness that the pre-war Golden Age was mythical. An article in the *Contemporary Review*, aimed at a cultured and educated audience, makes this point plain:

> The fact is that to the social grievances which almost culminated in 1914 in a war of classes in the United Kingdom, the citizen-soldier has added the many wrongs, or supposed wrongs, of the past four years.[81]

Authorities were strongly motivated by the concern that pre-war class conflict could merge with grievances accumulated during the war and produce a post-war crisis of unparalleled proportions.

Even so, this very obvious post-war distress should not obscure the fact that the wartime government had taken welfare seriously, and there had been a real and pronounced increase in welfare spending throughout the war.[82] From 1915 onwards the government had committed unprecedented resources to hospitals, pensions, grants, allowances and retraining schemes. The state did not simply leave welfare and health care to the free market or to private charity, and it was prepared to initiate change. It can be argued that servicemen and their families were not properly compensated for the sacrifices they had made, but nevertheless, the state did accept a far wider set of responsibilities than had previously been considered possible, and the link between warfare and welfare has long been made explicit.

Post-war welfare policies reflected these cultural shifts, and during the 1920s well-respected, socially conservative figures began to argue for greater state intervention in this sphere. Welfare had previously been the preserve of the Liberal and Labour parties but the plight of ex-soldiers ensured that the traditional right became vocal about the importance of state support too. Field Marshall Sir Douglas Haig, commander of the British Expeditionary Force for most of the war, made it clear that he was 'appalled' by the inadequacy of the state pension system.[83] The following exchange in the House of Commons indicates that it was hard to maintain a traditional opposition to state welfare in the post-war political environment. In 1922, Sir John Ross, the Lord Chancellor of Ireland, spoke harshly about the burden of public assistance and explained how the taxpayer was suffering as a result. He then continued in heavily ideological terms: 'Social reform . . . that is what it is called by those who like it; those who disliked it called it "socialism", those who detested it called it "Bolshevism".' In reply, Hilton Young, the Liberal member for Norwich, asked if any member desired a reduction in war pensions. Ross did not answer and the debate was effectively over.[84] It had become impossible to discredit state welfare completely, even by associating it with Bolshevism; all accepted the legitimacy of state support for veterans. Some Conservative and Unionist MPs were even prepared to accept a level of compulsion in post-war employment schemes for ex-servicemen. Employers willing to provide opportunities for disabled ex-servicemen could sign up to a voluntary register, which was administered by the state. Yet public disquiet continued because it was widely believed that too many employers were unwilling to cooperate and that some kind of a compulsory system was required. Major F. B. Cohen, the Unionist MP for Fairfield, Liverpool, acknowledged that the spirit of compulsion was 'foreign' to most British people, but also argued that employers should be compelled to take on a certain number of disabled ex-servicemen. The principle of voluntarism had to be sacrificed 'to help the man who fought'.[85] Dr Thomas James Macnamara, (Liberal, Camberwell North West), the Minister for Labour, resisted this pressure by arguing that such compulsory schemes had caused friction between employers and the government in Italy, Poland and Germany.[86] Yet the mere fact that prominent, socially conservative members of the elite were arguing for greater state involvement indicates a significant change in establishment attitudes towards state welfare. Thus, post-war governments were aware that veterans' welfare had to be taken seriously, yet at the same time they were reluctant to commit themselves to unlimited spending in this sphere. The period of reconstruction was a difficult one, and economic uncertainties were compounded by the trade depression that began to affect Britain's economy from the autumn of 1920. As a result, a large number of ex-servicemen feared – and often experienced – unemployment and poverty throughout the interwar years. Governments worried that these men would develop the habits of welfare dependency, and as the new Ministry of Health was also responsible for the Poor Law, the issues of health, welfare and the management of poverty became inextricably entwined.[87]

The government had been committed to a policy of reconstruction before the end of the war, and the slogans of the 1918 election promised a 'land fit for heroes'. Nevertheless, the heroes were not expected to be passive recipients of this new land, they were to play an active part in creating it. The Great War was the 'War for Civilization', but the military victory was only one stage in the creation of a greater civilization and the government was worried that a post-war Britain would be 'peopled by those who were crippled, half-crippled or showing little outward trace, though nonetheless secretly deprived of health'.[88] This was reflected in Lloyd George's comment that Britain was 'a C3 nation'.[89] The army used the term 'C3' to describe men with 'marked physical disabilities' or 'evidence of past disease'. Worryingly the National Service Medical Boards had categorized 31–32 per cent of examined men in this category: clearly this could not be the basis for a stronger, prouder, reinvigorated country.[90] The government's message to disabled veterans was plain: the state was prepared to recognize their contribution to the war effort and it accepted a level of responsibility for the care and treatment of disabled ex-soldiers. However, at the same time, official and semi-official comments were unambiguous about the ex-soldier's duties: with the exception of those men in truly extreme circumstances, the post-war veteran could not expect the state to provide for him fully, and any support he did receive depended on his ability to demonstrate that he was an appropriately masculine citizen, fully conscious of his responsibilities. The nature of war neurosis with its attendant patterns of recovery and relapse meant that shell-shocked veterans often found it especially difficult to meet these criteria.

The identity of the wounded veteran was not solely formed by his war experiences, but included his expectations of life as a civilian too. Britain was not a parliamentary democracy before the First World War; on the contrary, the franchise was extremely limited. Nevertheless, workers, even non-enfranchised workers, had been increasingly affected by the ideals of civil society since the late nineteenth century, and they had since become determined to secure the right to health and welfare provision.[91] Thus, wounded veterans were also citizens, workers, husbands, fathers, ratepayers and so on. In many ways the wartime welfare system was a clear response to the novel conditions of prolonged mass warfare, but state welfare was not completely unprecedented. It grew not just out of total war, but also out of the long tradition of state support for those in need. There had been relief for the poor in England and Wales since the sixteenth century and this collective care had required the recipient to fulfil certain categories.[92] Some of these categories were mechanical, such as the criteria for residency, whereas others were more clearly moral, such as the traditional distinction between the deserving and the undeserving poor. Developments in welfare since the nineteenth century, whether state- or charity-led, had been predicated on the model of the male breadwinner and female carer. In this way, welfare reinforced patriarchal values.[93] The 1911 Insurance Act, the centrepiece of pre-war Liberal reforms, was organized so that working men contributed payments so as to provide resources for periods of need. The assumption behind this legislation was that a man would only require welfare as a temporary respite while he was recovering his position as the family provider. During and after the Great War it became obvious that some men would never again be able to support their families without help, yet still the government continued to stress the expectation that all but the most extreme cases should aim for recovery, accompanied by retraining if necessary.

So although the ex-serviceman could legitimately perceive himself to be a citizen-soldier claiming his rights, those dispensing the welfare wanted to ensure that he occupied all the traditionally appropriate moral categories before gaining any benefits. The veteran had to demonstrate that he was committed to fulfilling his role as either family breadwinner or self-supporting single male. The state did accept responsibility for the care of wounded veterans, but key components of the state's responsibility were defined as follows:

a. the restoration of the man's health where practicable
b. the provision of training facilities, if he desires to learn a new trade
c. the finding of employment for him when he stands in need of such assistance[94]

The state's attitude towards disabled soldiers was voiced most clearly in *Recalled to Life*, a government-supported fortnightly magazine aimed at soldiers, sailors and those concerned with their welfare. At the same time as recognizing veterans' pension rights, the government made it clear that both honour and practicality demanded that a veteran should not live on his pension. Much has been written about war as a test of masculinity, but the wartime government presented reintegration into civilian life as a test of masculinity too.[95] In June 1917 the editorial proclaimed that 'a disabled sailor or soldier is not less of a man, but more of a man than he was before the war'.[96] Subsequently the magazine went on to emphasize the way in which the government had created opportunities for retraining, and printed stories about successfully rehabilitated disabled veterans. These stories were often presented in highly gendered terms as disabled men were given the opportunity to learn skills that set them apart from women workers. As one article made clear: 'It's the skilled men who are wanted. Men who can do *men's* work, and not those that do the work which can be done by women.'[97] Moreover, many men seemed disinclined to engage in apparently feminine occupations. Staff on War Pensions Committees complained that disabled men would not take the opportunity to learn military embroidery 'in spite of inducements and the prospects of good remuneration' it remained unappealing because it was 'women's work'.[98] *The Times* correspondent would not criticize these men for trying to maintain some personal dignity and concluded that this attitude was understandable 'in men rendered sensitive by disablement'.[99]

It was obviously possible for wounded men, especially those who were mentally wounded, to perceive themselves as unmasculine because of their disabilities. However, the gender boundary was maintained by those men who could learn new and appropriately masculine skills. The post-war welfare system was based on the belief that men, no matter how disabled, would maintain their position in the gendered hierarchy and would remain as family providers. Those in authority also attempted to bolster the status of disabled ex-soldiers by maintaining a clear boundary between the positions of those who had fought and those who had not. That this was not purely an issue of gender was made clear by Captain Tudor-Reese, the Liberal member for Barnstaple, who responded angrily to rumours that conscientious objectors had been employed to supervise the training of wounded veterans. In asserting that 'conscientious objectors were not entitled to associate with decent men', Tudor-Reese was working to ensure that all veterans retained a valued position in the post-war social hierarchy.[100]

So members of late wartime and post-war governments wanted to maintain the prestige of the veteran, but they also wanted to ensure that ex-soldiers were clear about their own responsibilities. In order to achieve these aims, the government used the pages of *Recalled to Life* to instruct men about the particular nature of wartime pensions. While stressing the veterans' rights and the duty of the state, articles also made it plain that life on a pension would be untenable. Using the words of a serviceman to convince other servicemen, the journal printed these remarks from J. A. Bennet, a sergeant at Queen Mary's Workshop in Brighton.

> Live on your pension, eh! But can you: think again, *can you*? Have you realised how the purchasing value of a sovereign has deteriorated as compared with pre-war times? It's only worth about 12/6 nowadays, and we can not say what will happen as regards price in the future ... Your pension is not meant to live on; it is a pension for services rendered, not a retiring pension. To live on your pension is out of the question, it would be a mere existence ... Do you want to be a respectable self-supporting citizen or a lazy good-for-nothing, depending on charity? Do you want to live comfortably, to have, and to save money, or lead a miserable, grovelling existence?

The message here is emphatic. This was not presented as an instruction from the government, which could have been construed as patronizing; it was presented as a man-to-man talk, as simple advice from one soldier to another. Bennet also pointed out the impracticalities of living on a pension, although he did so without implying any dereliction of duty on the government's part. It was impossible to live on a pension, not because the government had been miserly, but because Britain had suffered from inflation, and in any case, it was simply not that kind of a pension. That he had to be so explicit about the nature of the pension suggests that the government believed many men were genuinely unclear about the status and the function of their pension awards. Bennet finished with an appeal to self-respect and pride. Those disabled men who were not prepared to rehabilitate themselves would lead shameful lives, despite their contribution to the war. However, it was particularly difficult for mentally wounded veterans to retrain and thus remake their lives in this fashion because of the stigma and the misunderstanding surrounding mental illness. Mr T. Sanders, the Secretary of the Ex-Services' Employment Department, explained that many employers were willing to engage physically disabled men, but they were reluctant to consider the mentally wounded. 'The men we find employers fight shy of most,' Sanders told a reporter, 'are "nerve" cases – shell shock etc. It is easier to fix up a one-legged man.'[101]

The material and ideological limitations of the welfare system were compounded by bureaucratic difficulties. In 1919 the War Pensions Committees had stopped dealing with pension provision, and the responsibility had been transferred to local Labour Exchanges. The great majority of staff on the War Pensions Committees were extremely angry with this exchange of responsibilities and so failed to communicate properly with the Labour Exchanges. In addition, unemployed ex-servicemen were often resentful because they were not entitled to any allowances for three days after registering at the employment exchange. As a result, there was serious unrest among ex-soldiers in this period, and the Ministry of Pensions acknowledged that the turmoil was mainly due to 'want of co-operation' between government agencies.[102] There were also poor communications between the Ministry of Labour and the training agencies, all of which resulted in long delays for resettlement grants and training schemes. Complaints came from all over the United Kingdom, but unrest was particularly evident in large industrial centres, and caused authorities to become anxious about the revolutionary tendencies of disaffected ex-soldiers.

The pension officials' frequent lack of sympathy was also an issue, and significantly it was one which was taken seriously, although most officials were keen to point out that the problem was largely structural and so did not reflect a hostile attitude from their staff. The Ministry of Pensions in Birmingham blamed the way in which the discharged men had to deal with a variety of agencies. As a result 'each department is unable to take a comprehensive view of the needs of the man'.[103] The consensus was that applicants were treated sympathetically at an individual level but that lack of cooperation between medical staff, the Ministry of Labour, and Pensions Committees resulted in confusion, misinformation and delay. This problem also indicates the extent to which post-war difficulties were intimately connected with pre-war systems. The local committee in Portsmouth criticized the way in which the pensions and training agencies were based on the poor foundations provided by the pre-war Labour Exchanges, which dealt with the supply and demand of labour in a very limited way. Moreover, their premises were usually in very poor condition and their staff 'were badly paid and drawn from the wrong class'.[104] Staff at the local committee described the way in which 3,000 discharged men were registering daily at an exchange with insufficient space to accommodate 100. Men had to queue all the way down the main street in all weathers; furthermore, the number was expected to increase to 5,000. Understandably the men were pessimistic about their chances of finding employment.[105] These complaints indicate the context in which men were trying to re-establish their civilian lives. The authorities were dealing with ex-soldiers in a way which was reminiscent of the treatment meted out to the pre-war unemployed. For shell-shocked men who were easily confused, the system proved to be unworkable because of the widespread chaos in the offices. In the words of one government clerk, the claims section was a 'world of wildest melodrama'.[106] Those who felt nervous or mentally unstable were singularly ill-equipped to deal with this situation.

The *Labour Leader* had long protested about the way in which disabled soldiers and their families were treated, particularly in the context of the courts-martial controversy in 1917. Populist publications on both the right and the left tried to present themselves as the soldier's champion. The socialist *Daily Herald* ran a regular feature entitled 'Tommy's Troubles'. Men were encouraged to write in with their complaints – which were mainly connected with pensions and the minutia of demobilization – and the paper either advised them or contacted relevant bodies on their behalf. *John Bull* ran 'Tommy and Jack', a similar column which was 'conducted' by Haig, who had become President of the British Legion and the Remembrance League after the war. 'Tommy and Jack' publicized deserving cases of need among the veteran community. Sometimes they gave men and their families money from the Unity Relief Fund, and sometimes the British Legion intervened directly to obtain pension reassessments or retraining grants. Significantly, the shell-shocked man was a regular feature of this column; his mental condition did not dishonour him in any way. Yet it was not only those on the political extremes who were angry about the treatment meted out to veterans in general and shell-shocked men in particular. In the same year, an angry letter to *The Times* highlighted the plight of 'nerve shattered pensioners', and demanded, 'If they are suffering from curable disorders, why are they not cured?'[107] Despite the obvious social stigma attached to mental health problems, there was broad support, at least in principle, for state-funded welfare and rehabilitation programmes after the war.

The bureaucratic confusion that bedevilled the pension system made it hard to rehabilitate men successfully. However, the post-war pension system was also restricted by other problems, namely stringent financial restraints and contemporary establishment fears about class conflict. Collie, renowned for his preoccupation with malingering, highlighted the way in which class tension related to professional rivalry over the care and control of disabled men, and complained that, 'It is unfortunately the case that many low class GPs on the Panel of the National Insurance Act conspire with working-class patients to obtain false certificates, and to encourage this would mean a vast unnecessary expenditure of public money.'[108] Collie was not simply worried that the money would be wasted. He was afraid that the money would be wasted as the result of a class-based conspiracy which supported malingering. As a result, those formulating pension policies concentrated primarily on encouraging men to seek employment. If men were unable to find suitable employment, in some circumstances they could receive grants to help them to retrain or to develop a small business.

Problems in the system were aggravated by the motivations and internal workings of the medical boards. War-injured veterans had to appear before medical boards at regular intervals in order to ensure their pension entitlements, but the boards were often staffed by RAMC officers and were generally characterized by an atmosphere of suspicion. Even if individual doctors were highly sympathetic, the structure was one which frequently provoked distress and was highly unlikely to induce a sense of comfort and security in pensioners. The first pension recommendation could not extend beyond three months, a second examination could extend that period for a further three months, but any further extension had to be recommended by a medical referee.[109] The process was designed to discourage malingering; however, it also condemned the ill or wounded man to a continual series of highly formal medical boards, with all the accompanying strain and anxiety that such an examination entailed. In practice men were often awarded pensions for 6 or 12 months. Nevertheless, many pensioners spent the immediate post-war years in a position of real economic uncertainty, and although it was possible to appeal against a board's decision, the appeals process was long-winded and cumbersome. An appeal could also be a disheartening procedure. In 1922, of 1,391 cases coming before the Newcastle Appeal Tribunal, only 229 were successful.[110] This may well have been an extreme case, but in such circumstances many veterans were reluctant to embark on the appeals procedure.

All disabled men had to deal with this unwieldy system but shell-shocked men were in a particularly difficult position. Life was especially hard for those who did not develop serious symptoms until some time after the war. Bertram Cameron made a claim two years after being discharged from the army. In a letter to the Ministry of Pensions he described how he had begun to develop 'a shaky condition' during his service in France but that he had not claimed before 'as I quite thought a few months of civilian life would put me right'.[111] In such a situation the burden of proof was tremendous. Shell-shocked men were also at a disadvantage because of the prevalent medical assumption that psychological casualties had carried some kind of pre-war disposition. Doctors had to decide whether a man's disability was either attributable to war service or whether it had been merely aggravated by the war, and even where medical records indicate that a man's pre-war health was good, pensioners' conditions were deemed to have been only aggravated by the war. Such a judgement did not affect the amount of money a man received because financial awards were based upon levels of disability, but the whole process may well have affected morale and contributed to the impression that the government was not prepared to recognize the extent of men's war injuries.[112] In addition, pension awards tended to decline after each medical board, even if men claimed that their symptoms remained the same. So the situation was such that even if a man was awarded a pension, he could not rely on the government accepting full responsibility for his disability, and he certainly could not assume long-term financial support.

Although the welfare system was essentially state-led, discharged men could seek further help at a local level. Discharged disabled men appeared before local committees who were empowered to provide assistance from locally subscribed funds or to recommend that cases receive assistance from national funds. The committees were based on neighbourhoods rather than on any military or hospital-based units, and this was presented as a way of humanizing a potentially cold, bureaucratic system.

> These committees are as a rule, very human informal bodies. When the man comes in to put his case the chances are that some member of the committee knows him or his wife; a friendly talk ensues, and gradually the man's needs and wishes for the future are elicited, pertinent suggestions are made to help him, and he goes out with the feeling that he has friends who will see to it that the best possible is done for his welfare.[113]

This was not necessarily the case: local committees may well have also been hotbeds of neighbourhood intrigue and ancient, unresolved grudges. Nevertheless, they certainly had the potential for a level of compassionate familiarity. Yet this opportunity was largely denied to psychologically damaged men because such men did not go to ordinary local committees for advice on pensions or further treatment; rather, their cases were managed by a special medical board presided over by Collie. The board's headquarters were in London and it dispatched members to examine discharged neurasthenics in other towns.[114] It certainly can be argued that these committees may have had access to more specialized information than their local counterparts, yet it is also the case that their knowledge of the local community would have been less and that going to a 'special' medical board may well have attracted some stigma.

The shell-shocked man was part of the wider community of discharged disabled veterans, all of whom had to rely on a state that provided only variable or partial support. Yet this chapter has indicated that mentally wounded men came to occupy a special, and possibly peculiar, position in many ways. Shell shock could be seen as an honourable wound but shell-shocked men were often stigmatized as either mad or degenerate. Furthermore, neither the committee of enquiry nor the pension system could dissipate the popular association between the war, shell shock and injustice. This was the reason for the establishment of the Ex-Services' Welfare Society (ESWS), which was set up to help veterans who had been confined to lunatic asylums. So despite Lord Southborough's wishes, shell shock could not simply be forgotten and it remained politically controversial throughout the 1920s.

4

Lunatics and Lunacy Reform

*The Marquess of Lansdowne said he was convinced from what he had
heard from official sources that it was the policy of the War Office that
the treatment of nerve shaken soldiers should in no sense resemble that of
ordinary lunatics.*[1]

*Thus their hands are plucking at each other; Picking at the rope-knouts
of their scourging; Snatching after us who smote them, brother, Pawing us
who dealt them war and madness.*

WILFRED OWEN, 'MENTAL CASES', 1917

SHELL SHOCK AND LUNACY: WAR AND MADNESS

During the First World War military and political authorities persistently argued
that shell-shocked men were not mad, or that shell-shocked men should not
be treated as mad men. In stark contrast, by the late twentieth century it was
the norm to present shell-shocked men as mad, as 'men whose minds the Dead
have ravished'.[2] The Great War was interpreted as such a wasted, ineffectual
and inhumane struggle that it quite literally drove men mad. This attention to
the unprecedented brutality of the war is not completely misplaced: we are all
agreed that the trenches of the Western Front must have been fearsome. Yet the
relentless focus on the extraordinary nature of this particular conflict has served
to relieve modern commentators from a careful consideration of some of the
most painful and morally disturbing questions of the Great War: Should soldiers
on active service be punished for cowardice or desertion? And were all deserters
really suffering from war neuroses? The early-twenty-first-century commentator
can simply dismiss these questions on compassionate grounds and announce
that no death sentences should have been passed in such horrific circumstances.
In Britain, the Shot at Dawn campaign has argued that men who failed to fight
were suffering from psychological trauma and so should not have been executed.[3]
The current French response is similar. In November 2008, President Nicolas
Sarkozy, commenting on French soldiers who had been shot for cowardice in

the First World War, announced that the men were not cowards at all, they were simply men who been pushed to their limits.[4] The consensus is that the war had driven men to such extreme levels of despair that they should not be judged. Yet senior officers in the First World War did not have the luxury of almost 100 years of hindsight: a man who refused to fight – for whatever reason – was a serious problem. It was not possible consistently to take a sympathetic view of cowardice and desertion. After all, many men were pushed beyond all reasonable limits.

The political focus on the men who were executed is valid in itself but it obscures the history of those who were pushed to the limits and who survived the war. The tendency to think exclusively about those who did not survive dominates much war literature too. One key factor in the most revered literary depictions of the First World War, shell shock and despair, is that little attention has been paid to life after the war. The most influential war poetry is largely rooted in the wartime experience. In prose, the characters of Septimus Smith and Harry Penrose both die – albeit for very different reasons. In *All Quiet on the Western Front*, Paul Bauer does not live to see the end of the war; in fact the essence of the tale is that he, and by extension all veterans, simply cannot live in a post-war world because they have been too damaged. Recent depictions of the First World War continue with this theme, and Barker's Billy Prior similarly fails to survive the conflict: like Bauer, he too dies towards the very end of the war.[5] There is a slight twist in Faulks's *Birdsong*: Stephen Wraysford, the central character, disappears from the story after the war and his history has to be rediscovered by his descendants. He lives but cannot give testimony.[6] Overall, the literary interest in the shell-shocked soldier in wartime is not matched by an interest in the shell-shocked serviceman afterwards.

THE EX-SERVICES' WELFARE SOCIETY

It is this now neglected subject, namely the condition of the shell-shocked man after the war, that motivated the initial founders of the ESWS. This chapter will highlight the early campaigns of the ESWS in some detail. Although many charities attempted to provide for veterans in distress, the ESWS was the only one designed specifically and exclusively to cater for veterans suffering from psychological injury. As a result, the organization clearly plays an important role in the history of the post-war treatment of shell shock.[7] By looking at the work of the ESWS we can see what happened to men who did fall foul of official welfare provision, and we can assess the conditions faced by those trying to create support for mentally wounded veterans. What is clear from a study of the ESWS is that there was a high, albeit variable, degree of both public and official sympathy for the plight of mentally wounded veterans. However, the ESWS aimed to do more than garner public support to compensate for the scanty state welfare system: the society had been created in response to widespread concerns about the fate of ex-servicemen in lunatic asylums, and it aimed to challenge government policy on this issue. As a result, the ESWS became embroiled in some serious public and private disputes. These disputes had a detrimental effect on the society's development because it was difficult for it to achieve a real level of respectability as long as it was associated with controversial topics. So the inadequate treatment of shell-shocked veterans cannot be solely attributed to the financial stringency of unsympathetic post-war governments, although this was clearly a factor. It was also the result of a system that relied heavily upon a close relationship between state welfare and private charity at a time when the key aims of the charity concerned were in direct conflict with government policy.

The ESWS tried to encourage support for both lunacy reform and mentally broken men. As a private charity it had to encourage public support, but it had to do so without causing the government too much embarrassment. By claiming that shell-shocked veterans were in dire need, the ESWS was obviously implying that the state system was inadequate. This may well have been the case but provoking government hostility could only be counter-productive for an organization that really needed to establish an effective relationship with the Ministry of Pensions. The post-war welfare system was not simply organized on the relationship between the veteran and the state; governments – whether Coalition, Labour or Conservative – were committed to maintaining the role of the charitable sector. There were strong financial reasons for this approach: post-war welfare was expensive and the British economy was weak. In addition, there was an ideological commitment to charity as a force which would humanize the state sector. The following extract from *Recalled to Life* indicates how this combination of charitable and state support would create a harmonious balance:

> With such a combination there is every prospect that the care of those who should be sacred to us will not be stereotyped into a dull process of issuing doles over a counter, while the occasionally foolish and harmful actions of unthinking sentimentalists will be curbed by the orderly dispositions of enlightened officials and men of science.[8]

This is a highly idealistic view of the relationship between the state and the voluntary sector. It also ignores the fact that private charities also needed government support, or at least approval. A history of the newly established ESWS demonstrates that it was very difficult for a private charity to flourish while it opposed government policy. The words of Major George Tyron, the Conservative Minister of Pensions, are telling '... the value of the work done by such a society would depend upon it being in the hands of reasonable and well-disposed persons'.[9] As far as ministry officials were concerned, ESWS committee members were not 'reasonable and well-disposed persons'.

LOOKING AFTER MY MOTHER'S SON

> . . . they laid on My Mother's Son
> More than a man could bear,
> What with noise and fear of Death,
> Walking, the wounds, and cold,
> They filled the Cup for My Mother's Son
> Fuller than it could hold.
> They broke his body and his mind,
> And yet they made him live,
> They asked more from My Mother's son
> Than any man could give.[10]

Rudyard Kipling wrote 'My Mother's Son' to publicize the work of the ESWS in 1919, and his words reflect the way in which the ESWS initially tried to present shell-shocked veterans to the general public and to government ministers. To begin with the veteran was presented as a boy; he was a mother's son rather than a trained adult soldier. Secondly, the physical imagery is stark and it conveys one simple message: some men were asked to bear more than was humanly possible during the war. This is of course the narrative that modern commentators repeat each Armistice Day but with one significant difference: for the ESWS, shell-shocked men were not the tragic symbols of a futile war; on the contrary, they were real men who had taken part in a worthwhile struggle and who now needed practical help to rebuild their lives. Given the well-entrenched stigmas surrounding insanity and nervous breakdown – as well as the enduring confusion between shell shock and madness – the society initially wanted to educate people about the nature of war neurosis as well as protect the interests of the veterans themselves.

Although the wartime government had instituted a statutory pension system, many believed that ex-servicemen required further protection. Government grants, re-education programmes and training schemes were all designed to help men who had already begun the process of creating their lives anew. Those who could not easily do so may well have felt that they were not receiving the debt of honour and gratitude that they were due. It was not only shell-shocked men who felt aggrieved: all veterans were susceptible to such sentiments. Bitterness was especially acute when it seemed as though those who had not served in the war were receiving preferential treatment. This grievance – or perceived

1. Men relaxing in the lounge at Eden Manor, c.1929.

2. Men working in the garden at Eden Manor, c.1929.

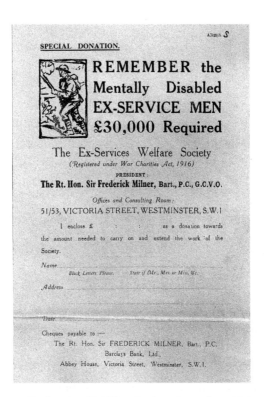

3. Ex-Services' Welfare Society Appeal, c.1926.

4. Ex-Services' Welfare Society publicity photograph, c.1928.

5. The Thermega stand at the Ideal Home Exhibition, Olympia 1929.

6. The King of Greece visiting the Thermega workshop, 1929.

grievance – was expressed often and openly in parliament and in the mainstream press in the early 1920s. Captain Charles Loseby, a barrister and the National Democratic party MP for Bradford East, argued that ex-servicemen should automatically receive representation on professional governing bodies. They deserved this representation because they had volunteered to fight, little realizing 'that during their absence worthless individuals would seize the opportunity to filch their practices and official positions'.[11] Loseby had been gassed in 1915 and then wounded at Cambrai in 1917. As a veteran, a barrister and an MP, he was ideally placed to speak about ex-servicemen with both authority and expertise. Yet he tended to sensationalize. Most men had not volunteered to fight; they had been conscripted. Loseby's words – and he was not alone – have contributed towards one of the central myths of the First World War: that the British Army was dominated by young naive volunteers, all blithely and blindly sacrificing their young lives for no good purpose. Loseby's words are also an uncomfortable reminder that one of the most significant tropes of European fascism, that of the overriding political importance of the front-line community, was also present in the British parliament. Haig, a figure on the conservative rather than the radical right, shared Loseby's views up to a point, but expressed them in more moderate language. He insisted simply that no man who went to fight for his country should be in a worse position on his return to civilian life.[12]

Aside from this general concern about the returning ex-serviceman, there was a particular fear that ex-servicemen in asylums were being especially neglected. Milner argued that shell-shocked men were 'a class the government had done the least for'.[13] Certainly the state system had not developed rapidly enough to meet the needs of mental casualties, and private charities had similarly been unable to keep up with wartime demands. The Mental After-Care Association made a direct correlation between shell shock and the 'increase of lunacy' since 1917, and the organization was obviously overburdened by the end of the war.[14] There was a clear gap in non-governmental support for shell-shocked veterans and so in January 1919 a group of women met to form the executive committee of a new charity. The Ex-Service Men's Welfare Society was subsequently registered with the London County Council in May 1919, and in the following July it was officially renamed the Ex-Services' Welfare Society because the original title seemed too long. The society was organized specifically to cater for the needs of mentally wounded veterans, but its title betrays no hint of any language that could imply psychological injury. This remained the case until 1957 when the name was changed to the Ex-Services' Mental Welfare Society. Nevertheless, despite the reticence of the first official titles, the society was eager to discuss publicly the needs of shell-shocked veterans. Publicity material was very open about the men's condition, referring to mental disability and neurasthenia on a regular basis. However, members of the ESWS committee rarely referred to 'shell shock'. In their publicity, their minutes and their correspondence, they used terms such as 'nervous breakdown' or described the men as 'mentally broken'. The term 'shell shock' was scrupulously avoided, although it was clearly still part of popular discourse.

For the early committee members it made sense to insist that the ESWS should initially focus on lunacy reform at the same time as insisting that mentally broken men should not be part of the lunacy system. In April 1919 the society stated that its object was, 'To make such provision as shall be necessary for those cases of acute nervous and mental breakdown as would otherwise be sent to asylums (including those cases known as GPI) [General Paralysis of the Insane].'[15] The inclusion of men with GPI was potentially controversial. It was accepted that GPI only occurred in those who had been affected with syphilis, and was usually regarded as being directly due to syphilis. Yet the stricken men may well have fought in the war and their families often attributed the condition to war service. In the immediate post-war years some blurring of these categories was acceptable. Dr Mapother accepted the principle that GPI 'may be accelerated by the strain of war'; Dr Hurst, in more forceful tones, argued that, 'There is no doubt at all that active service had led in certain cases to a much more rapid development of the disease than would have occurred otherwise. In some cases the disease might have always remained latent.'[16]

The ESWS aimed to set up homes which would provide care, treatment, recreation and a level of vocational training to mentally broken men, and so ensure that no veteran – regardless of his pre-war history – need fear the asylum. This willingness to challenge government policy and the associated commitment to 'the People's Lunatic' can be seen as part of the English radical tradition.[17] Yet the original founders of the ESWS were mainly from the upper middle class and they sought support from the established elites; their central aim was always to maintain the respectability of the veteran. The ESWS can be seen as an example of the fractured, often confused, face of radical post-war activism. Certainly the organizations that the ESWS initially contacted for support indicate both a high level of social conservatism as well as some acceptance of the newly emerged radical right. The early organizers sought help from, among others, the British Empire Union (a far-right group that had merged with the Anti-German League in 1917), the Patriotic League, the Catholic Women's League, the Women's Freedom League and the Federation of Women's Village Institutes. The early ESWS executive committee was radical in that it was sometimes populist and often prepared to be provocative. Yet it was also keen to attract the approval of establishment figures. Certainly most committee members were socially and politically conservative in all spheres other than their support for veterans' rights. The founders were women and the early executive committees were dominated by women. Yet the women of the ESWS remained tied to male power structures.

In December 1918 the founders of the soon-to-be-established ESWS decided to form women's committees to support soldier candidates in the forthcoming general election. They did not choose to lobby the established political parties, let alone put themselves up for election to stand for the cause of veteran welfare. They genuinely believed that the soldier's voice – the voice from the trenches – was more valuable than any other.[18] This was a common motif in interwar European societies: the belief that the veteran's voice should be especially privileged was unparliamentary and undemocratic but certainly not uncommon.

THE KING'S UNIFORM AND THE PAUPER ASYLUM

Chartfield, the first ESWS home, was established on Putney Hill in south London in 1921. Its aim was to provide mentally wounded men with an alternative to the asylum. Some families were genuinely unable to cope with the mentally broken son or husband who had been returned to them, and dispatched their own war-shocked loved ones to the local asylum.[19] However, for a number of reasons, a great many ex-servicemen and their families were very angry that ex-servicemen were being sent to such places. Most importantly, the government was publicly committed to honouring the war victims and to creating homes fit for heroes. In the words of Dr Christopher Addison (Liberal; Hoxton, East London), the first Minister for Health, 'It was vital that this class of men should escape the stigma and disabilities of being classed as lunatics.'[20] Yet asylums were routinely described as 'pauper asylums' and the public displayed a 'ghoulish fascination' with the mentally wounded inmates; even Boards of Guardians sometimes treated asylum patients with derision.[21] Doctors also sometimes shared in these prejudices and were often so poorly trained that they were afraid of the mentally ill and 'had visions of acutely maniacal persons dancing up and down the corridors'.[22] Clearly the lunatic asylum was the complete antithesis of the home fit for the hero, and mentally wounded men were being classed as lunatics. Secondly, the discourse of health was strongly hereditarian in the 1920s, and so asylum treatment humiliated not just the veteran but his entire family.[23] In 1921 William Robinson, the Senior Assistant Medical Officer at the West Riding Asylum in Wakefield, returned three ex-service cases to their homes. The men were all mentally wounded and none of them had shown any real signs of recovery; nevertheless, their relatives had insisted upon their release.[24] The families may have been moved by simple compassion – it must have been pitiable to see mentally wounded men in these inhospitable institutions – or it may have been that the sense of collective shame was overpowering. Whatever the reasoning, the message was clear: the asylum was no place for an ex-serviceman. Finally, the conditions in asylums were particularly poor in the immediate post-war years. According to the Second

Annual Report of the Board of Control, by 1915 42 per cent of asylum medical staff had volunteered and been accepted for military service. These men were frequently replaced by inexperienced and untrained workers, and it was often impossible to replace mental nurses at all. Furthermore, many mental hospitals became overcrowded during the war because nine of the larger asylums had been turned into war hospitals.[25] Conditions improved slightly after the armistice but the Geddes Axe of 1921 effectively halted all capital expenditure. This mattered because maintenance work had been neglected during the war years and the associated costs had increased considerably as a result of inflation.[26] So not only did many believe that asylums were the wrong places for mentally disabled veterans, at this particular time many asylums were in a state of disrepair and so were doubly unsuited to the needs and rights of returning veterans.

This public concern was displayed in populist commentary from both the political left and the right throughout the early post-war period. In September 1919 the *Daily Herald* reported that lunatic asylums were worse than prisons and claimed that inmates were 'ravenously hungry'.[27] *John Bull* used even more inflammatory language by claiming that Tommies were being 'tortured' in local asylums, and that, 'A wave of burning indignation at the disgraceful treatment of these helpless heroes has swept over the country.'[28] Traditionally more moderate – even more conservative – voices also expressed concern about asylum conditions. The 1919 Report for the Board of Control indicated a great increase in the mortality of asylum patients during the war, and Commissioners attributed the high death rate to the 'reduction in quantity and deterioration in the quality of the food supplied to patients'.[29] Clearly there was a long-standing concern that mental patients were not receiving proper care, and this was exacerbated by fears that some patients had been allowed to enlist for combat. In the words of an editorial in *The Times*, 'Have we been sending some of our lunatics into the Army, and starving the others?'[30] In 1922 the *Morning Post* also drew attention to the shortcomings of local asylums, and printed a highly detailed article about cruelty towards ex-service patients.[31]

This controversial situation worsened when the Ministry of Pensions decided to withdraw allowances from 700 ex-service mental patients on the grounds that their complaints had not been due to, or aggravated by, war service. An article in *The Times* expressed the views of many: the government's actions were not illegal but they were deeply unjust.

> There must be, for most people, deep misgivings in the thought that these men, who wore the King's uniform and are now victims of the most tragic of all human afflictions, are to enjoy no longer that small mercy which distinguished a 'service patient' from a pauper 'lunatic'.[32]

Obviously it was possible for veterans to succumb to mental illnesses that were entirely unconnected to their war service. A man may have been predisposed towards mental illness or his illness could have been triggered by some event that happened after the war. Yet expressions of concern from across the political spectrum indicate that many people wanted all mentally ill veterans to be treated as though their illness had stemmed from the trauma of combat, whether this was technically the case or not. This may be an illogical position but it clearly indicated a lack of general confidence in the diagnostic procedure, and a widely held belief that the medical-military authorities had misdiagnosed some cases. In brief, veterans were to be given the benefit of the doubt.

POST-WAR IMAGES OF SHELL-SHOCKED MEN

This public concern for shell-shocked men in lunatic asylums was accompanied by more negative accounts of the mentally wounded. Images of the shell-shocked ex-serviceman as morally unsound, or even downright dangerous, began to appear in the press after the war. As early as 1918, *Recalled to Life*, a publication that purported to support servicemen and ex-servicemen, published an article describing the tendency of neurasthenic ex-servicemen to 'get into trouble':

> These patients easily get into trouble; they issue false cheques, are hopelessly unreliable and extravagant etc and yet are not sufficiently irresponsible always to justify confinement. Moreover they have such a poor make up that psychological treatment is very difficult. All psychological treatment depends upon the essential moral worth of the individual.[33]

T. W. Standwell, a devotee of 'physical culture' and who was well known for his mail-order body-building courses, noticed a real – and as far as he was concerned, welcome – change of attitude towards the shell-shocked man after the war.[34] In a lurid article entitled 'Are you a potential post-war criminal?', he wrote that that he had been the subject 'of much indignant abuse' when he had first insisted that the cause of shell shock should 'not be sought in the strains and stresses of the military bombardment, mine explosion or air raid deluge but in the prior lives of those afflicted'.[35] Yet by January 1920 Standwell was confident that the public mood had changed, and that this change was a direct result of the outrages committed by apparently 'shell-shocked' men.

> We open our morning papers and turn instinctively to the report of the latest post office raid, bank brigandage, or revolting outrage – in the full knowledge that when the criminals have been arrested it will be explained that they have been victims of

shell-shock, or that they have in any case passed through war experiences . . . The
early excuses that these present criminals were war heroes, whose exuberances must
be forgiven because they had been 'through it' will no longer wash.[36]

In a similar vein, the *Daily Herald* reported the story of a man in Blackpool who
had thrown his five-week-old baby into the sea. The man had been suffering
from shell shock and consequently was certified as insane.[37] But it was not
only in the popular press that shell shock was associated with criminality and
deviance. Squadron Leader W. Tyrrell, who had served in the Royal Air Force
medical services, noted that a man's character changed at the onset of shell
shock and 'the previously well-behaved man perpetrates petty crimes . . . indeed
a sudden recourse to minor crime by previously well-behaved men was one of
the promontory signals of impending breakdown'.[38] Tyrell had himself suffered
from shell shock but made it clear that he recovered quickly and then went on
to serve at the front for two and a half years: his was clearly not the sort of shell
shock that manifested itself in petty crime.

Outrage at the behaviour of shell-shocked men obviously tied in with the
contemporary medical view of shell shock as a symptom of degeneracy. Robinson
insisted that large numbers of shell-shocked men had never been in the firing line.
He made strong links between shell shock and crime, alcohol and syphilis, and
concluded that the majority of service patients would have become patients in
mental hospitals whether there had been a war or not.[39] Alongside this fear about
the moral worth of the shell-shocked ex-serviceman, or the anti-social behaviour
he might inflict on others, there was a suspicion that unscrupulous men were
pretending to be shell-shocked when they were not. Certainly Norgate, who was
concerned with the effects of the war in Bristol, complained of scoundrels who
used shell shock as an excuse when caught.[40] There is no evidence to indicate that
this behaviour was widespread, but it clearly did happen on occasion.

In February 1918 *John Bull* ran an article calling for 'a hero's release'. Fred
Hines of Wellington in Somerset had joined the army under age, had fought at
the battles of Mons, Marne and the Aisne, and had been wounded in action many
times. On his discharge he was described as 'honest, intelligent and willing' but
two weeks after being released from hospital he was sentenced to three months
in prison for the alleged theft of a bicycle. *John Bull* condemned the sentence
outright, 'We say at once and without hesitation that the sentence was brutal
and unmerited. Hines was unfortunately under the influence of a little drink and
a deal of shell shock.'[41] Hines exemplified all the positive attributes associated
with shell-shock victims: he had volunteered for the war and had not waited
to be called; moreover, he had volunteered when under age, demonstrating a
youthful and idealistic heroism, and he had been physically wounded. Hines had
suffered from frost-bitten feet, he had been injured in his side, nearly all the calf

of one leg had been removed, and he had lost one rib and fractured another. By emphasizing his physical injuries, *John Bull* was reassuring its readers that Fred Hines's shell shock was undeniably honourable: clearly he was no coward. Yet for those who were poorly disposed towards the concept of psychological war wounds in general, this kind of reporting was disturbing because it seemed to imply that men who had been mentally wounded at the front should be given greater moral leeway than other citizens, or that rogues could 'claim' shell shock when there was really no justification for it. This was just what Standwell was complaining of when he insisted that there should be no extravagant leniency towards men who had 'been through it'.

At this point it is also worth mentioning that not all post-war nervous complaints were attributable to combat. Private Arthur Christmas was thrown from a horse when he was on Home Service and consequently was diagnosed as suffering from neurasthenia and nervous debility, and awarded a small pension.[42] This is obviously the sort of case that could arouse suspicion in those worried about malingerers. Also, the fact that Christmas was categorized along with those suffering from nervous collapse as a result of service at the front, should make us wary of making generalizations about the way in which nervous complaints were routinely confused with cowardice. Shell shock was definitely a clear symptom of mental strain in the trenches, and most shell shock cases were classed as some kind of nervous complaint. Nevertheless, not all nervous complaints were the result of trench warfare.

LUNACY REFORM AND POLITICAL CONFLICT

The immediate post-war years were clearly characterized by public sympathy for, and suspicion of, the shell-shocked ex-serviceman. The ESWS wanted to encourage public sympathy and allay the accompanying suspicions and fears. By physically removing men from the asylum system, they hoped also to remove all public misgivings: the shell-shocked man would no longer be seen as 'a potential post-war criminal'. Yet lunacy reform was a contentious issue and Loseby, one of the key figures in this campaign, was controversial too. As has been said, Loseby's legal background and his war record lent him some credibility. However, as an MP standing for the National Democratic Party (NDP), he was in a marginal position. The NDP, formerly the right-wing British Workers' League, was established in 1916 to act as a 'pro-war counterpoise' to the Labour party.[43] It had strong roots in the Labour movement but was deeply opposed to the pacifism of some Labour members and so had a policy of standing against Labour candidates. The NDP was short-lived, but it displayed all the hallmarks of the new post-war radical right: non-Marxian socialism, extreme patriotism, imperialism, the veneration of the veteran. Much of the NDP's financial support came from trade unionists but it also received money from some of the social elite, most notably Viscount Alfred Milner, a somewhat divisive figure who combined some progressive views on domestic policy with a zealous and neo-Darwinist commitment to Empire.[44] Loseby sat as an MP from 1918–1922, and by 1921 his general interest in veteran welfare had developed into a specific concern for ex-servicemen in asylums because, in his own emotive words, 'these men are wretched and they are kept behind bars.'[45] Loseby was not just concerned about the fate of these men; he was also motivated by the belief that there was a 'constituted opposition' to the ESWS, and by extension, to all those who fought for veterans' rights.[46] In response, Loseby created a small advisory committee of MPs to investigate the question of ex-servicemen in asylums. At the same time, he introduced a deputation of ESWS representatives to the Minister of Pensions and presented their case for them.[47] As a result of this commitment, Loseby was invited to become part of the ESWS executive committee.

The plight of ex-servicemen in lunatic asylums caused much public anxiety after the war because, contrary to expectation, the numbers increased. Although the strains of active service were over, the transition to civilian life was very stressful. For most servicemen, the idea of home, and the reality of parcels and letters from home, maintained morale on the fighting front. Yet after demobilization, many ex-servicemen returned to far from ideal domestic lives. They may well have come home to problems of employment, housing or health; there were often significant changes in familial and social circles. In addition, some veterans had to battle to establish their own pension rights, rights which they had been assured of when fighting.[48] Life on active service, despite its anxieties, may well have provided men with a level of security that was lacking in the ordinary home. Robert Graves wrote what has come to be seen as a scathing portrayal of the Great War – *Goodbye to All That* (1929) is central to the canon of disenchantment literature – yet he still demonstrated a tremendous pride in his own regiment and a great fondness and respect for the men he fought alongside.[49] Ironically, once men had been demobilized, they may well have felt more emotionally vulnerable. It is also the case that the army had discharged many mentally broken men although post-discharge care was clearly weak.[50] So, for more than one reason, the numbers grew, and official figures released by the Board of Control indicate an increase of almost 40 per cent between the beginning of 1920 and October 1921.

Macpherson disagreed with these statistics and said that by October 1921 the number of ex-servicemen in asylums was closer to 6,000.[51] Nevertheless, whether one agrees with the Board of Control or with MacPherson, a significant number of ex-servicemen were clearly being held in public asylums during this period.

In November 1921 Loseby arranged a meeting in the House of Commons to

Table 2 Numbers of ex-service personnel in public asylums[52]

Date	Numbers
1 January 1919	2,506
1 January 1920	4,673
20 October 1921	6,435

discuss the question of ex-servicemen in public asylums. He opened the meeting by explaining his primary concerns, the first of which was that the Ministry of Pensions was withholding treatment allowances from men unless they agreed to be treated in asylums. These allowances could amount to as much as six guineas a week and so this was clearly a matter of some material importance to many men. Of even greater significance was the way in which the ministry seemed to be manipulating pension rights so as to force men into particular types of care. In Loseby's words, 'I think it is also an undisputed fact that a man who refuses treatment offered to him by the Minister of Pensions is liable to have his pension completely stopped.'[53] Not only could this situation be construed as unethical, it seemed to contradict government statements of support for disabled men. Also, it seemed almost to guarantee that the number of ex-servicemen in asylums would continue to grow. This highlights an intrinsic weakness in official welfare policy at the time. A system in which state responsibility is to be supported and supplemented by private charity can only work if both government and the relevant charity are agreed on a common plan of action, or at least a unified response. However, in this case, government ministers seemed to believe that some mentally wounded veterans could only be treated in lunatic asylums whereas the ESWS believed that it was always deeply wrong, and medically inappropriate, to put an ex-serviceman into an asylum. The official explanation for the government's commitment to asylum treatment was that some mentally broken men needed to be isolated, both for their own sake and for that of others. Consequently, MacPherson spoke against the ESWS in the House of Commons, on the grounds that the society was proposing to mix neurasthenic cases with the insane.[54] Loseby insisted that this was not the case, and argued that the society had opened Chartfield simply to provide non-asylum curative treatment for those patients who would otherwise have been sent to asylums.[55] MacPherson's comments were quite incongruous given that one of the most common complaints about the local asylums was that they were guilty of mixing together patients of different categories, or in the words of one patient's father, asylum inmates were being 'indiscriminately herded together'.[56] One can therefore suggest that it was not clinical practice but the control of resources and the government's prestige that really lay at the root of MacPherson's concerns. In the House of Commons he had certainly made it clear that he did not want to

send ex-servicemen to a charity institution.[57] Given the extent to which charities
provided care for ex-servicemen at this point, his remarks can only mean that he
did not want to send ex-servicemen to this particular 'charity institution'.

This public meeting indicates the difficulties faced by the ESWS in its early
years. Everyone present made a clear commitment to the care of the ex-soldier.
Many of the participants had fought in the Great War, and for all of them the
wounded ex-soldier – whether mentally or physically wounded – was deserving
of support. This was a respectable cause on which all could easily unite. Yet this
cause became rapidly less respectable when it became part of the wider lunacy
reform campaign and when the ESWS expressed a critical or hostile attitude
towards the Ministry of Pensions. By criticizing the ministry, ESWS members
were essentially accusing ministers of failing in their duty towards men who had
fought. Loseby used the meeting to argue that the ESWS 'has established what
we believe to be an experimental but model institution'.[58] He then called on Dr
Montagu Lomax to speak. Lomax was a GP who had come out of retirement
to help the war effort, and during the years 1917–1919 he had worked in the
Prestwich Asylum in Lancashire. He had been so shocked by his experiences there
that he had written a book to denounce the practices within the asylum system.[59]
He exposed the dreadful material conditions in which inmates had to exist: they
were often cold, hungry and poorly clad. He also made plain the links between
the asylum, the workhouse and the prison, arguing that the asylum was one of
the state's punitive institutions. The crux of his complaint was that patients were
not treated; they were simply denied their liberty.

On a general level, Lomax insisted that the whole asylum system was 'rotten
to the core'.[60] More specifically, he argued that, contrary to official protestations,
there was no special treatment for ex-service patients. One of the reasons for the
social stigma attached to asylum patients was that many of them were technically
paupers and their fees were paid by the local county or borough. Ex-servicemen
were officially in a different position: the Ministry of Pensions paid their fees at
a higher rate and they were classified as private patients. Yet Lomax was scathing
about this official position:

> The government allows these men a suit of clothes of their own to distinguish
> them from the paupers, and they also give them 2/6 a week, £6 a year. That 2/6 is
> supposed to keep the man in luxuries, but he does not get them; it is handed to the
> ward charge who buys him a few cigarettes and one or two apples, and makes a bit
> in the process too. And that is all the distinction that the ex-soldier has to separate
> him from pauper lunatics.[61]

Lomax painted a grim picture of asylum life and argued forcibly for material,
moral and organizational change. Yet his harsh words simply alienated some of

his listeners. Lieutenant Colonel Nathan Raw MP (Coalition Unionist; Wavertree, Liverpool) was a doctor with much experience of the lunacy system, having worked at the Mill Road Infirmary in Liverpool for over 20 years. Raw insisted that there was a very high recovery rate in asylums and he rejected Lomax's complaints about lack of liberty and callous treatment. Raw argued that a degree of physical restraint was necessary in some cases: for example, when insane patients were either suicidal or homicidal. Yet, he went on to say, when restraint was not necessary it was not used, and the great majority of lunatics were not confined but were able to 'go into the open highway for long walks'.[62] He then denounced Lomax's proposals on practical grounds, arguing that it would be impossible to create enough new institutions to deal with the large numbers of ex-servicemen currently housed in asylums. Raw had the advantage of being able to argue from a position of authority – he clearly had far more experience than Lomax – and he effectively dismissed Lomax's arguments.

> I want this meeting to understand – and I am speaking now with authority – that you can not undertake to treat ex-servicemen, or anyone suffering from diseases of the brain, with any specific remedy. A great many of them are incurable, they are dangerous to society and dangerous to themselves, and I think the general attack which Dr Lomax has made today, which is based on an experience of about two years, on the attendants in this country, numbering very many thousands, is really disgraceful.[63]

This angry exchange indicates the way in which a discussion about shell-shocked men and lunacy reform could easily become polarized and acrimonious. Raw did not advocate the treatment of all mentally wounded ex-servicemen in asylums. On the contrary, he thought that very few mentally wounded soldiers should actually be classified as insane and that they should mainly be treated in mental wards attached to general hospitals.[64] He also thought that the treatment offered at Chartfield was 'excellent'.[65] In many ways, Raw held views that were quite close to those held by Loseby and other members of the ESWS but he was alienated by the sensationalism of Lomax's stories.

By this stage MPs were no longer discussing the possible role of the ESWS; they were simply having a dispute about the alleged abuses in the asylum system. This gave Lomax extra publicity, but it did not help the ESWS at all. Frederick Roberts MP (Labour, West Bromwich) concluded the meeting by saying that he was concerned about the care of ex-servicemen but if he thought he had been invited to discuss the general reform of the lunacy laws he would not have put off other engagements to attend.[66] Reports certainly indicated that Lomax dominated the event. A short article in *The Times* even implies the meeting had been arranged specifically to provide Lomax with a platform.[67] Dr Davis Waite, the Chairman of the ESWS, indicated some disquiet in a letter to Loseby the following day. While thanking Loseby for arranging the meeting, he concluded that 'the result was a little unsatisfactory – Dr Lomax sidetracked us badly and while he perhaps made out a case for enquiry regarding the conduct of lunatic asylums generally – the ex-serviceman in particular became rather a side issue'.[68]

APPEALING FOR HELP AND PROVOKING ANTAGONISM

Despite being 'sidetracked' by Lomax and his campaign for lunacy reform, the ESWS retained its interest in the issue, particularly with regards to ex-servicemen. The executive committee attempted to organize a deputation of metropolitan mayors to urge the Ministry of Health to exempt all ex-servicemen from certification.[69] It also maintained a fairly consistent level of communication with the Ministry of Pensions, with peers in the House of Lords, with members of the House of Commons and with the National Council for Lunacy Reform (NCLR). This particular commitment resulted in long-standing onerous obligations, and in order to oblige the continually cash-starved NCLR, the ESWS even agreed to house one patient whose mental condition was definitely not attributable to war service.[70]

A real and committed opposition to the certification of ex-servicemen caused some serious practical problems. The society had particular difficulties with Mr. Wadkin, an ex-officer, who had received after-care and financial support from the ESWS in 1923. The ESWS private papers are discreet but it was clear that Wadkin was experiencing – or perhaps provoking – marital difficulties. These difficulties, the nature of which was never made specific, were so severe that his wife asked the committee for help at the beginning of 1924. By this stage, committee members felt that they could do nothing 'for this class of case', and advised Mrs Wadkin to see a family medical man with a view to placing her husband under restraint.[71] One can only infer that Mr Wadkin had been violent towards his wife. In the meantime, the society continued to give Mrs Wadkin a high level of support. In June she was given an emergency payment of £5, and Stanley Thompson, the ESWS Secretary, accompanied her to the magistrates' court where she attempted to obtain a separation order from her husband. This was the most extreme option available at the time given that divorce on grounds of insanity was not possible until 1937. However, the magistrate refused to issue the separation order and so Thompson applied to the Master of Lunacy, believing that certification was necessary in this instance. The Master pointed out that the ESWS could not consistently press for Wadkin's certification while appealing to the public to remove all ex-servicemen from lunatic asylums. Thompson and the rest of the committee realized the Master of Lunacy was making a sensible point – or at least an unanswerable point – and Wadkin was allowed to stay at Eden Manor, the society's new home.[72]

The ESWS commitment to lunacy reform also provoked some very real problems of presentation and management. In particular it ensured that relations between the society and the Ministry of Pensions remained potentially rancorous. In November 1923 the entire executive committee publicly complained about the treatment received by ex-service personnel in both 'private and pauper lunatic asylums'.[73] Furthermore, they argued that treatment throughout the UK was inadequate:

> We are assured that our country, in its treatment of its mentally affected, is far behind such countries as Germany, France, America, and Switzerland, which have made a study of the treatment of insanity on scientific lines for many years past.[74]

These complaints were immediately rejected by Charles Craig, the Parliamentary Secretary to the Ministry of Pensions, who hotly defended both the asylum system and the extent to which the government supported its mentally broken war veterans.[75] This disagreement was followed by a series of articles in the *Morning Post*, articles that could only be interpreted as attacks on the ESWS.[76]

The author of these articles acknowledged that there had been some justification for the criticisms levelled at the asylum system in the years immediately after the war. He then went on to insist that the situation had changed since then and he responded to all of the complaints that had been raised by ESWS publicity: the quantity and quality of food in asylums, the level of financial support and the staffing arrangements. The tone of each article was designed to discredit those who had expressed any doubts about the condition of ex-servicemen in asylums, and he described those who complained as 'persons whose intentions have been admirable, but whose information has not always been accurate'.[77] In the final article, the tone changed and the journalist adopted a much more outspoken and critical approach, implying that the ESWS raised money from asylum inmates, 'One society, for instance, which proclaims sympathy for the insane derives a proportion of its income by regular circularisation of lunatics in asylums.'[78] Although the ESWS was not mentioned by name, members of the executive committee believed that they had been insulted and wrote a letter of complaint to the *Morning Post*. The journalist replied that he was not trying to be unfriendly; he simply wanted to allay public anxieties. Given that the ESWS had not been named there was little that committee members could do other than issue a public statement declaring that they did not take money from asylum inmates.[79] The committee was unaware that Roberts, who had become the Labour Minister of Pensions, had participated in the journalist's investigations. Nor were they aware that the Ministry of Pensions continued to monitor ESWS activities. In a private memo on the '*Morning Post* investigations', the Ministry's secretaries summarized the articles and Robert's responses, and noted that they 'very satisfactorily disposed of the charges made by Sir Frederick Milner and his associates'.[80] So ESWS committee members were right to suspect that they were being impugned; however, they had no idea of the level of hostility involved.

Despite these difficulties, the ESWS was becoming more financially sound by the mid-1920s, and it opened a new home, Eden Manor in Beckenham, in October 1924. Committee members were optimistic and they paid £100 to publish new appeals in *The Times*, the *Daily Telegraph*, the *Morning Post* and the *Daily Graphic*. The appeals featured a picture of the Duke of Connaught opening the new Sir Frederick Milner Home, and it explicitly presented the ESWS home as a viable alternative for the '5,000 ex-Servicemen in Pauper Lunatic Asylums'.[81] The appeal also stressed the normality of these men before their military service:

> The Ex-Services' Welfare society (Patron HRH Prince George) is establishing recuperative homes for the care and cure of these mentally-broken ex-Servicemen who answered the call clear-brained, normal men and who sacrificed that without which life is but a husk of aimlessness'.[82]

In this instance, the ex-servicemen were not 'Mothers' Sons' but 'clear-brained normal men'. In addition, the society produced a small pamphlet, detailing its aims and asking for support. At first the 1924 campaign appeared successful in that it generated a good response from the general public.[83] However, this publicity soon evoked more problematic responses, and involved the society in disagreements that continued for almost a year. One of the appeals appeared in St Columba's Church of Scotland magazine. The language was uncompromising, and highly critical of current government policy:

> *Mentally-broken 'service' men*
>
> It is startling and humiliating that no fewer than 6,000 ex-servicemen are today in pauper lunatic asylums. Not only is this a serious slight to our defenders, but their being grouped with the normal class of pauper lunatics is a hindrance to their recovery and a stigma handicapping their later return to honourable employment. Sir Frederick Milner has made noble efforts to provide recovery homes for them elsewhere.[84]

Lieutenant General Sir Alymer Hunter-Weston read this appeal and was furious. Hunter-Weston had been elected as the Unionist MP for North Ayrshire in October 1916. He also had the prestige of an extensive military career, having seen active service in India, Egypt and South Africa, and he had received the *Croix de Guerre* and the Legion of Honour during the Great War. Describing himself as a 'plain, blunt soldier', he had long been committed to ensuring that the army received sufficient respect and support from the civilian world.[85] In addition, Lord Southborough had approached Hunter-Weston personally and requested that he sit on the Government Committee of Enquiry into shell shock.[86] It is possible that Southborough's request stemmed from the fact that as well as commanding men, both at Gallipoli and on the Western Front, Hunter-Weston had been himself been invalided out with nervous strain. In the event, Hunter-Weston did not sit on the committee due to his commitments in Ayrshire, but he obviously felt that his knowledge of mentally wounded soldiers was self-evident. He became so angry about the 'misleading and needlessly offensive' appeal that he immediately alerted George Tyron. Hunter-Weston then contacted the Rev Archibald Fleming, the editor of St Columba's Church of Scotland magazine, and told him that he had unwittingly published false information.[87]

Hunter-Weston argued in the much the same vein as Nathan Raw during the House of Commons meeting in 1921. He stated that ex-servicemen were classified as private patients and that their fees were paid by the Ministry of Pensions. He insisted that ex-servicemen received 25 shillings a week plus allowances for their families, and that asylums were regularly inspected by Ministry medical officers in conjunction with the Board of Control. He also maintained that only those men in real need of asylum treatment were so detained; other cases were removed to more appropriate institutions. As a result of Hunter-Weston's interventions, there was a bizarre three-way correspondence between Hunter-Weston, Fleming and Everard Howard, Chairman of the ESWS. Strangely, there was no direct communication between Hunter-Weston and Howard. Fleming acted as intermediary and forwarded letters from one to the other. As in 1921, the primary issue, namely whether or not mentally wounded men should be treated in local asylums, became sidetracked and the correspondence was primarily concerned with patients' diets and with general living conditions. As a result, these letters clearly indicate the sorts of conditions that some mentally wounded ex-servicemen, as well as many mentally ill civilians, had to endure.

In his role as chairman, Howard visited many local asylums to visit ex-servicemen and to ensure that they were being properly cared for. When describing these visits to Fleming and Hunter-Weston, Howard consistently stressed the sanity and the respectability of the veterans he encountered. His first example was the son of a clergyman whose stipend could not stretch to a private institution. The patient complained about the 'bad language and filthy habits' of the other inmates, and Howard's letter made it clear that asylum life offended the young man's sense of dignity and morality.[88] Howard's second, more detailed description of an asylum visit contains the following account of a wounded ex-serviceman:

I visited an asylum recently and saw a very pathetic figure, a badly wounded soldier,

seated outside a ward which looked on to the Airing Court where some 100 or so
poor unfortunate lunatics were wandering round and round, some shouting, others
wandering in their minds, but all walking round breathing God's atmosphere, the
only recreation these poor deranged people had! I spoke to the ex-service man and
asked if he was happy. He gave a faint smile and the short conversation I had with
him proved to me that he was quite conscious of his surroundings, and the scene
before him was not calculated to make his mind happy.[89]

In his first draft, Howard described the man as having lost a leg. In the final piece,
this specific disability was replaced by the more general comment that the soldier
was 'badly wounded'. Why did he make this change? Possibly he wanted to protect
the patient's privacy by avoiding any details that could lead to easy identification.
What is more obvious is that Howard, like many other commentators, was keen
to draw attention to the physical wounds of mentally broken veterans. A physical
wound proved that the man had been in serious combat and it suggested bravery:
the physically wounded soldier had not shirked from his duty. So Howard was
ensuring that this man's mental collapse could not be dismissed as cowardice.
More widely, emphasizing the physical injuries of mentally wounded veterans
was also a way of refuting the old wartime prejudice that 'the wounded appear
to be comparatively immune to shell shock'.[90]

In this letter, Howard also indicates some sympathy for the 'poor unfortunate
lunatics', namely those patients without a service history.[91] The policy of the
ESWS was to remove ex-servicemen from asylums but the society had to do so
without seeming callous about the fate of the civilian patients who were so clearly
going to remain. Loseby had previously addressed this issue in two ways. First, he
claimed that conditions in asylums were unsatisfactory for all patients – Lomax's
book had made this plain. Secondly, he insisted that while asylum treatment was
inadequate for all patients, it was doubly unsatisfactory for the ex-soldier 'with
his special claim on the gratitude of the public'.[92] However, Howard avoided the
issue of the soldier's 'special claim' altogether, and made one clear point only:
mentally broken ex-servicemen were not insane and so they did not require
asylum treatment. In yet another account of an asylum visit, Howard described
how a mentally wounded soldier was distressed at being labelled as a 'lunatic'
and he complained that:

I have no sane or healthy person to speak to all day long, day after day and week after
week! Is it fair for a sane man – and no Doctor can deny that I am at the present time,
to be cooped up all this time with these poor wretched creatures?[93]

After having established the principle that ex-servicemen should not be treated in
asylums, Howard went on to describe the general deprivations of asylum life. He

was particularly concerned about the poor quality of institution food, a subject that had long provoked criticism. Hunter-Weston claimed that asylum patients were well nourished because the institutions had unlimited access to their own garden produce. Yet Howard dismissed this claim and sent him the following details of a typical asylum diet:

Breakfast: 2 rounds of bread and margarine or dripping. Tea.

Lunch: Cut of a joint (meat tough). Vegetables. A little rice.

Tea: 2 slices of bread and margarine. Tea.

Supper: Porridge or cocoa without milk.[94]

Howard then went on to provide less anecdotal evidence to indicate that the above description was a representative one. He calculated that 48.5 per cent of asylum breakfasts consisted of only a beverage with bread and margarine, and that 49.5 per cent of all patients were given only bread and margarine for tea.[95] There was little evidence of either fresh garden produce or dairy products in the average daily diet of an asylum patient. These concerns were not new: Lomax had also been appalled at asylum food, describing it as ill-selected, badly cooked and unappetisingly served.[96] *John Bull*, in typically vitriolic style, later insisted soldiers had been better fed in the trenches than they were in local lunatic asylums.[97] Yet Howard's investigation dated from 1925: the shortages of the war years and the difficulties of the reconstruction period should have been long gone. Of course they were not, and the details of an asylum patient's diet gives us some idea of the lives of those who were poor or ill, or both, in the interwar years. George Orwell, writing less than ten years later, gives us dire descriptions of food in the casual wards of the local workhouses, and portrays a harsh world in which the destitute were accustomed to living on 'tea and two slices'.[98]

It is not just that the food was poor, general living conditions were unacceptable too. In the Glamorgan Mental Hospital at Bridgend, men occupied rooms devoid of artificial light and were often without any heating facilities at all. There were also tales of physical cruelty, and of attendants abusing their positions by stealing the inmates' pocket money. Howard was keen to provide as many details as possible and so prove that the original ESWS appeal had been justified, but Hunter-Weston grew tired of this correspondence. In March 1925 Fleming reported that Hunter-Weston had become 'nettled about the voluminousness [*sic*] of what I sent to him last!', and he also refused to meet Howard, clearly wishing to avoid being drawn any further into the controversy.[99]

Hunter-Weston seemed to grow bored with his quarrel. Yet no sooner did Hunter-Weston cease being a problem for the ESWS when an even bigger row erupted. Major William Colfox, MP for West Dorset (Conservative Unionist) began to notice the ESWS campaign literature, and he responded with even more ferocity than Hunter-Weston. Like Hunter-Weston, Colfox was from the established military elites and he too had been decorated for services during the Great War: he had been awarded the MC for gallantry in 1920. He had also served as Parliamentary Private Secretary to the Minister of Pensions in 1920, so could claim to speak with some authority on the subject of state welfare for ex-servicemen. Colfox took particular exception to the term 'pauper' being used in reference to ex-servicemen in asylums, and he directly accused Milner of misrepresenting the truth:

> You of all people who have been in repeated communication with the Ministry of Pensions and who know the true facts, must understand what a harrowing and totally false impression such words must make on those who are less well-informed on the matter than yourself.
>
> It is really monstrous that anyone in your position should repeatedly circulate these falsehoods, apparently with authority.
>
> You state that I have contributed money in answer to previous Appeals – if this is true, I very much regret that I should have been one of your dupes.[100]

Milner was ill – by this stage he was 75 years old, in poor health and very deaf. Consequently Howard was forced to deal with Colfox's increasingly vociferous complaints. The arguments developed along now familiar lines: the quality and the quantity of inmates' food, the question of segregation, and the general standard of living. In addition, Colfox began to attack Milner personally and to cast doubts upon the integrity of the ESWS. More specifically, he accused the society of misleading the public about the sorts of services it could provide. Colfox pointed out that the ESWS was legally unable to care for men who had been certified, and he argued that, 'The public ought to be informed that your society are [sic] legally unable to care for these certifiable cases.'[101] This was of course the central problem facing the ESWS: the society wanted to provide an alternative to the asylum but the law clearly stated that patients who had been certified had to be treated within the official asylum system. As far as ESWS committee members and supporters were concerned, the way to resolve this problem was simple: ex-servicemen should not be certified. Yet Colfox interpreted ESWS actions as malign and accused the society of misusing public funds. For ESWS committee members, this was too similar to the claims made by the *Morning Post* in 1924, and no charity would welcome such allegations twice in one year. One letter from Colfox ends with an ill-tempered and sarcastic conclusion as the MP pointed out that it was not wise:

to make use of ex-servicemen and their misfortunes to provide comfortable salaries and occupations for designing people not unduly hampered by conscience. I must congratulate your Society on having obtained a large sum of money without having overstepped the law with regard to fraud and false pretences.[102]

These accusations were grave. The ESWS contacted its solicitors and, despite his illness, Milner wrote Colfox a long and conciliatory letter in an attempt to defend the ESWS and mend relations.[103] As a result, Colfox withdrew the personal comments about Milner's lack of integrity, but he still insisted that the society was wrong to claim that over 5,000 ex-servicemen were living in pauper conditions in lunatic asylums.[104] In addition, unbeknown to Howard, Colfox was keeping the Ministry of Pensions aware of the correspondence. Private memos indicate that the Ministry remained wholly sympathetic to Colfox throughout the entire episode, with George Chrystal, Secretary to the Ministry of Pensions, going as far as to refer to 'our fight with Milner'.[105]

In some ways it is unsurprising that the ESWS was criticized by Conservative MPs and by the traditional military elites. People in these groups were temperamentally inclined to support the status quo and to argue that ex-servicemen were not being treated badly. Yet the ESWS received criticism from the political left too. The *Daily Herald*, a newspaper supported by the Trades Union Congress, also objected to the 1924 Armistice Day appeal on the grounds that it would cause unnecessary distress to the relatives of mentally ill ex-servicemen, and that the ESWS was guilty of being both callous and incorrect.[106] The ESWS committee initially dismissed the *Daily Herald* article as the product of simple editorial prejudice. Yet the situation was more complex than it first appeared: the *Daily Herald's* criticisms were actually rooted in its support for the first Labour government, which had held power from January till October 1924. The editor made this clear in a private interview with Stanley Thompson, the secretary of the ESWS. Reporting back to the committee, Thompson admitted that he had 'obtained no satisfaction' from the editor who 'clearly showed an antagonism to a policy of the society which might lead to an attack on the party of the late government'.[107]

Ramsay MacDonald's 1924 Labour administration was a short-lived minority government. Nevertheless, Labour MPs were, for the first time, in positions of real ministerial responsibility and so were ultimately accountable for the care of wounded ex-servicemen. Of course all politicians professed a deep commitment to veteran welfare, but Labour members in particular argued that they had demonstrated the greatest care for vulnerable, mentally wounded ex-servicemen. During his short term in office, Roberts arranged for the state to accept responsibility for an extra 700 mentally ill ex-servicemen. These men had previously had their allowances withdrawn because their complaints had been classified as not attributable to war service. Despite the fact that these men could not be characterized as mentally broken war heroes, the state paid for their asylum fees so that they could be treated as private patients like all other ex-servicemen.[108] So, as a result of its support for the Labour government, the *Daily Herald* opposed the ESWS campaign. The *Daily Herald's* support for mentally broken ex-servicemen, whether the wounds were attributable to the war or not, was a cause which the ESWS also championed. Consequently such a breakdown in relations can hardly have been anything other than disappointing. Once again the ESWS had failed to manage the debate effectively and so had alienated potential supporters.

THE LOSS OF ROYAL PATRONAGE AND A CHANGE OF DIRECTION

This disapproval of the Ministry of Pensions was clearly unhelpful to the ESWS; criticism in the press was similarly unwelcome. Yet of even greater importance was the way in which the emphasis upon ex-servicemen in 'pauper asylums' alienated royal patronage. As the campaign literature indicates, the ESWS valued high-profile and elite support. The society wanted to make it clear that it was supported by figures of the very highest authority and social standing. In practice this entailed maintaining a fine balance between supporting veterans and criticizing government policy, a balance the society patently failed to maintain following the publication of the 1924 Armistice Day appeal.

Shortly after the 1924 Armistice Day, Sir Frederick Ponsonby, the Keeper of the Privy Purse at Buckingham Palace, wrote a letter of complaint to the ESWS. Ponsonby had two main grievances: he complained that the ESWS pamphlet had contained inaccurate statements about ex-servicemen in lunatic asylums and, more seriously, he complained that the role of the King had been misrepresented. The pamphlet claimed that the King had donated money to the ESWS but Ponsonby was adamant that this was not the case. He argued that the King should not be associated with any attack on the government and that the pamphlet should be withdrawn. Furthermore, he announced that if it was not withdrawn he would advise Prince George to withdraw his patronage and he would also advise all members of the royal family to refrain from being associated with the ESWS in any way. Howard at once apologized and complied with Ponsonby's demand. Yet despite these efforts Prince George withdrew his patronage and the ESWS was no longer allowed to use the King's name in any publicity. In addition, the letter from Prince George's equerry was so undiplomatic as to be positively insulting, 'His Royal Highness has been advised by Sir Frederick Ponsonby that it is most inadvisable that he should be in any way associated with a Society, the objects of which are to attack the Minister of Pensions.'[109]

The whole episode indicated how easy it was to lose support, even when there was widespread public and political support for the general aims of the ESWS. Committee members were especially embarrassed about the way in which the Armistice Day pamphlet had to be withdrawn, as clearly the withdrawal implied that the ESWS was somehow in the wrong. This was certainly the opinion expressed by Tyron at the Ministry of Pensions. In response to questions in the House of Commons, Tyron made it clear that he agreed with the *Daily Herald's* criticisms of the ESWS publicity, thus shedding even further doubt upon the society's claims.[110] Howard tried to limit some of this damage by sending explanatory letters to a number of national newspapers but none of them were printed. *The Times* was prepared to consider publication if Howard could provide a very short letter but by this stage the committee had decided that it was not a good moment to reopen the topic, especially given that they were disadvantaged by having such a limited space in the press.[111] Perhaps Howard was aware that his explanation was not wholly credible. He insisted that the society's publicity had not contained inaccurate statements and also that the ESWS would 'not resort to subterfuges'.[112] He then went on to describe the indignities suffered by ex-servicemen in asylums but he offered no explanation at all for the decision to withdraw the offending pamphlet. As a result, he did nothing to dispel the view that the pamphlet must have contained libellous material.

ESWS embarrassment was compounded by the attitude of the British Legion. There had always been a close relationship between the British Legion and the ESWS, and in its early publicity the society had encouraged all ex-servicemen to join the Legion. British Legion representatives sat on the Executive Committee, and in 1923 the ESWS had gone to great lengths to express public support for a British Legion circular detailing the poor treatment received by ex-servicemen in mental institutions.[113] On a more general level, the British Legion had consistently and publicly provided support for mentally wounded veterans. The Legion made representations to the Ministry of Pensions on behalf of such men, and gave money to mentally damaged men and their families in times of need. Consequently, it was a serious blow to the ESWS when the British Legion publicly withdrew its support. At the Standing Joint Committee for Ex-Service Patients, the British Legion representative expressed satisfaction with the government's work for ex-service mental patients, and the organization went on to make a public statement with reference to the recent publicity of the ESWS. This statement announced that, 'The British Legion disassociated themselves entirely from the expressions contained in a pamphlet issued by the ESWS. This pamphlet was possibly the basis of the statements which have appeared so generally in the public press.'[114]

These local difficulties with royal patronage and the British Legion indicate the extent to which veterans' charities in Britain relied upon either traditional or elite support networks to survive. Shortly after its foundation, the ESWS had decided that popular 'box collections' were ineffective and that substantial donations could only come from the economically or politically powerful.[115] However, this is not simply a question about resources but about the role of veterans' organizations in Britain. In France the *ancien combatants* played an effective and autonomous role at both local and national level, and in Germany large, politically active and highly visible veterans' societies organized mass demonstrations to demand their rights throughout the 1920s.[116] Yet in Britain, the British Legion worked so as to limit the radicalism of veterans' groups or service charities. It has been argued that, in comparison with the continental experience, veterans' movements have been relatively insignificant in British political history.[117] Yet the history of the ESWS indicates that the British Legion was not politically insignificant, but that its significance lay in its ability to ensure that service charities did not disturb the political consensus.

The furore provoked by the 1924 Armistice Day appeal prompted deep regret and anger within the ESWS. In a letter to Howard, Loseby described the situation in colourful, typically dramatic language and warned the chairman that he was 'surrounded by enemies'.[118] It is possible that Loseby was indulging in some hyperbole at this point but it is also clear that the society was not developing well. As a result, Milner insisted that the ESWS change direction, despite its morally sound position. In an informal, handwritten note to Howard, Milner tried to reassure the chairman about the loss of royal patronage. He claimed that Ponsonby was 'a very pompous individual' and suggested that the whole business had been motivated by personal vengeance. Yet at the same time Milner insisted that Howard must let the matter drop and sever all royal connections for the time being.[119] On a more formal level, Milner also wrote a note, clearly designed for the entire committee to read, outlining the necessary procedure for the future.

He began by stressing that he had not wanted to become president of the ESWS in the first place. He reminded committee members that he suffered from poor health and did not have sufficient time for the work; consequently he was not in a position to accept responsibility for the committee's activities. He had only agreed to become president because he thought that the society's work was very valuable and he was aware that his name would be useful for fund-raising.[120] It was certainly the case that Milner had initially refused the presidency and had offered to become a patron instead. He changed his mind only when committee members persuaded him that there was no real difference between the roles of patron and president. Milner had clearly been annoyed by all the negative publicity and his letter to the committee carried a veiled but still discernible hint: if they did not organize themselves more thoroughly they might well lose his support too. Milner was clearly trying to make the committee work in a more politically sophisticated manner. He pointed out that the offending pamphlet 'although undoubtedly true was injudicious'.[121] Moreover, that the ministry had met the ESWS to a certain degree and so a conciliatory approach would be more successful in the long term.

There is evidence that a majority of the committee took Milner's advice seriously and began moving in a less confrontational direction. Not all members of government ministries were automatically hostile to the demands of service charities, as the initial interest in Loseby's parliamentary meeting demonstrates. Furthermore, many committee members no longer wanted to place themselves in opposition to the Ministry of Pensions, as indicated by an incident in March 1925. Thompson had paid a visit to Chartham Asylum where there were eight ex-service patients, none of whom were officially treated as ex-service patients despite the assurances made by the Labour government in the previous year. In response, Thompson unilaterally decided that the ESWS should award all of the men 2/6 weekly, that being the sum that the Ministry of Pensions routinely awarded recognized ex-servicemen. The rest of the committee were deeply angered by Thompson's judgement. Not only was he being financially reckless, but also he was publicly opposing the Ministry of Pensions when the society had just been advised to gain more parliamentary support, and had decided to try to get on to the Ministry's list of approved homes.[122] Consequently, the committee would not agree to give extra funds to the patients in Chartham, and the issue led to Thompson's resignation.[123] Losing Thompson was a blow to the society in many ways because he had been an active and enthusiastic committee member since 1923. Yet he was also the member who by this stage had maintained the most consistent opposition to the Ministry of Pensions, and his departure did allow the organization to develop a more workable relationship with the ministry.

Part of the reason for the committee's growing desire to appear more amenable to the authorities lay in the way that the firm commitment to lunacy reform had begun to alienate not only potential supporters but those who could offer real expertise. Dr Edward Mapother had been a well-qualified asylum doctor before joining the RAMC in 1914. He later commanded the neurological division of Number Two Western General Hospital in Stockport and maintained an active interest in war neurosis and clinical psychiatry after the war.[124] The ESWS was keen to gain the support of such a well-respected figure, yet when Mapother agreed to work for the society in 1925 he insisted that his association be limited by very strict conditions: he was prepared to see patients, but he was not prepared to pronounce on whether or not symptoms were attributable to or aggravated by war service; he would not enter into any controversy with the Ministry of Pensions or the Board of Control; he would not accept any official connection with society; and he would not allow any publicity to be attached to his name.[125] Moreover, Mapother went to the effort of informing the Ministry of Pensions of the restrictions he had placed on his working relationship with the ESWS.[126] Given Mapother's position, is it unsurprising that he insisted on working according to his own conditions; nevertheless, his responses do indicate a genuine level of suspicion. Clearly he was afraid that his name might be misused in some way, and his strong statements indicate the extent to which the ESWS had alienated those on whom it relied for help.

The change in the committee's attitude was made clear later in that year, when all committee members responded cautiously to a scandal involving the Ministry of Pensions' Hospital in Orpington, Kent. One patient at the institution claimed that a doctor had hit him and had taken out a summons to that effect. In response, other patients took the opportunity to complain about a whole host of issues: mainly food, clothing and personal liberty. Recalling Lomax's and Loseby's earlier words, the patients insisted that 'we are treated like convicts'.[127] As part of the process of gaining support for the injured man, five hospital patients approached the ESWS offices in Victoria and received help with drafting a letter, which they then forwarded to the *Daily Graphic.* Members of the ESWS committee were prepared to offer some help but they shied away from any controversial publicity. An ESWS barrister was briefed for the case but two committee members asked the editor of the *Daily Graphic* to delay the publication of the letter. In the meantime, the men were asked to frame the letter in their own words and to send it in themselves, without any obvious or public reference to the ESWS. The committee's comments at this point are revealing, as minutes record that, 'The committee thought it advisable that the society should not figure too prominently in the case as the statements made by the men might be exaggerated.'[128]

Consequently, the ESWS continued to support mentally damaged ex-servicemen but the committee became more reluctant to court controversy. The *Daily Graphic* articles mentioned that the men had sent a petition to the ESWS but made no mention of the way in which the society was providing the men with financial support.[129] Even more significantly, committee members were demonstrating a level of suspicion for the first time. Prior to this case they had supported ex-servicemen's claims unconditionally, yet by the end of November 1925 they were clearly trying to maintain a balanced position between the wounded ex-servicemen and the Ministry of Pensions. By the following year the position had shifted even further, and the ESWS was explicit about disassociating itself from lunacy reform, announcing that, 'It was the general feeling of the Committee, that enlargement on the treatment of ex-servicemen in asylums be eliminated as far as possible in the new booklet.'[130] By the mid-1920s it had become clear that it was impolitic to associate the plight of mentally wounded men with the broader issue of lunacy reform. Some ex-servicemen did remain in local asylums and there is no doubt that their conditions were often pitiful. Yet the ESWS shifted its attention to those who could more easily be reintegrated into society; in short, to those who could most effectively be mended. It is this process of re-integration and respectability that forms the basis of the next chapter.

5

No Longer 'Nerve-Wracked Boys'

That is the help beyond all others. Find out how to make useless people useful, and let them earn their money instead of begging it.[1]

CAPTAIN A. K. WATSON, HONORARY TREASURER OF THE ESWS

By the mid-1920s, the ESWS was paying less attention to lunacy reform. As a result, the society devoted more time to the development of new homes and associated activities for mentally wounded men. Wittingly or otherwise, the ESWS did continue to aggravate the Ministry of Pensions, but the overt commitment to lunacy reform had alienated so many potential supporters in the early 1920s that committee members became determined to adopt a less provocative stance. They aimed instead to capitalize on their good relationships as the decade developed. The following chapter charts the changes in the ESWS as it moved away from the controversies of lunacy reform: by 1929 the ESWS was no longer just trying to rescue wrongly incarcerated veterans, it was providing respectable work for decent men. As part of this process, the ESWS stopped presenting mentally broken men as wretched victims of the war and started to present them as veterans deserving more respect than pity. Shell-shocked men were carrying the memory of the war in that they were literally unable to forget their wartime traumas, but in order to gain widespread popular and, especially, political support, the veterans had to carry these memories in a way that emphasized their status as respectable, hard-working and suitably masculine men. These images of shell-shocked men have not endured; on the contrary, the shell-shocked man is now the most tragic and the most emblematic of all the Great War victims. However, an exclusive focus upon shell shock as an emblem for war conceals an important part of the post-war history of shell shock, namely the extent to which mentally wounded veterans were presented as masculine, respectable citizens.

THE DEVELOPMENT OF THE EX-SERVICES'
WELFARE SOCIETY

Despite its troubled beginning, the ESWS was a firmly established charity by
the mid-1920s and it was involved in some extensive development work by the
end of the decade. Chartfield closed in 1922, yet while the society lacked a home
of its own it paid for its patients to receive care at private nursing homes. The
ESWS then opened Eden Manor in Beckenham in 1924, and in 1926 purchased
both the Long House in Ashstead and a hostel in Leatherhead. In the following
year a sheltered workshop was attached to the hostel, and in 1930 Eden Lodge, a
Home adjoining Eden Manor, was opened. In 1930 the society developed a new
initiative: a complex of 12 houses designed to accommodate veterans, their wives
and children. In the press, all these establishments were usually referred to as 'Sir
Frederick Milner Homes'.

It was difficult to set up a new charity in the 1920s. The paucity of official
help for all war veterans meant that there were many private charities attempting
to bridge the gap in state welfare provision. Consequently, the ESWS had to
face serious competition for limited public help. It is of course difficult to
assess public attitudes towards shell-shocked veterans accurately. Most of the
population may well have been involved in the Great War, but not everyone
had the same war experiences; certainly there was no unified public response
to the war. As Terraine has noted 'the patriotic widow who loses all her sons is
a part of Public Opinion; so is the Conscientious Objector; so is the profiteer'.[2]

By the same token, public attitudes towards shell shock were similarly diverse.
There were members of the public who thought that the shell-shocked veteran
was a malingerer or a criminal, but there were also those who believed that he
was a poor misunderstood boy and those who saw him as a genuine war hero.
The initial ESWS rhetoric stressed the importance of creating a broad network
of support, embracing a range of classes and of political positions. Yet this was
not the case in practice, and by the late 1920s it was clear that the society had
developed by relying heavily on elite support to attract funding and publicity.
By 1928 there was a strong connection between the ESWS and the Conservative
party, despite the high-profile quarrels with MPs Hunter-Weston and Colfox.
This reconciliation was largely welcome, but such an overt political association
had its drawbacks too. According to Howard, 'Certain members of the press had
enquired why we had only had Conservative Vice Presidents if the society was
non-political'.[3] Committee members agreed that this was a problem and that
the organization should represent all political opinion; nevertheless, the ESWS
remained dominated by Conservatives.

As with the Knutsford campaign at the beginning of the war, the ESWS
initially attracted a lot of high-profile public attention. There were a number

of prestigious names at the first ESWS Drawing Room meeting in January 1919, and committee members certainly believed that having Milner's support was invaluable. The way in which the society presented itself also indicates the importance members had always attached to occupying high-status venues. The annual report from 1922 includes details of a meeting at Lady Perk's House in Kensington Palace Gardens, a fete at Claridges, two balls at Grafton Galleries and a concert at Cam House.[4] It is a real indication of the way in which the society saw itself that advertisements for ESWS events were often placed in the 'Court Circular' column of *The Times*. This obviously fits into the traditional pattern of upper-middle-class charity work. Even when arranging popular events, the ESWS arranged high-profile support. At a fund-raising matinee at the Palace Theatre, Sir Harry Lauder sang and made an appeal, and the Queen agreed to be patron.[5] The society wanted support from social and political elites, and from established bodies such as the Red Cross, the Ministry of Pensions, the Board of Agriculture and the Labour Ministry. There was a level of internal contradiction in the society's attitude at this stage. The ESWS did want to challenge official policy, and most committee members did not want the Homes to become ministry institutions. On the other hand, committee members clearly wanted establishment endorsement and approval.

The ESWS also wanted a high level of popular support, but the society's records indicate the sort of ambiguous reception that shell-shocked men could face in post-war Britain. This ambiguity mattered, partly because a charity requires strong and consistent public contributions, but also because the government believed that neurasthenic men really needed a high level of popular backing. Major Herbert Evans, a Chief Inspector at the Ministry of Pensions, asserted that 'the public can be of great assistance by helping the men suffering from this disability to surmount their difficulties and make light of their complaints'.[6] Unfortunately the general public did not always feel able or willing to provide such assistance. There is evidence of a reluctance to accept shell-shocked men into the local community during the war, and this reluctance continued into the post-war period. In 1917 an owner who had been willing to let his property for the care of wounded veterans withdrew his permission as soon as he realized that the purpose was to house neurological casualties.[7] A Captain Hardcastle-type figure may well have been harmless, but nobody really wanted to live next door to him. As a result of this type of incident, society members were worried that people would object to having a home for shell-shocked men in their neighbourhood. Their fears were not unfounded. In 1920 when the ESWS was trying to lease Chartfield, neighbours became unhappy once they realized that the house was going to be used for mentally disabled servicemen. Mrs Clarke met the locals and was able to persuade them not to raise any formal objections, but the owners of Chartfield were intransigent and did not allow the property to become licensed as a nursing home.[8] There are also indications that the society found it difficult to attract financial support. Box collections became simply unviable and an experiment with selling the Pignall inventions at Selfridges was singularly unsuccessful.[9] The ESWS even found it hard to persuade employers to participate in training schemes for recovering men.[10] The ESWS papers do not suggest that the organizers encountered any serious or explicit hostility towards mentally wounded veterans, but they do indicate popular responses were mixed and that fund-raising was difficult in the immediate post-war years.[11]

CHARITY, POLITICS AND CLASS

The competitive fund-raising environment was one of the reasons for the highly sensational nature of some of the ESWS campaigns: committee members simply wanted to ensure that their campaigns were noticed. Since 1919, emotionally charged ESWS publicity presented the public with stark visions of the mentally broken ex-servicemen amidst incurable lunatics. As in the following letter from Milner, the contrast between the wretched victim of the war and the hopeless madman was paramount:

> All around he [the shell-shocked veteran] sees tragic cases of incurable lunacy, and hears their demented cries night and day. So far as he can foresee his future, it is an eternity of horror among the unfortunate people ... *And his bitterest thought must be that his fate is the 'reward' for giving up all to serve his country in the Great War!*[12]

Leaving aside the fact that this sensationalism alienated many potential supporters, there were two problems with this type of publicity. First, the distinction between the mentally broken veteran and the lunatic was not always as clear as Milner's words imply. Robert Laurie's unfortunate history makes this point plain. In 1924 Laurie, an ex-serviceman, was in Hanwell Mental Hospital and his mother was eager to have him transferred to one of the special asylums funded by the Ministry of Pensions. When writing to the EWSW to ask for help, Helen Laurie described her son as 'making good progress'.[13] Yet the Medical Superintendent of Hanwell Mental Hospital disagreed and described Laurie in the following terms:

> Robert Alexander Laurie, re-admitted 11 July 1924, is suffering from Dementia Praecox. He is dull, slow and foolish, lacks interest in himself and is untidy and slovenly in his habits. He does no work and cannot apply himself to any work, when apparently willing to do it. He takes no interest in current events and rarely if ever reads the daily paper.[14]

Was Laurie recovering well, or is the doctor's harrowing picture more accurate? We cannot answer that question with any certainty, but Laurie's story certainly indicates that it was not always possible to make a clear distinction between the honourable mentally broken ex-serviceman and the hopeless lunatic.

Secondly, the ESWS had continually emphasized the sheer numbers of men being held in lunatic asylums: publicity material constantly drew attention to the 5,000 or 6,000 ex-servicemen who required urgent and immediate help. Yet this constant attention to the numbers meant that ESWS achievements would always appear weak in comparison with the problem it had identified. As the Ministry of Pensions noted in 1924, the ESWS had raised £4,000 but had only provided accommodation for about 20 men. In comparison, the government had provided care for over 50,000 cases at the cost of approximately £1,000,000: obviously the government was providing much more care than the ESWS and was doing so far more efficiently. The government could, and did, use these figures to highlight the reckless extravagance of the ESWS, but of course the backbone of ESWS complaints had always been that the government relied on inadequate asylum care simply because it was cheap. However, while ex-servicemen were undoubtedly being placed in local asylums, these were not the only official options available: 44,000 men had been treated outside of the local asylum system.[15] In addition, in 1923 the Ministry of Pensions had established two 'special asylums', one at Kirkburton in the north of England and another, Old Manor, near Salisbury in the south. The institutions had been designed specifically 'for any case which shows distinct promise of improvement under special treatment', and they were accommodating a total of 450 men by December 1924.[16] It was one of these special asylums – Kirkburton – that Helen Laurie had in mind when she asked for her son Robert to be transferred from Hanwell, a local asylum. There were also a number of neurological hospitals and outpatient clinics around the country that were funded by the Ministry of Pensions: at the end of 1924, 800 men were receiving treatment in these hospitals and 750 were receiving outpatient treatment.[17] The hospitals and the clinics all offered a mixture of psychotherapy and occupational therapy.

Clearly it would cost a great deal to house all of these men in ESWS homes, or in anything similar. The house at Beckenham was spacious. A picture of the Eden Manor lounge shows us neatly dressed men reading newspapers and listening to the gramophone; their clean house-shoes do not disturb the polished parquet.[18] We can see bookshelves, flowers and a painting; we also know that the Ladies' House Committee paid great attention to household details and ensured that there was a plentiful supply of tablecloths, napkins and antimacassars.[19] The room was clearly designed to encourage bourgeois domesticity and to distinguish the Frederick Milner Homes from the pauper asylum. There were also ample grounds so that the men could relax in the garden or enjoy horticultural projects;

a picture of men picking fruit in the garden of Eden Manor is positively bucolic.[20] One can of course argue that veterans deserved this type of treatment, but the fact remained that ESWS activity had only provided homes for a tiny proportion of mentally wounded men throughout the 1920s. As the cost of government treatment continued to rise, ministry officials were able to make comparisons, which cast the ESWS in an unfavourable light:

> Against the £3,005,000 per annum which the Ministry expends and the thousands of beds it has provided, the society's claim to consideration is 30 unneeded beds in an unnecessary institution, together with an unlimited supply of incorrect and misleading literature.[21]

The ESWS committee began to realize that a continual focus on the '6,000 ex-servicemen' being held in asylums was not always effective. In addition, throughout the 1920s it became more and more obvious that the bedrock of ESWS support was going to come from come from the political right. The ESWS was reluctant to nurture relations with the left-wing press because support from the left tended to produce the kind of political conclusions, which were anathema to the largely conservative, pro-military committee. A letter in the *Swindon Advertiser* fiercely supported Milner's campaign and went on to argue that wars 'are not waged for the people but only by the people, to the financial gain of the few and the downfall of the many'.[22] ESWS committee members were embarrassed. Milner supported the Conservative government and was openly hostile to the Labour party, and no one at the ESWS wanted to inflame left-wing and pacifist tendencies.[23] However, it is also the case that the left-wing press, although not entirely indifferent to mentally wounded veterans, certainly afforded the issue a far lower priority than did the newspapers of the right. *John Bull*, for example, featured articles on shell shock regularly in the 1920s whereas more left-wing papers such as the *Daily Herald* or the *Labour Leader* focused less on mentally wounded veterans and more on the general problems facing destitute soldiers, such as pensions or housing.

This tendency to the political right was reflected in the society's attitude towards class. The history of wartime shell shock has already indicated the importance of class in terms of both diagnosis and treatment. Post-war procedures were similar in that working-class veterans consistently received substandard treatment from a government determined to maintain the social structures of pre-war Britain.[24] In many ways this is unsurprising. We have already indicated how the medical-military profession was resistant to change, and mental health care was an area in which class boundaries had traditionally been very clearly marked. Advertisements for private mental health care homes were usually explicit about the particular class of patient they wished to attract. St Andrews

Hospital for Mental Diseases in Northampton insisted that it offered treatment 'For the Upper and Middle Classes Only' as did 'The Coppice' in Nottingham.[25] The ESWS commitment to lunacy reform was in many ways a class-based issue, as was the society's commitment to provide decent funerals for all men in their care.[26] In both cases the primary motivation was to ensure that old soldiers were not being treated as paupers. ESWS donors reflected this traditional approach. In 1920 a potential supporter wrote to the ESWS explaining that he wanted to make out a legacy for the society; however, he would only do so if he received assurances that the money would be used exclusively for the care of an officer. The committee agreed with his request and accepted the money.[27] This determination to maintain class distinctions existed uneasily alongside the worker radicalism of the period, and resulted in a high level of class consciousness among voluntary organizations. This is best demonstrated by the National Federation of Discharged and Disabled Soldiers and Sailors (NFDDSS), which limited its work to the rank and file and to officers who had risen from the ranks.[28]

The NFDDSS commitments indicated a high level of class consciousness combined with a recognition that class divisions were not as straightforward as they might appear. Clearly the distinction between officers and other ranks did not neatly reflect civilian class divisions, a situation exemplified in the 'ex-officer problem' which persisted throughout the interwar period.[29] The current historiographical focus on the distinction between officers and other ranks provides a distorted picture of class privilege among veterans after the war. Even contemporaries were unclear about the class status of officers, and in 1920 Haig called for greater support for ex-officers on the grounds that many of these men did not come from the privileged backgrounds normally associated with the officer class. On the contrary, he declared that 90 per cent of ex-officers of the national army had risen through the ranks 'at the call of leaders'.[30] They therefore deserved support because, unlike the pre-war officer class, they were not independently wealthy, they had accepted commissions out of a sense of duty and they had clearly not been motivated by personal gain. Haig's comments can be seen as part of a wider discourse of front-line camaraderie in which the combatant/non-combatant division was held to be more meaningful than divisions of class or rank. The ESWS initially constructed itself on this prevalent commitment to wartime comradeship and tried to appeal for support by reflecting this. Policy statements on this issue were consistent and clear: the ESWS existed 'for ex-servicemen of all ranks and all services (including the mercantile marine) their dependants and relatives'.[31] Furthermore, to make this commitment possible in real terms, ESWS fees were set so that they related to the man's ability to pay.

Yet alongside this genuine dedication to equality of treatment, the ESWS was also committed to maintaining boundaries of class or rank. The society itself aimed to provide services for all ranks but no one expected officers and men to share the same intimate physical spaces. By 1920, committee members were planning to establish units of 35–40 beds for ex-officers and of 45–50 beds for men from the other ranks.[32] It was widely believed that a more democratic approach would be unpopular with officers, although Loseby attempted to make the distinction less stark by proposing one home for officers and men of a similar education, and one for all other men from the other ranks.[33] Loseby's proposal would have resulted in genuinely arbitrary – and possibly quite odd – distinctions. His plan was not implemented, but committee members remained consistently confused about the society's real approach towards class division. During discussions about the purchase of a new house, Griffin insisted that any new home should cater for both officers and men, and he complained that Chartfield had been an elitist institution because it had cared only for officers. Yet Griffin's concerns were quite unfounded because Chartfield had always been open to both officers and men from the other ranks. However, it was difficult to make a clear and simple distinction between officers and men. The ESWS distinguished between regular army officers, officers promoted from the ranks and temporary officers;[34] in short, there were three different categories of officer. This was complicated, but the society was reluctant to abandon this distinction, and continued to describe and classify men according to their service rank. So by 1930 the ESWS was still categorizing some men according to their position in the services, although the men concerned had been demobilized and many had been leading civilian lives for over a decade. Committee members and staff were not trying to make their homes into service institutions and the commitment to military rank can best be understood as a device to remind men of wartime comradeship. By celebrating wartime service identity, the ESWS was minimizing the possibility of post-war conflict.

SOCIAL CONSERVATISM AND GENDER

By the mid-1920s the ESWS was losing the elements of radicalism that had marked the original society. This development was facilitated by a series of personnel changes on the executive committee. In Dr Mapother's words:

> The personnel of the Executive Committee has recently been almost entirely changed, the wild people who used to dominate it have been discarded or reduced to insignificance and the management now seems to be in the hands of very reasonable and capable businessmen.[35]

These changes resulted in better relationships with key bodies such as the Board of Control, and there were serious attempts to facilitate a working relationship with the Ministry of Pensions. Mapother was right in that the personnel changes radically altered the nature of the committee. It became a group led by businessmen and military figures whereas originally the committee had been largely, although not exclusively, organized by women. For the first three years, the committee was dominated by Mrs Clarke, the honorary organizer. She was the most active and vocal member of the committee, she personally guaranteed the mortgage on Chartfield, negotiated with government ministers, wrote letters to *The Times*, and was very much responsible for the initial creation of the organization. Mrs Clarke was certainly energetic and prepared to be provocative. Yet the society's early radical tendencies diminished and its public face became more and more conservative, as is indicated by its advertising practices. ESWS advertisements and features appeared most often in the *Gentlewoman*, *The Times*, *The Sunday Times*, the *Daily Mail*, the *Daily Express* and *John Bull*. This particular range of newspapers can be seen as offering a spectrum of right-wing opinion, from the socially conservative and pro-establishment to the rabidly populist. By 1922 the ESWS was receiving a great deal of its publicity from the *Gentlewoman* because the journal often waived its standard fees and asked the society to pay for printing costs only.[36] The *Gentlewoman* was clearly aimed at refined middle-class ladies and so by associating themselves with it, committee members were presenting the ESWS as a traditional, philanthropic organization rather than a radical or challenging one. It had long been accepted that that the philanthropic world was an acceptable and comfortable place for women, and studies of the voluntary sector in this period have given much importance to the role of women as providers of philanthropy.[37] Yet as we have already said, the women committee members did not attempt to challenge male power structures. Right from the outset it was clear that women would defer to their male colleagues on important issues. At one stage Mrs Clarke insisted that leading members of the nursing profession should sit on the executive committee in advisory positions. This was hardly an outlandish suggestion but Major Thwaites, the society's doctor, disagreed and so deferred the matter without any discussion. The issue was not raised again, and no explanation was given.[38]

After the loss of Chartfield in 1922, the committee's early radicalism became even less visible. The loss compounded the ESWS's economic problems and committee members tended to blame Mrs Clarke for financial mismanagement and poor book-keeping practices.[39] The whole episode resulted in Mrs Clarke being forced to resign.[40] This was the point at which the organization became much more masculine. There were always women on the committee, and for most of the decade there were more women than men. However, from 1922 there was a clear male hierarchy and it was men who dominated at meetings, made key resolutions and adopted the most public roles. After the establishment of Eden

Manor in 1924, the women's energies were directed more towards the home, and a Ladies' House Committee was established. Initially the members wanted the House Committee to play an important role, but the women lacked confidence in their own power and almost apologized for making decisions about the range of treatments to be made available at Eden Manor. Committee-meeting minutes record that 'the committee realised that in making suggestions connected with the medical side of the society, they were placed in a very delicate position'.[41] As time went on, the Ladies' House Committee increasingly dealt with smaller, more domestic questions such as furnishings, repairs, entertainments and outings. Moreover, it is significant that women did not sit on the far more influential Finance Committee. It is also the case that the House Committee had ceased to be a 'Ladies' Committee' in all but name by 1926 when Surgeon Rear Admiral Axford of the Executive Committee began to sit in on meetings. These meetings were originally attended by at least five women about once a month, yet by 1929 there were generally long gaps between meetings and often Isabella Kirkland Vesey, the chairman [sic], was the only one present. More and more it seemed as though she was doing all the work associated with the House Committee, and it was Axford rather than one of the other women who tended to accompany her on her visits to Eden Manor. The Ladies' House Committee was eventually dissolved altogether in 1929. In its place, Colonel Wood was appointed, and charged with making weekly visits to Eden Manor so that matron could refer matters of household management to him.[42]

Women had lost control of this organization despite the fact that charity work was a traditionally female sphere. One explanation for the decline of female influence could lie in some of the early responses to shell shock. Women's established roles had long been somewhat marginalized in the treatment of shell shock. While it was widely accepted that middle-class ladies would visit sick and wounded servicemen in hospitals, this practice had been actively discouraged in many shell-shock institutions. Collie was convinced that much damage could ensue from 'kindly intentioned philanthropic lady visitors'.[43] It was not only the lady visitor who was viewed with suspicion: Dr Brock, a temporary captain in the RAMC, was concerned that mentally damaged men could become over-dependent on their own wives if allowed to spend too much time with them, and would consequently fail to develop the will power required to conquer their illnesses.[44] Given that shell-shock treatment was based on practices in civilian mental health hospitals, female nurses had only a limited role to play too. Although some women did nurse war neurosis cases – as the Southborough report indicates – on the whole doctors were unhappy about female nurses associating too closely with shell-shocked men. At Dykebar War hospital, nurses played only a minimal role and their duties were largely connected with the kitchen and the dining hall rather than the patients.[45] The Great War has often been presented as an event that provided new opportunities for women in the workplace. Yet as far as shell shock and women's work was concerned, the effects were far from emancipating. There were greater numbers of mentally ill men and serious staff shortages in mental hospitals, but women were still not welcomed into mental health nursing. Mental health nursing remained a resolutely male sphere well into the mid-twentieth century.

The language of front-line camaraderie and the 'old soldier' discourse may well have challenged female authority with regards to charity and philanthropy. As has been said, after the Great War many conservatively inclined establishment figures began to call for state aid in a manner that would have been unthinkable had the needy not been war veterans. With men like Haig involving themselves in high-profile charity work, public welfare became a very suitable masculine activity – as long as it was directed towards old combatants. As far as the ESWS in particular was concerned, the organization developed in a way that made it far removed from a traditional ladies' philanthropic society. This was particularly the case after 1925 when, under the influence of Sir Ralph Millbourn, committee members became determined to see the organization succeed as a business rather than simply a charity. This attitude was summed up by Captain Watson, the honorary treasurer, in a speech to the AGM in 1929, 'It [the work of the committee] is far from being a pastime – this is a real man's job. That is what is expected here. If you are prepared to take off your jacket and work, you are all right here.'[46] The implication was clear: women's work was a mere pastime.

This gender bias did not just affect women on the committee; it also had an impact on women who may have needed treatment. A discussion about the society's position towards women claimants indicates another way in which ESWS radicalism had become diluted over the years. In 1920 the society had announced that its remit included the care of women who had suffered a breakdown as a result of military service.[47] Yet in April 1923, Miss Vaughan, a new committee member, asked whether or not women could apply to the ESWS for help. No one on the committee could remember any prior commitment to women, and Miss Vaughan had to write to the London County Council to find out what had been written on the original society deeds.[48] Obviously no one had paid much attention to the problems of mentally wounded women during these years, although by October 1923 it had been established that 71 ex-service women nurses were being held in local asylums.[49] Nevertheless, the formal commitment towards care for women remained. A 1924 publicity leaflet referred to '6,000 Ex-Service Men and Women Nurses in Lunatic Asylums', and records do demonstrate that the ESWS supported Nurses Clappen and Lovejoy, women who required long-term mental health treatment as a consequence of their war service.[50] However, it was not possible to keep women in any of the society's homes, and although ex-servicewomen were entitled to work in the industrial workshop at Leatherhead, the women actually working there in the late 1920s were the wives of neurasthenic ex-servicemen, not mentally wounded nurses.

OFFICIAL APPROVAL AND FINANCIAL IMPROVEMENT

So from the mid-1920s the ESWS became increasingly more conservative, possibly more cautious, on issues of class and gender. This was partly as a response to the discord created by its strong identification with lunacy reform, and partly due to the realization that the society could become much more successful if it gained strong establishment approval. The biggest identifiable change within the ESWS can be seen in its attitude to the Ministry of Pensions. The society's initial policy was in direct opposition to the ministry, and a determination to maintain this opposition resulted in key resignations in 1923. Yet the society had adopted a far milder approach by 1925, and was even trying to get its name on the Ministry of Pensions' list of approved establishments by this stage.[51] However, relations were still fractious. Later that same year, ESWS solicitors wrote to the Board of Trade asking for permission for the society to go through the process of incorporation. At first the Board of Trade had seemed agreeable, and then it had written to say that incorporation could not be granted. The ministers at the Board of Trade genuinely had no objections to the plan, but they bowed to pressure from the Ministry of Pensions and refused to grant the relevant licence. This was a grave blow to the committee members who wanted the society to adopt a more formal status, and wanted also to protect individual members from the possibility of litigation. Nevertheless, they decided to make no complaint or comment about it; instead their response was simply to leave the matter to Milner who had many friends in the Commons and so had the opportunity to influence people informally.[52] Clearly there was a growing belief that negotiation was better than opposition, and this may well have been a response to Milner who had strongly advised a change of attitude as a result of the loss of royal patronage in 1924.

The ESWS tried to maintain this non-confrontational approach to the Ministry of Pensions. In 1926, Howard and Millbourn met Colonel George Stanley MP (Unionist, Willesden East) and Sir Lisle Webb, the Director General of Medical Services, to establish a working relationship between the ESWS and the ministry. During this meeting Millbourn explained that the ESWS no longer aimed to remove all ex-servicemen from asylums; rather, it wanted to raise money to help those men who had no choice but to remain in asylums.[53] Negotiations then collapsed because Stanley believed that a recent ESWS pamphlet was still hostile to the government. Committee members were disappointed and decided to send Stanley a conciliatory letter.[54] The Ministry of Pensions displayed even more antagonism the following year by effectively cancelling the annual ESWS boxing tournament even though arrangements had been made, publicity had been distributed and members of the royal family had publicly proclaimed their support. The committee drafted explanatory letters to ministers and the press, but then decided not to send them because they did not want to appear provocative and, bearing in mind the scandal of 1924, they did not want to draw the King into any controversy.[55]

Unbeknown to ESWS committee members, the Ministry of Pensions consistently communicated with other government departments, private companies and members of the public to ensure that they did not cooperate with the ESWS. A few examples will suffice. In 1923, Milner contacted a previous donor, Sir John Butcher, to ask him for another donation. Butcher wrote to the Ministry of Pensions for advice before making a second donation, and was told that 'there was not a great deal of solid fact' behind the ESWS appeals.[56] The ministry was no more supportive in 1927 when Tyron wrote to Worthington Evan at the War Office, requesting that he remove the ESWS from the officially approved list of Friends, Associations and Societies. Although the ESWS had become less confrontational by this stage, Tyron still described it as a body that had caused his department 'serious mischief'.[57] Moreover, officials at the Ministry of Pensions did not restrict themselves only to dissuading potential donors: government officials also instructed the Metropolitan Police to monitor the ESWS offices in Victoria and the ESWS home at Beckenham. However, this obviously intrusive behaviour provided the Ministry of Pensions with no ammunition. The police report concluded that the work in the society's offices was 'carried on in a very satisfactory manner'; police comments on Eden Manor noted that, 'Several patients are always in residence and the place is quietly and respectably conducted.'[58]

ESWS committee members were unaware of this level of official hostility. Yet at the same time as being discredited by the Ministry of Pensions, they were developing far better relationships with local asylums. Annual reports in the late 1920s make some very positive comments about changes in asylum practice, and ESWS committee members established particularly good links with staff at Broadmoor asylum and at the Scottish Board of Control.[59] In addition, the society was growing considerably less critical of the government in general. The annual report of 1927 commented that, 'Whatever criticism may be leveled at our State Departments, it must be remembered that the aftermath of a war always brings in its train problems of unemployment and misery, which no Government can adequately compensate.'[60]

This more constructive approach towards the government was accompanied by the society's growing financial success. Table 3 indicates the way in which income from appeals grew enormously in the latter half of the decade, confirming Milner's belief that it was more useful to seek establishment support than to court controversy.

Table 3 ESWS Income, 1926–1930[61]

Year	Income from appeals etc.
1926	£25,428 1s 6d
1927	£33,148 8s 3d
1928	£40,349
1929	£55,044
1930	£49,937

There was a general increase in income, year on year, the exception being 1930 when income fell slightly. Yet this decline can be explained by a particularly generous one-off donation of £10,000, which had artificially inflated the 1929 figure. Normal fund-raising procedures in 1930 had still raised more money than they had in the previous year. This financial success is even more striking when compared with earlier years: in 1921 and 1922, for example, donations had amounted to less than £5,000 annually.[62]

By 1925 the ESWS was paying far less attention to the campaign for lunacy reform. The committee still gave donations to the NCLR, but were far more specific about the way in which their money could be spent, and members clearly wanted to control the relationship between the two organizations.[63] As a result of this change of direction and a healthier financial situation, the ESWS was able to develop a far wider, and less controversial, range of activities. There has been little research into the condition of mentally wounded men who did not receive official help or treatment. By definition, these men were less likely to have their experiences recorded than men who had undergone repeated interviews with pension officials and doctors. Yet ESWS records provide some insights into the lives of these men because by the time they came to the society's attention, they had often been without official support for months or even years.

Initially the primary aim of the ESWS was to establish homes for neurasthenic ex-servicemen. Yet providing care homes was only one aspect of the society's work, and although their homes were both important and hugely symbolic, a far greater number of men benefited from the services set up to deal with men who were outside the care of ESWS institutions. During the period between the closure of Chartfield and the opening of Eden Manor all of the society's resources were committed to supporting men in this way. However, even after the homes started to become properly established, the society continued to devote significant funds to this type of work. Table 4 indicates where and how the ESWS allocated its expenses in the years 1926–1930.

Table 4 ESWS Expenditure, 1926–1930[64]

Year	Ex Gratia payments and clothing	Further assistance, relief, hostel accommodation	Dental treatment	After care	Legal aid	Assistance and relief expenses	Total
1926	£1425	£168	No details	£247	£133	£800	£2,773
1927	£2,599	£303	£224	£296	£3,215	£1,688	£8,325
1928	£4,089	£491	£168	£324	No details	£2,689	£7,761
1929	£3,200	£333	£144	£284	No details	£3,101	£7,062
1930	£3,961	£562	£152	£294	No details	£3,729	£8,698

During this period the number of staff increased and specialisms developed as the society began to organize its workers into seven discrete departments, namely advice, employment, pensions, legal assistance, financial assistance and relief, medical and asylums. By 1926, ESWS staff occupied four rooms on the second floor of 122 Victoria Street, London, at a rental of £250 per annum.[65] These rooms were not grand, but they were a great improvement on the previous premises at Craven Road, Paddington where staff had been crammed into a tiny office perched above an outlet for Aerialite and a rather shabby general store. As a result of this expansion and organization, men travelling to the society's offices were able to receive specialized help from a team of about a dozen dedicated staff, and as can be seen from the figures in Table 4, throughout the latter half of the 1920s ex-servicemen continued to need help with clothing, accommodation, medical and legal expenses. It is worth noting that the society stopped publishing the amount it devoted to legal expenses after 1927, although it continued to give money for legal fees throughout the 1920s. Some men asked for help only once, perhaps to find a job or claim a pension, whereas others needed help over a number of years, especially those with families to support. Some men found it very difficult to re-establish independent lives: for example, Mr Meyrick, one of the society's first patients, was still living in a society home in 1929. It is widely accepted that mental health problems caused by combat in the Great War continued throughout the 1920s. However, it was the opinion of the ESWS that many men remained undiagnosed in the immediate post-war years and only had their symptoms belatedly recognized. As late as 1928, the society reported on the 'ever-increasing call on the society's resources' and commented that 'whilst in cases of physical disablement the question has by now become regularised, the mental and nerve cases are only being revealed as time goes on, calling for increased facilities for treatment'.[66]

MENTALLY BROKEN MEN IN THE LATE 1920S

In some respects, mentally wounded veterans were in a worse position at the end of the decade than at the beginning. Official provision remained inadequate, and by 1929 severe economic conditions were making the matter worse as the Depression meant that mentally wounded veterans needed more help. Neurasthenic ex-servicemen had always found it difficult to re-establish themselves in the post-war job market, and by 1930 the ESWS was pessimistic about the future, believing that conditions for ex-servicemen were very unlikely to improve due to 'conditions of life in the country at the present time'.[67]

Some examples from throughout the 1920s and beyond indicate the difficulties faced by neurasthenic ex-servicemen. In 1924 Mr Ford was a patient at the Ministry of Pensions' neurological hospital in Saltash, Cornwall, a specialist institution designed to provide men with occupational treatment.[68] Although he was officially receiving care from the state system, he travelled to London and arrived at the ESWS with no undergarments and no coat over his waistcoat. To make matters worse, Mr Ford's wife was ill and the couple had a small child whom they were unable to care for properly. How he had made the journey is unclear, but it had certainly been a difficult one and he had obviously been desperate for help. The ESWS gave Mr Ford £2 6s for a room and board, and also gave him clothes and boots.[69] This was not an isolated case. Not only had Mr Ford previously received £3 to alleviate similar difficulties, but the ESWS continually had to provide men with very basic items of clothing such as boots, jackets and underclothes. It is also important to note that these men were not all homeless or existing outside of the state welfare system. In particular, there was a real problem at the Ministry of Pensions' hospital in Saltash where records indicate that many patients had complained about a lack of clothing.[70] Those who had received no official help at all were in an even worse position. One ex-soldier had been taken prisoner during the war after suffering severe facial injuries. While he was in captivity, his left eye was removed, and he underwent several other operations too. He then developed severe nervous troubles and remained unemployed after his release. This man was eventually admitted to an ESWS home in September 1928, after having spent a decade suffering from an untreated nervous complaint.[71]

As well as the numerous cases in which men and their families were provided with money, shelter and advice, the ESWS also advised men how to claim for pensions or how to claim for an increase in their pension. The society had some particularly notable successes in this area, even when making new claims in the later 1920s. One example involves a man who had made a claim on account of nervous trouble in 1920. His claim was rejected and he then went to Australia and did not make another claim until six years later. This second claim was also refused and no further one was lodged until 1928 when the official time limit to do so had expired. The ESWS successfully represented this man at a tribunal where he was given an award at the 60 per cent rate plus allowances for his wife and child. He was later admitted for treatment and given the maximum allowances.[72] It is worth emphasizing that the man had applied for a war-related pension in 1920, but received neither pension nor treatment until 1928. However, he was luckier than Private Frederick Fahey. Fahey had been shell shocked in 1918 and invalided to Lord Derby's mental hospital in Warrington, Lancashire. In June 1919 he was discharged from the army and granted a small pension (at the 30 per cent rate) in recognition of the fact that his mental instability had been aggravated by war service. The pension continued until March 1920 when Fahey was described as 'quite recovered', yet he clearly had relapses and suffered from severe episodes of mental derangement from the summer of 1930. By 1940, Fahey's wife was clearly unable to cope – the family was living in Trinidad with five children and no income – and so she was pleading with the ministry for a pension. Her efforts were quite futile and the Ministry of Pensions simply refused to grant Frederick Fahey or his family any further assistance. In a handwritten note for the Colonial Office, the medical officer commented that, 'This strikes me as rather a hard case but the Ministry of Pensions have the last word in these matters and we can only regret that nothing can be done.'[73] We are not able to judge the extent to which the breakdowns Fahey suffered in the 1930s were linked to the mental instability he had suffered during the war. However, Fahey's story does indicate why mentally wounded men and their families sought help from the ESWS: Mrs Fahey tried to negotiate with the Ministry of Pensions by herself and she was swiftly and soundly rejected.[74]

The ESWS was aware that many families received an unsympathetic hearing from the Ministry of Pensions, and so committee members publicized their successful pension claims widely. A good pension award could guarantee real stability for a man and his family, and as far as the society was concerned it was a very cost-effective way of providing care. An initial input of time, money and expertise could result in a long-term commitment by the state, whereas providing money for services such as hospital care or dental treatment was a short-term solution only. These successes also indicate the extent to which the society's relationship with the Ministry of Pensions had changed. From the mid-1920s the ESWS no longer wanted to present itself as an opponent of the Ministry of Pensions; on the contrary, it aimed to present itself as a respectable and influential partner.

MALINGERERS, CRIMINALS AND BOYS

As part of its fund-raising and publicity campaigns the ESWS was eager to present itself as a reputable organization, and so a good relationship with the Ministry of Pensions was obviously crucial. However, the society also wanted to present mentally wounded veterans as respectable too. There had always been a level of popular sympathy for shell-shocked men, whether they were officers or men from the other ranks, yet this initial sympathy was tinged with three unhelpful associations: some still persisted in seeing shell-shocked men as malingerers; in the post-war period some began to be afraid that shell-shocked men were criminals; and even those who were highly sympathetic often thought of shell-shock sufferers as boys rather than as wounded men. Throughout the 1920s, the ESWS aimed to negate or discredit these associations and replace them with more positive ones.

Much has already been said about the belief that shell-shocked men were all malingerers. These suspicions were held largely but not exclusively by the military elites, and as a result the ESWS had always been keen to present the counter-image of the shell-shocked man as a malingerer. For this reason, the society had initially argued that it was asylum life which made men feel insecure and rendered them unfit for productive work.[75] The early determination to establish work schemes was partly to demonstrate the moral quality of the men they served, and to indicate that they were essentially hard-working men who had lost the habit of work as the result of inappropriate institutionalization. However, by 1928 the society began to change its approach towards mentally wounded men and started to claim that some of them were not of sufficient moral fibre for sustained work.[76] This shifting analysis can be seen as producing an attitude that was less supportive of mentally broken veterans as a whole. By 1928 the ESWS was attributing a level of blame to the afflicted man by associating his condition with innate character weaknesses, in much the same way as had many physicians and army officers during the war. However, this changing attitude was also a method by which the society strengthened its protection of its own men. Rather than deny that there was any relationship between mentally wounded men and malingering, they concentrated on demonstrating that their own men were not malingerers. No man within the care of the ESWS could be accused of malingering because the society simply did not tolerate that kind of behaviour. The ESWS had essentially narrowed its goals by the end of the decade. It was less concerned with challenging widespread representations of mentally wounded veterans, an admittedly difficult task, and more concerned with constructing an ethically sound organization, which would ensure that its own men would be perceived as morally blameless.

The associations between shell shock and malingering were stubborn and had a long pedigree. Closely related to the belief that shell-shocked men were either cowards or work-shy, was the concern that shell-shocked men were innately criminal. As we have already noted, this issue did not become prominent until after the war but it was a subject that caused ESWS committee members a great deal of anxiety. ESWS papers indicate that concerns about the potential post-war criminal were not simply sensationalism; nor could the society easily disassociate itself from criminals in the way that it did with malingerers because the ESWS did devote considerable time and resources to mentally ill men who had broken the law. Committee members and staff had to acknowledge that some mental illness could lead to criminality, but at the same time they had to avoid pandering to degeneracy theorists who argued that nervous collapse inevitably indicated moral susceptibility. Throughout the 1920s the society had to deal with a variety of behaviours that could effectively be categorized as criminal. Many of these incidents could be managed informally and privately, although others obliged the ESWS to deal with the courts and so involved more publicity. It has already been indicated that legal expenses became invisible in the annual reports published after 1927, although these same reports indicate that the society was still providing men with some kind of legal assistance. Committee members did not want to draw too much attention to this aspect of the work for fear of provoking an adverse reaction. These fears were not unfounded and we can see the sort of scandal that could result from court cases by looking at the notorious Hume Spry case. Frederick Hume Spry was an ex-officer suffering from neurasthenia and he claimed that he had been wrongly certified because his wife was having an affair with his doctor: he insisted that the two of them had conspired to put him away. The trial attracted widespread media attention in February and March 1927, and the ESWS was deeply implicated in the affair. ESWS solicitors acted for Hume Spry, Hume Spry's sister was married to Major Thwaites, an ESWS doctor, and Mrs Thwaites gave evidence in court.[77] Tyron was furious at the ESWS for supporting a man who had 'caused such difficulties' for his department.[78] Sadly, the Hume Spry case reinforced the ministry belief that the ESWS was continually involved in unsavoury controversies.

So, where possible, the ESWS preferred to deal with criminal cases informally and outside of the court system. In December 1925, the society found employment for Mr Nunn, a former patient. Shortly afterwards, Nunn absconded, having stolen £5 from his new employer. He then returned to Eden Manor where the doctor diagnosed a nervous breakdown and said that Nunn could not be held responsible for his own actions. As a result, the society repaid the money for him and the employer issued no charges.[79] This may sound petty today, yet we need to remember that £5 could buy a man a winter coat in Selfridges in 1925 and in interwar Britain it was possible to receive a custodial sentence for stealing a bicycle. Inevitably, the ESWS itself was sometimes the victim of minor criminal

behaviour. On one occasion the matron sent a patient out to pay the butcher's
bill and the man disappeared with the money. Committee members did not
want the police to become involved, and so they simply instructed the matron to
avoid giving money to the patients in future.[80] Often, however, it was impossible
to avoid going to court, in which case the ESWS was prepared to provide funds
where necessary. In addition to this financial contribution, the society's solicitors
would often provide services for free. The main aim was to ensure that mentally
ill ex-servicemen avoided a jail sentence if at all possible. A case in point involves
Mr. W. S. Cleal who joined the army aged 16, and was described as having an
excellent character before the war although he developed an 'extraordinary
irresponsible character afterwards'.[81] He was arrested for forgery in 1925 and
while he was standing trial at Gloucester Assizes, the Central Association for
Mental Welfare contacted the ESWS to ask if the society would put Cleal in a
home if he were to be acquitted. The committee agreed to put him in a private
mental hospital as a voluntary boarder at ESWS expense. An ESWS barrister
defended him, and as a result Cleal was bound over into the care of the society for
two years.

As well as having its own barristers and legal team, the ESWS developed
good working relationships with Police Court Missionaries. Whereas early
ESWS campaigns had often focused on challenging established procedures, by
the mid-1920s committee members were far more concerned about becoming
part of the establishment. They developed ways of working with the courts in a
practical manner, and stressed not only how successful they had been, but also
the extent to which magistrates and judges were grateful for ESWS intervention.
The society did not want to create the impression of having avoided the law or
of having enabled ex-servicemen to evade their responsibilities; rather it wanted
to emphasize the way in which it was helping the criminal justice system as well
as the disabled man.

> Magistrates have always praised the efforts of the Society to help the neurasthenic
> man who is found in an unfortunate position at the police court. Members of
> Parliament and newspapers have constantly referred cases to the Society for its
> guidance.[82]

The ESWS emphasized this support to save the society from being accused
of unfairly protecting the post-war criminal. ESWS publicity also attempted
to minimize any incidents in which ex-servicemen were involved. Reports
continually referred to 'misdemeanours' rather than crimes and described
formally accused men as being 'in unfortunate positions'.[83] The society perceived
and presented such men as possible rather than actual criminals, and argued that
criminal tendencies were merely the symptoms of mental illness. A statement

from a Police Court Missionary indicates the degree to which some court officials had accepted this view:

> It was after the War when the boys came back and the glamour had passed away that the results of their War service was shown by disordered nerves and breakdowns ... The blinded man is a tragic figure; the limbless man is a tragic figure; but the mentally disabled and the injured in mind is the greatest tragedy of all.[84]

Once again, the reference to 'the boys' emphasizes the vulnerability of the soldiers. This statement clearly reflects the view that veteran criminal behaviour could be part of an illness, and that mental illness was as much of a war wound as the loss of a limb. So criminal behaviour could be justly perceived as a war wound, and this was the message portrayed in publicity to celebrate the tenth anniversary of the ESWS in 1929. One story featured a mentally wounded veteran who had fought bravely in the war but had received only a small pension afterwards. The article goes on to say that the man's mental instability meant that he was bound to gravitate towards crime and he was eventually sent to Broadmoor. Yet in this instance the man's criminality is presented as a form of personal suffering and sacrifice rather than a danger to society at a large, and he is quoted as saying, 'I would go through all my war sufferings again ... even if it brought me to my present position.'[85] The narrative is framed in such a way that the veteran appears to be the primary victim, not those who were the target of his criminal activities.

ESWS obligations to veterans sometimes resulted in committee members having to make difficult moral decisions. The ESWS commitment to marriage was sorely tested in September 1927 when Mr J. P. Vakshort, a mentally wounded ex-serviceman, appealed to the committee for a loan because he needed a barrister to defend him at a forthcoming bigamy trial. The committee agreed to the loan because Millbourn had sufficient confidence in the man to act as guarantor, and because members were agreed that 'the man had received provocation from his wife'.[86] As with some other criminal cases, the ESWS committee can be seen as minimizing the gravity of the situation here. The minutes initially refer to Vakshort as a man who had 'got into difficulties', a highly understated way of describing a man standing trial for bigamy.[87] However, what is even more significant is the way that Vakshort's crime was excused by his wife's behaviour: clearly she was not treating him with the respect he deserved as both a veteran and a man. The ESWS's support for Vakshort may sit oddly with its publicly proclaimed support for marriage as an institution – annual reports repeatedly cited the way in which ESWS work had re-united estranged married couples; however, it accords well with the organization's commitment to ensure that that mentally wounded veterans should always be treated as honourable men.

The society's attitude towards malingerers and its work with those accused of crimes was part of a process designed to present 'unfortunate' men as respectable war heroes and decent citizens. However, there was a further, albeit more subtle problem associated with presenting shell-shock sufferers in such a manner: namely the extent to which they had so often been described as boys rather than grown men with adult responsibilities. Referring to soldiers as boys was an effective technique given that it produced a measure of public sympathy, but it was also potentially emasculating, and was not a good basis for establishing long-term support for mentally wounded men, their wives and children. We have already mentioned the widespread tendency to represent all soldiers as boys, especially on war memorials. There were clear reasons for doing so. Certainly the young men who went to war in 1914 were very conscious of their own youth and of being part of a vigorous and masculine 'youth movement'.[88] Many of the soldiers in the trenches perceived themselves as boys, and all soldiers were routinely described as 'boys' or 'lads' in press reports. This practice was even more pronounced in shell-shock cases. During the war, the press overwhelmingly presented the shell-shocked soldier as a boy, generally as a nerve-wracked boy. In 1917 much attention was given to the case of Stewart Stanley, a private soldier in the Royal Scots Fusiliers.[89] Stanley had been accused of desertion while on active service, had been found guilty by court martial and was executed on 29 August 1917. In the House of Commons, Philip Snowden (Labour, Blackbourn) attacked the military justice system because it had not taken into account that Stanley had recently been invalided home with shell shock. As a result he was executed because 'when he was on his way to the trenches a shell burst close by him and being already completely nerve-shattered he walked away from his regiment'.[90] Stanley was 21 years old and so clearly an adult, but all those opposed to his execution emphasized his youth and consistently referred to him as a 'boy' or a 'young lad'. Using words which presage the late twentieth-century caricatures of the First World War, James Hogge (Liberal, Edinburgh East) asked the House: 'How is it that young lads of tender years who have failed in their duty are shot and that generals are promoted?' In addition, the *Labour Leader* published a 'touching letter' written 'by the boy to his mother'. The letter certainly highlights Stanley's anxieties, as he confessed to his mother that, 'I am lying here waiting for a General Court-Martial, and I am just about broken-hearted, thinking on what they are going to do with me.'[91] This is a moving story in itself but the *Labour Leader* was clearly emphasizing Stanley's relationship with his mother to highlight his filial piety and to make it clear that he was primarily a son and a dependent, not an autonomous adult.

Shell-shocked men were presented as boys rather than wounded men for a variety of reasons. Mental health problems robbed a man of complete masculinity, and one can interpret shell shock as a potentially emasculating condition.[92] It is also the case that the image of the madman has long been held to have been unattractive. The victimized mad woman was a cult figure for romantics in the late eighteenth and early nineteenth centuries, yet the early twentieth-century madman was widely held to be either dangerous or ridiculous.[93] Consequently, it was very hard to present an acceptable image of a mentally wounded man whereas the nerve-wracked boy was a much less sinister and far more sympathetic figure. There is also evidence that many shell-shock sufferers did display infantile behaviour, and the initial treatment at the Maudsley Hospital responded to this desire to return to a child-like state. On admission, men were given a bath and warm milk, and were fed on easily digestible foods for the first few days.[94] Furthermore, it was easier to forgive a boy for some of the indiscretions associated with shell shock than it was to forgive a grown man, and it was also easier to argue that a boy, as opposed to a man, could be swiftly rehabilitated.

The associations between shell shock and boyish weakness were certainly pervasive in the early 1920s. In a parliamentary debate over the Lunacy Laws, Colonel Leslie Wilson, speaking for the government, announced that, 'The best way to deal with shell shock cases was to secure a limited number of seaside boarding houses, with the most grandmotherly landladies they could get, properly certified by the Ministry of Health.'[95] Wilson's call for 'grandmotherly landladies' indicates one widespread belief about shell-shock sufferers, namely that they were poor boys in need of mothering. Some medical authorities also continued to hold this view well into the post-war period. Dr Somerville, the Medical Officer at a Ministry of Pensions' Hospital in Durham, explained shell shock to a medical audience in 1923, describing the shell-shock sufferer in the following terms, 'What the war has done for its anxiety neurotic victim is this: It has battered the courage out of him and left him in the condition of a frightened child.'[96] Sufferers themselves used this language too, and a patient complained to Somerville that the condition left him feeling 'like a bloomin' kid'. [97] These feelings were no doubt the result of the strong sense of disempowerment that often accompanies mental breakdown. Nevertheless, the men concerned were largely adults and not boys, however vulnerable they may have felt.

Behind these images of nerve-wracked boys lay grown men who had to rebuild their lives, find jobs and support their families. Although the young soldier is obviously a highly sympathetic figure, the situation was in many ways far more problematic for older men given that they normally had wives and families to maintain at the same time as trying to regain their mental health. One example illustrates the difficult circumstances that some of these men had to manage: Mr Davis was a mentally wounded ex-serviceman who had been discharged from an asylum in July 1922. By the following year his condition had worsened and he had been returned to the institution. In the meanwhile, the Ministry of Pensions had suspended the payment of his pension, leaving Mrs Davis and their four young children without any visible means of support.[98] Mr Leeks was in an even more vulnerable position. He had volunteered at the age of 54 and served five months in the trenches. As a result he lost the sight of one eye and suffered from paralysis. By 1925 he had no money and no job, so the ESWS agreed to give him a £1 a week for three months.[99] This was not a long-term solution to his financial problems and his employment prospects were obviously highly limited. Clearly some very young men did suffer from nervous collapse as a result of combat during the Great War; however, an over-emphasis upon the illnesses of very young men has obscured the equally valid stories of older men and their families.

The image of the shell-shocked soldier as a war-wracked boy was not only unrepresentative, but it was also unhelpful in many respects. Claiming that innocent boys were suffering needlessly was no way to secure government support. It was also an approach likely to alienate the top echelons of the military profession who were sensitive to charges of not providing properly for veterans. In the years immediately following the armistice it made sense for the ESWS to publicize the plight of young men who had been consigned to local asylums. However, by the later 1920s it had become far more profitable to publicize the way in which the society was helping men and their families. Not only were the images more suitable in terms of attracting high levels of support, but as time went on it became increasingly more difficult to present shell-shocked men as boys anyway.

The ESWS concern for respectable masculinity was expressed in the importance the committee attached to the question of shaving. In Howard's long correspondence with Fleming and Hunter-Weston, he was determined to prove that men were being poorly treated in asylums. To provide an example of this inadequate treatment he cited the Wiltshire County Mental hospital in Devizes where none of the men were shaved, and those who wished to remove their beards were forced to resort to using a pumice stone.[100] Howard raised the issue again when attempting to persuade Colfox that it was wrong to keep ex-soldiers in asylums.[101] The virulence of Colfox's reply indicates that he too held it to be an important matter. He flatly refused to believe that asylum patients were forced to use pumice stones, although he acknowledged that in some circumstances shaving may have been forbidden 'on account of the patient's mental condition'.[102] The Ministry of Pensions was also irritated by this claim and dismissed it as 'a hardy annual of this society'.[103] Shaving was important because it was an activity carried out by all grown men, and it was a symbol of both adulthood and respectability. Some respectable men had beards or moustaches – most obviously the King – but their beards were notably well trimmed and maintained in good order. However, the male lunatic was popularly perceived as unshaven, an image reflected in Kipling's 'My Mother's Son' when

the normally clean-shaven patient is confronted with his bearded reflection in
the asylum looking glass:

> They pushed him into a mental Home,
> And that is like the grave:
> For they do not let you sleep upstairs,
> And you're not allowed to shave . . .
> And no one knows when he'll get well –
> So there he'll have to be:
> And 'spite of the beard in the looking glass
> I know that man is me.[104]

Even the family is shell shocked

A comparison between the publicity of the early 1920s and that issued at the end
of the decade indicates the extent to which the ESWS wanted to turn attention
away from images of the young, unkempt veteran in the asylum. 'My Mother's
Son' encapsulates all that is vulnerable about the incarcerated man, and the actual
cases which the ESWS chose to highlight at that time reflected similar themes. In
1922 the society was contacted by the father of an ex-serviceman. The Board of
Control had told him that if he did not agree to certify his son they would take the
matter into their own hands and force the young man into a county asylum. The
ESWS decided to print the correspondence between the father and the Board of
Control, and circulate it among Members of Parliament.[105] This provided useful
publicity for the society because the Board of Control appeared to be acting in a
heavy-handed manner, and the ex-serviceman was obviously in distress, as was
his father. It was appropriate publicity at the time because the ex-serviceman was
a completely passive victim: he had no voice at all and it was his father and the
Board of Control who were the principal actors in the drama. Yet by the end of
the decade the ESWS did not want either Members of Parliament or the general
public to see shell-shocked men as purely passive victims. They wanted to show
that the men were employable, and they wanted to establish homes for mentally
wounded war veterans who were also married men. In 1923 Somerville insisted
that, 'All war anxiety neurotics are either completely sexually impotent or almost
so.'[106] ESWS homes for married men were an attempt to refute such claims and
to make it clear that neurasthenic ex-soldiers could enjoy a normal, healthy,
heterosexual relationship.

The ESWS firmly rejected any medical theories based on privileging the
wholly masculine environment, and constantly encouraged wives and relatives
to maintain as much contact with the mentally ill man as possible. Funds
were used to enable wives to visit their husbands when treatment was taking
place far from home, and wives were often invited to social events in at Eden
Manor – the society's support of the bigamous Vakshort should not be taken

to imply a flippant or irreverent attitude towards marriage as an institution. Yet marriages clearly were destroyed as a result of war neurosis. Mental illness and the attendant risks of unemployment, poverty and possible separation placed great strains on relationships. This was especially the case when ex-servicemen were in the process of continual assessments and pension reviews, as this procedure provoked great economic insecurity.

WORK, IDENTITY AND THERAPY

The ESWS wanted to destroy the associations that linked the war neurotic with the malingerer, the criminal or the vulnerable boy. The way in which they chose to do this was by emphasizing the extent to which the ESWS was a society which promoted work and created real work opportunities for veterans. Work was central to masculine identity, many doctors believed that work was excellent therapy, and work also provided men with financial security. Not only was work crucial to masculine identity but there was some symbolic link between fighting and working in that they were both essentially male activities. If shell-shock victims had failed as men, it was important not to mother them as boys, but rather to find some way of enabling them to demonstrate their adulthood and their manliness. So by completing honourable masculine work, shell-shocked men were recovering the masculinity that they may have lost when they initially became mentally ill.

The belief that work was the defining feature of a man's life was reflected in the strength of the work ethic in official circles. Collie made this stance plain when, in 1918, he wrote that, 'I have always believed that hard and continuous work is the only way to be really happy, and that work in one form or another is the only salvation for those who are suffering from functional nerve disease.'[107] Collie adopted an extreme and uncompromising position but there were others who believed in the therapeutic value of work too. Elliot Smith believed that shell-shocked men could benefit from being engaged in useful work; however, he did stress that the work must be genuinely interesting, and that for some men, work alone may be insufficient to deal with mental conflict.[108] This commitment to work as a good in itself, combined with a medical belief in the therapeutic value of work, produced a growth in the practice of occupational therapy during the war, although this development did not completely eradicate all faith in the rest cure. In 1919 a Village Centre installed 'sleep baths' for neurasthenic men. In these 'sedative baths' up to 150 men were encouraged to spend long periods lying in hammocks in warm baths in order to 'soothe their jangled nerves'.[109] Yet the ESWS showed little interest in this kind of treatment, and consistently demonstrated a commitment to the therapeutic and curative value of work.

There was a wide consensus on the therapeutic value of work but the issue still prompted serious disputes between doctors and officials from the Ministry of Pensions. Doctors, who were keen to maintain their professional autonomy, wanted to use work as therapy and maintained that in certain cases work should be seen as part of a treatment package. Alternatively, government officials insisted that a man capable of work should be denied treatment allowances. The commissioner of medical services in Birmingham was very worried about the rule that stated that a pensioner should not be assessed by a medical board while he was under treatment, arguing that 'a pensioner may remain on treatment allowances for years without his case ever being investigated by a board'.[110] His attitude reflected that of Collie's. He was not solely concerned about waste and inefficiency, but was fearful of the way in which the work-shy could deliberately use the system to promote their own idleness. These were concerns that had dogged the medical treatment of shell shock during the war, and they continued unchanged into the 1920s. The resulting conflicts produced serious inequities in the system and the harmful results are well illustrated by the two following cases from the John Leigh Memorial Hospital in Altrincham, Cheshire.

Patient A. was a man suffering from 'psychasthenia'. He had improved to the extent that he could work all day long in the carpenter's shop, and he realized that he was well on the way to a complete recovery. A medical board examined him minutely, and much to the man's surprise, awarded him 100 per cent disability allowance. In the days immediately following the medical board's review he developed all kinds of new symptoms that he had never had before, and at the end of the week he told his doctor that the treatment was not working and that he wished to be discharged. The doctor was convinced that the man's behaviour was entirely motivated by the knowledge that he had a guaranteed pension. Patient B. was also described as 'psycasthenic', and the doctor estimated that his disability level was at 100 per cent. Nevertheless, he was reviewed by a medical board, examined in only a few minutes, and had his disability level reduced to 50 per cent. He was aware that his far healthier fellow patient had been awarded a more generous pension, and believed the whole system to be quite unfair.[111]

These examples indicate that there was a high level of subjectivity involved in diagnosing and defining shell shock, and that the wartime conflict between the medical profession and other authorities dealing with wounded men remained unresolved. The question of psychological disability was far more complex than that of physical disability, where hard and fast guidelines existed, for example, with regard to the loss of limbs. The cases also imply a level of inconsistency in the approach of the medical boards, as Patient A. was examined with far more rigour than Patient B. Such situations indicate why so many doctors were so keen to separate the question of pensions from that of treatment, even if it did risk men avoiding boards for years. More importantly, in terms of the way in which people

remembered post-war health care, this sort of unequal treatment contributed to
longer-term perceptions of official injustice and unfairness towards wounded
soldiers generally, and shell-shocked soldiers in particular. Dr Mapother
reported similar problems when dealing with men working under the auspices
of the ESWS. While engaged in work, their symptoms appeared so minimal that
pension officials were inclined to believe that the men were quite well, and it was
sometimes difficult 'to get justice done'.[112] These concerns indicate the extent to
which some attitudes towards shell shock had remained unchanged during the
interwar period. As late as 1930, war-neurotic ex-servicemen were facing the
same issues that had dogged them during the war – quite simply they still found
it difficult to prove that they were really ill.

While work was clearly important for identity, and there was a widespread
agreement that it was central to the recovery process, it is also the case that
work was important for financial security. This became increasingly important
throughout the 1920s as the interwar period was characterized by continually
high unemployment, and the Ministry of Pensions identified the development
of 'economic neurasthenia', a condition whereby men suffered from neurotic
relapses in response to a position of economic uncertainty.[113] As ministers
increasingly tried to relieve the state of financial burdens, mentally wounded
veterans found it even harder to find work. By the same token, voluntary
associations like the ESWS became even more anxious about their fund-raising
abilities. ESWS committee members were always aware that mentally wounded
ex-servicemen faced very serious difficulties in the job market. Their initial
concerns were based around the importance of work as a source of male pride,
and a belief in the value of work as therapy. As a consequence, the ESWS
consistently tried to develop specific projects for mentally wounded men. One
of the committee's first proposals suggested trying to place mentally disabled
men within certain specified trades such as the concrete-block or freshwater-
fish industries.[114] Nor were ESWS resources just directed towards institutional
activity. Ex-patients often asked for donations or loans to enable them to establish
their own businesses, and the society was usually prepared to meet these requests.
For example, in 1927 the committee agreed to lend an ex-officer £100 so that
he could repay loans and establish a pig-farming business.[115] Those who could
not go out to work were encouraged to take part in occupational therapy within
the home. Men worked in the gardens and the conservatories at Eden Manor,
and they learned to make fancy leatherwork or objects from raffia. This is not as
trivial as it sounds: basket-making may well be an occupational-therapy cliché,
but by the late 1920s the men were making wicker chairs, which were popular
in golf and tennis clubs.[116] There were also chickens and pigs at Eden Manor so
that men could develop animal husbandry skills.[117]

However, none of these activities, although no doubt useful and laudable in themselves, provided much long-term material security for men within ESWS homes, or for the organization itself. Of course all charities are vulnerable in this way but the ESWS was especially so for two reasons. First, the ESWS faced unpredictable long-standing costs as a result of its commitment to the care of incurable men. Secondly, as time went on, it started to become obvious that even curable men could sometimes achieve only a partial recovery. Even with very good treatment, some men were simply not going to recover sufficiently to enter the job market, and by 1925 the ESWS acknowledged that men who were fit to leave were 'not fit by nature of their disability to compete in ordinary commercial life'.[118] So by the mid-1920s, mentally wounded veterans appeared to be in a weak economic position, and although the ESWS was becoming financially stronger, it was also facing more demands as time went on. As far as most committee members were concerned, there were two obvious ways to secure a stable financial future. The first was to establish a colony, or sheltered workshop. This was discussed several times throughout 1925, and committee members sought advice from local businessmen and from the director of a colony for disabled soldiers in Scotland. However, they eventually thought that a colony would be too expensive to establish and seemed to dismiss the idea altogether.[119] A second option was to develop work schemes with local employers. If patients worked locally they could receive money, work experience and possibly even job training. They could contribute to their keep and because they would be occupied all day or sometimes for the entire week, in turn they would make fewer demands upon the staff at the home. Sometimes private arrangements with employers were successful, such as when a Sussex poultry breeder agreed to take on three ESWS men as pupils.[120] Yet these arrangements were necessarily small scale, highly vulnerable to fluctuations in the economy and reliant on the goodwill of employers.

By this stage the ESWS was adopting a far more realistic, possibly more cynical approach towards the employment of veterans. In the initial post-war period many were arguing that employers should consistently privilege the ex-servicemen in the job market. Loseby had insisted that this was not just a moral position, it was practical too, and he urged the government to 'remember that those who served them best in the time of crisis were also the best fitted to grapple with the difficulties of the present position'.[121] This argument was based on the belief that it was the finest men who had gone to fight whereas the inferior ones had stayed at home, and that men had learnt valuable lessons from the experience of warfare. Yet life in the trenches did not necessarily fit a man for a variety of employment situations, despite Loseby's rhetoric to the contrary. The ESWS had a firm policy of employing disabled ex-servicemen wherever possible but often with poor results, as when committee members hired a cook through the Disabled Sailors' and Soldiers' Association (DSSA) – the cook was so incompetent that they decided never to hire anyone through the DSSA again.[122] If the ESWS found it hard to employ disabled ex-servicemen, it was clear that a large number of employers would find the problems insurmountable. There is also some evidence that able-bodied men became resentful when employers took on wounded veterans. Millbourn tried to take on such men in his own company but was forced to admit that 'we cannot take in a lot of cripples – the men won't have it.'[123] Presumably the men were concerned that the veterans would be unable to carry their full share of the workload. It is also possible that many men simply did not want to be reminded of the war or to face the physical consequences of the war on a daily basis. So despite their reservations, ESWS committee members decided to establish an industrial colony because they had become increasingly convinced that it was the only way to satisfy the separate but interdependent needs of mentally wounded men, their families and the ESWS as an organization. Sheltered employment could provide for the men's cultural, therapeutic and material needs, while at the same time it would turn the ESWS into more of a business. As a result, the society would be less reliant on donations and be more in control of its own finances.

THE ESTABLISHMENT OF THERMEGA

In the autumn of 1926, committee members started to discuss the possibility of creating a self-supporting industrial workshop alongside one of their homes. The society needed to find a product that disabled men could manufacture and that could be sold for a profit. In March 1927 the chairman visited the owners of a patented electric-blanket company in Bavaria and recommended that the committee purchase the patent immediately. The purchase was completed by June, by which time the society had applied for patent rights within Great Britain and the British colonies, and had arranged for a German instructor to familiarize ESWS men with the assembly process. Workshops were organized at the society's home in Leatherhead, and in September 1927 Thermega was established as a subsidiary company. The presence of a German instructor is not as odd as it first appears. The British Legion had adopted policies designed 'to shake hands' with ex-enemy organizations since 1923, and the ESWS action can be seen as part of a wider movement towards post-war comradeship between combatants of all nations.[124]

There were two key characteristics of Thermega. To begin with, the company was dedicated to providing 'employment or facilities for employment under special conditions for persons suffering from neuroses or neurasthenia'.[125] In addition, Thermega alone held the patent rights for the electric blanket within Britain and the Empire, and so the industry was protected. As a result, the workers were free from competition with able-bodied men, a factor which the committee had gradually come to accept as necessary. So the establishment of Thermega involved a recognition that mentally wounded ex-servicemen could not compete in the marketplace, alongside a refusal to withdraw those men from the world of respectable, productive work. However, it should also be added that it was not possible to employ only mentally wounded ex-servicemen at Thermega. At first, neurasthenic ex-servicemen were employed as travelling representatives, but this policy was abandoned because the men were too liable to break down under the strain of the job. The committee quickly decided that only fit men could be employed in such roles, and asked the Officers' Association to recommend candidates.[126]

The development of Thermega was not just an extension of previous work projects and the ESWS's long-standing commitment to providing vocational opportunities for ex-servicemen; in many ways it signalled a completely new direction for the society. Most crucially, Thermega was to operate on 'a strictly business basis'.[127] By this stage, the executive committee was dominated by men from the business community, the most influential of whom was the chairman, Sir Ralph Millbourn, who had enjoyed a successful career as a stockbroker. For the first time, the society's ex-servicemen were producing a product that was viable on the commercial market. Millbourn was aware that although previous ventures were considered as 'work', they were actually relying upon their customers' sense of charity and goodwill. This was certainly the case with the ill-fated Pignall inventions, the toy-making and the craft work, because people were encouraged to buy the goods principally to support ex-servicemen. Horticultural work had been well organized at ESWS homes, but the society was in no position to compete commercially in this sphere, and the produce was mainly used in the society's homes. So Thermega was a financially viable enterprise in a way that previous work schemes were not.

The development of Thermega did not just alter the financial circumstances of the ESWS but also had an impact on the culture of the organization. As far as Millbourn was concerned, the ESWS had entered a new phase whereby men had left the 'hobby stage' behind and were now committed to a really feasible business plan.[128] For the first time, work teams were organized in a rigorous manner. A small group of 10–15 men was initially selected for the work. They were those with the lowest level of disability and with the highest level of morale so as 'to foster the right spirit'.[129] There were initially no piece-rates, but the men were able to earn bonuses because the society wanted to replicate the work environment of non-sheltered industry as far as possible. In addition, the committee decided to withdraw supplies of pocket money and cigarettes to men who had started earning with Thermega. The aim was to encourage men to be independent and to enable them to think of themselves as workers rather than as patients.

The committee even decided that the new matron should be categorized as a 'Lady Superintendent' and that she should not wear a nurse's uniform.[130] This cultural change affected men in all the ESWS homes, not just those working for Thermega. With the establishment of the industry, policy changed so that those men who were likely to be a permanent charge on the society, that is, those men who were unlikely to recover, were to be boarded out to country places. The society would still pay for their care, but for the first time the intention was that the primary ESWS home would, like Collie's Homes of Recovery, be occupied only by the curable.

The ESWS attitude towards its own image changed during the 1920s, reflecting the different way in which the organization saw itself and the different way in which it wanted the general public to see mentally wounded ex-servicemen. Executive committee members had of course always been aware of the importance of good advertising. Right from its inception the society had committed scarce resources to advertisements in national newspapers, it had organized pamphlets and ballots, and it had even paid people to act as fund-raisers. Early ESWS publicity had been very focused on the war itself. Appeals were launched on key dates such as the start of the Gallipoli campaign or Armistice Day, and images were used to evoke memories of the war too. Publicity leaflets from the mid-1920s urged people to, 'Remember the mentally disabled ex-servicemen,' and included an image of a typical British Tommy marching forward, rifle in hand.[131] Yet although this encouraged people to remember the soldier's sacrifice, actually wounded men were noticeably absent from much ESWS publicity. Photographs focused instead upon visiting dignitaries, such as Frederick Milner or members of the royal family. One high-profile campaign from the later 1920s featured a stylish young woman and a Great Dane posing in fashionable locations around London. The dog was wearing a collecting bag, which clearly states that the collection was in aid of mentally disabled ex-servicemen – but the men themselves remained invisible.[132] Axford, in particular, initially insisted that the men should not be used in publicity material, but his wishes were eventually overruled by other committee members.[133]

The public image of the ESWS began to change with the development of Eden Manor. As well as pictures of domestic ease, the men were shown at their daily tasks, making nets, looking after pigs, basket-making. There is an escapist air to these images: the men have been returned to a rural idyll or a domestic paradise and are far removed from the rigours of the everyday commercial or industrial world. Were these helpful scenes or was this a vision of the ex-serviceman as 'the New Womanly man'?[134] Certainly domesticity and respectability loomed large, but images became increasingly more masculine by the end of the decade, and tended to focus much more upon the men in the workshops. When Thermega became operational, Millbourn decided to dedicate far more resources to advertising. The committee even arranged for Gaumont Films to make a short documentary of the men working in the workshop at Leatherhead.[135] This advertising boost was partly to ensure sales of the product and partly to present a particular image of the ESWS and of the ex-servicemen: Thermega was not just about electric blankets, it was also about the role of neurasthenic ex-servicemen in civilian society. During this period the ESWS became increasingly careful about the society's public image. In 1928, and again in 1929, committee members refused to take part in publicity campaigns with Papworth Village Settlement.[136] The Village Settlements were too redolent of wartime arrangements for wounded men, and they were too associated with the idea of broken men in need of care and treatment. Committee members wanted exposure which indicated how far men had moved away from their injured wartime identities; in effect, how far broken men had been mended. They were particularly pleased with the publicity generated at events such as the British Industries Fair where Thermega ran a successful stall in 1929. In the same year, the Thermega electric blanket was displayed in the 'House of the Future' at the *Daily Mail* Ideal Home Exhibtion at Olympia.[137] The displays associated the once mentally wounded men with order, new technology and consumerism. As well as raising the profile of the company and its main product, the advertisements indicated ways in which the neurasthenic ex-serviceman could contribute towards the domestic home in a suitably masculine manner. This was a real change of emphasis: the picture of men in the lounge at Eden Manor shows them passively accepting the comforts of domestic life, whereas Thermega advertising indicates how the same men were actually creating the comforts of domestic life. Another example of the way in which the ESWS wanted to disassociate itself from the war can be found in the title of the new company, which was founded in 1928. The committee had originally decided that the industrial section would be entitled 'Sir Frederick Milner Industries', but the committee later agreed on the name 'Remployed Ltd'.[138] The later choice of name was much more clearly associated with men returning to work, whereas an organization named after Milner would remind people of disabled soldiers.

The men who appeared in ESWS photographs in the late 1920s began to look less and less like disabled veterans, let alone war-wracked boys. Images in ESWS pamphlets still included traditional pictures of important visitors, but the dignitaries were generally shown alongside men who were operating machinery, as in the photograph in which the King of Greece watches the men assemble electric components in the Thermega workshop.[139] There was a further subtle shift in the nature of ESWS publicity. Committee members had always sought support from the royal family – Queen Alexandra was the first one to write her name in the Visitors' Book at Eden Manor – but they were able to present the relationship between themselves and the royal family in a different light by

the end of the 1920s. The ESWS made a point of giving electric blankets and
pads as gifts to the King and Queen, most notably during the King's illness in
1928.[140] This gesture indicated that mentally wounded men were no longer
pauper lunatics asking for help; rather they were skilled working men who could
provide a necessary service. This image was reinforced in the AGM reports, which
emphasized the way in which electric blankets were being used for the sick and
needy in both private homes and hospitals. Once again, the early post-war images
had been reversed, and mentally broken men were not portrayed as being needy
themselves; rather, they were the ones who were providing for the needy because
they no longer wished to be seen as 'broken men'.

6

Shell Shock and Veterans' Voices

> *How many of our men swung the lead with shell shock; and on the other hand how many men were ruined for life, and perhaps their own hospitals had helped in the disaster because someone thought that they were swinging the lead. The numbers will never be known but the fact remains that there are still numbers of poor men who might almost say that they had been wounded by their own folk. The fact also remains that there must be a good few no doubt prosperous ex-soldiers who can chuckle with how they got out of the Army with shell shock.*[1]

EDWIN BLOMFIELD, 1931

To commemorate the first Armed Forces Day on 27 June 2009, Bolton Council announced that Private James Smith, a local man who had been executed for military misconduct in 1917, was to have his name added to the Roll of Honour in Greater Manchester. This is no doubt a comfort to Smith's relatives who have long argued that Smith was a brave soldier suffering from shell shock, not a coward or a miscreant. More broadly, this type of recognition affords a sense of satisfaction to the authorities and to the wider public at large: we are righting the very obvious wrongs of our forebears.

There is nothing that marks the conceptual distance between our own world and that of the First World War as our divergent attitudes towards shell shock. Historical empathy seems almost impossible. From the standpoint of the early twenty-first century, mentally wounded soldiers were shot in cold blood and this cannot be right. Yet from the perspective of medical and military observers at the time, shell shock was no straightforward, easily identifiable, morally neutral diagnosis. 'Shell shock' was a confusing term that did not help anyone to distinguish between men who were suffering from mental breakdown, men who were genuinely exhausted and men who were 'swinging the lead'.

Edwin Blomfield's words give us some insight into the mind-set of a shell-shocked man after the First World War. Blomfield was a New Zealander who was living in England when the war broke out and he joined the New Zealand Army as a private soldier in 1915. He saw action in Gallipoli and on the Western

Front. There is no such thing as a typical shell-shock sufferer, but Blomfield was a soldier from the ranks who remained mentally broken long after the war was over – if not typical, his experience was certainly common. Blomfield's words aptly express some of the contemporary complex responses to shell shock. Most obviously, he was sure that some men had been mistreated. More specifically, he was convinced that some mentally broken men had actually been made worse by 'their own hospitals'. This was certainly the most serious issue for mentally broken men at the time: they were not overly worried that the signs of mental breakdown could lead to unwarranted execution; rather, they were genuinely scared that the signs of mental breakdown could lead to a total nervous collapse because this, in turn, could lead to a lifetime of humiliation and anguish, possibly even a lifetime in the local lunatic asylum. Yet Blomfield also worried that some men had been 'swinging the lead'; had in fact been shamming shell shock and so essentially cheating their comrades who had stayed at the front. To a soldier like Blomfield, mentally broken and disillusioned though he was, the suggestion that all who disobeyed orders were shell-shocked and therefore heroes would have been met with total incomprehension.

So how do we bridge this gap in comprehension? Those of us opposed to capital punishment cannot condone the death penalty regardless of whether or not a man was mentally broken, cowardly or even criminal. Yet the anachronism of the retrospective pardon, judging those responsible by the standards of our own times and by our own conceptions of 'shell shock', takes us not one jot closer to appreciating the experiences of the shell-shocked man. It is a process that is high in compassion, possibly high in moral self-congratulation, but certainly low in historical understanding. It is for this reason that I have tried to look at the way in which men, and those responsible for their care, tried to cope with the condition that they called shell shock.

Men tried to manage shell shock in ways that were often messy, unjust and inefficient. We cannot help but shudder at the colonel who hit a mentally broken soldier on the head with a stick or the men who poured boiling tea over their mute comrade. There are, of course, compassionate stories too. Leaving a man behind when he was too traumatized for yet another wiring party may seem like a small gesture, but it was clearly an act based on genuine warmth and sympathy. The history of the ESWS tells us a little about the complicated world of the shell-shocked man. Sometimes he was seen as criminal, sometimes a malingerer, sometimes simply a poor boy. In the main, most obviously in the late 1920s, the mentally broken man could be seen as honourably wounded, respectable and capable of full, or at least partial, recovery. Most shell-shocked men were not 'shot at dawn'.

Of course these images of the respectable, hard-working, mentally broken veteran prompt a further question. Is this what shell-shocked ex-servicemen wanted? The history of mental health treatment – from curing the mad to moral management – is one of domination and manipulation.[2] Did ESWS committee members force a particular agenda onto powerless subjects? This is possible. The ESWS certainly wanted to maintain traditional social hierarchies. One photograph from the annual report of 1928 is very telling: Milner and Millbourn stand over a mentally broken ex-serviceman who is stitching an electric blanket on a sewing machine. The man is nameless; he is seated and facing away from the camera while Milner and Millbourn stand erect – they are clearly in control.[3] The words in ESWS publicity leaflets are similarly telling. Describing the men in their care, ESWS committee members wrote that, 'After years of hopeless drifting they have recovered their self-respect and independence.'[4] These are not the men's words; this is a judgement from those in charge of them. Did the initially radical ESWS become part of a process of silencing dissent? Did it serve to quieten the rage of shell-shocked men and their families? If so, the ESWS was acting in accord with most other ex-services' societies: mainstream British veterans' movements were sometimes critical of government policy, but they were never intrinsically opposed to the state. None of this is to deny that men in the care of the ESWS received high-quality treatment or that many of them were able to rebuild their lives. It is simply to emphasize that mental health care in the 1920s was characterized by a lack of what we now consider to be an important component of all health treatment, namely individual agency.

When it came to 'telling the shell-shock story' during the war and in the 1920s, the words of shell-shocked men were simply not prioritized. Of course occasionally they did speak up. The men from the 'Home of Recovery' in Golders Green were very vocal about their hostility towards general hospitals and the so-called 'cheery chap'. The men who complained about the hospital in Orpington were similarly forthright. Yet by and large men internalized the values of the prevailing culture. In the words of Donald Hankey, a young officer who was killed on the Somme in October 1916, the ordinary fighting man 'has learnt to endure hardship without making a song about it'.[5] We deem such wordless endurance as deeply unhealthy, possibly even suspect, but we need to recognize this behaviour as a contemporary coping mechanism: the expression of trauma does not always promote recovery. However, as a result of this reluctance 'to make a song', it is not easy to find the words of ordinary shell-shocked men, and once found they are not always easy to understand. Blomfield's tale tells us only that shell shock was sometimes mistreated and sometimes dubious. Esplin's story makes it clear that he was dismissed as 'one of the barmy ones'.[6] His words lead us to believe that a mental wound was shameful and that he was perceived as sexually inadequate, quite unlike the 'battle-stained heroes' for whom the women were eagerly waiting. Yet physical injuries could be shameful too. Blomfied, who was also physically wounded during the war, was deeply embarrassed because his wounds were septic and they had a bad smell. In some ways he seems more humiliated by what he sees as his ugly, damaged body than he does about the 'dubious distinction' of shell shock.[7]

A physical injury did not necessarily turn men into romantic 'battle-stained heroes'. By the same token, a mental wound did not automatically render a man permanently 'barmy'. An officer, providing evidence before Southborough's committee, described his own shell shock and how he 'knew the thing was coming on for months before it actually arrived'. He then explained that he was able to return to duty after six months and had no further difficulty controlling himself.[8] This man's words emphasize first his own self-control – he struggled for months before breaking down – and secondly, his own powers of recovery. In his case, shell shock was a weakness conquered. When looking at how men described the onset of shell shock, the Captain Hardcastle model does not seem too far amiss. Army Form W3436 was introduced in 1917 and on these forms 'the men frequently said their condition was due to being blown up by a big shell or something of that sort'.[9] Yet information from the men's own units generally failed to confirm their statements. Why did these men say they had been blown up when they had not? Possibly they were genuinely confused and unable to remember events properly. After all, it is not unreasonable to assume that a traumatized man might be somewhat bewildered. On the other hand, the men's descriptions could lie in the recognition that there was both sympathy and respect for the soldier who had been blown up or buried alive. It is understandable that men may have wanted to attribute their own nervous collapse to a sensational, war-like event rather that to a slow wearing-down of the nerves. These men were presenting their breakdowns in the best and the most dignified possible way, and all of their comments indicate the importance that they attached to the honourable and respectable wound. We need to remember that the images that arouse our compassion – the startling suicide of Septimus Smith; the old soldier with a shattered memory, living a half-life in a nursing home; the 'men whose minds the dead have ravished' – are not the images that mentally wounded soldiers wanted to associate with. Shell shock was significant to the men of the First World War not because it indicated mental collapse in the face of unimaginable horrors, but because it signified the drama of the battlefield.

Given the soldiers' determination to present shell shock as a real and honourable battle wound, why has the dominant public memory of shell shock become one in which we associate shell shock with victimhood, frailty and futility? The answer could lie in a natural sympathy with mentally broken men. Some of the descriptions of shell-shocked soldiers, particularly those in lunatic asylums, are genuinely piteous. There is also a very evident sense of collective guilt in response to concerns about possibly unwarranted executions. To emphasize this guilt, and the attendant responsibility to redress wrongs, it has been men's mental vulnerability that has been emphasized, not their active participation in battle. Given the obvious horrors of trench warfare and mental breakdown, it seems almost callous to turn our attention to the men who 'coped' with shell shock or to those who managed to live with it.

Yet we need to pay attention to these other parts of the shell-shock story because the figure of the mentally wounded soldier is now so central to modern understandings of warfare and its effects. The shell-shocked soldier of the First World War is important not just because we sympathize with his plight – which was admittedly dreadful – but because he now symbolizes the traditional inability to talk about war or to effectively communicate the essential reality of armed conflict. Hewitt tried to explain these difficulties:

> When you get a story from the front line they're – whoever's telling you – is inclined to glorify it that little bit. You take the glory part about it and you miss the ugly part that is not said. In no circumstances in my opinion can anyone tell you what war is like unless they're actually in the front line . . . unless they've been in the front line they cannot tell you. And even if they do tell you, you cannot grasp the thing, what it is, it's impossible to convey by word the actual scene in the trenches. Impossible. Without feeling. And then, if anyone tells anyone of it, unless they'd been there they wouldn't understand'.[10]

Of course the soldier's tendency to 'miss the ugly part' did not stem from the First World War. The near-impossibility of talking about war without glorifying it, without turning it into romance, is one of the themes of Tolstoy's *War and Peace*. This impossibility could well explain a veteran's silence: if your words can only turn war into romance, it might be better just to remain silent. However, what is significant about First World War narratives is that since the late 1920s there has been an ever-intensifying emphasis upon 'the ugly part'. In words, which can appear baffling to a modern reader, Falls, an old soldier himself, condemned those writers who were excessively gloomy when describing their war experience:

> Every sector becomes a bad one, every working party is shot to pieces, if a man is killed or wounded his brains or his entrails always protrude from his body; no-one ever seems to have a rest. Hundreds of games of football were played every day on the Western Front, by infantry as well as other arms, but how often does one hear of a game in a 'War Book'?[11]

So, on the subject of war stories, Hewitt complains about the tendency to glorify and Falls complains about the tendency to relentless misery. There is a potential problem for the non-combatant historian here. What can we do if we really can glean nothing from the stories of old soldiers? Of course, as Richard Holmes has already observed, our roles as historians would be decidedly limited if we only considered our own lived experiences.[12] Our aim is not to recreate the First World War or the experience of First World War shell shock (admittedly impossible tasks), but to try to understand how those war experiences were discussed, interpreted, internalized and, sometimes, forgotten or marginalized.

It is the histories of those men who lived with shell shock – the mentally broken men who were, to one degree or another, mended – that have been most seriously marginalized. We can only speculate as to why this has been the case. Is it, as Gray and Oliver have suggested, part of our current preoccupation with catastrophe?[13] Are we simply more interested in sensational stories about boys being 'shot at dawn' than in the histories of those men who managed to live with their neuroses? That is certainly part of the answer. It is also because later generations began to identify with the shell-shocked soldier, or rather, with the shell-shocked soldier who refused to fight. This figure, rooted in historical reality but gradually mythologized, reinforced and reflected popular and political perceptions about the First World War. Lloyd George famously stressed the collective unwillingness to go to war in 1914. No one wanted this conflict, but the European powers somehow 'slithered over the brink into the boiling cauldron of war'.[14] The shell-shocked soldier has now become a popular extension of the European Great Power slithering into an unwanted war: he did not want to fight so much that it drove him mad.

Yet this figure of the shell-shocked soldier who would not or could not fight sits uneasily alongside aside those soldiers who endured years of warfare and yet were very proud of their war service. As we have seen, mentally broken men did not just display anti-war symptoms. Sometimes these men were violent to their comrades; sometime they became reckless warriors; sometime they came home and mistreated their wives or mothers. Others simply needed a brief rest before returning to the front to carry on fighting. These stories have been neglected because, as Stephen Badsey has observed, the perceived uniqueness of the First World War has led us to believe that it can only be understood through personal emotional responses or through art and literature.[15] If we search for an understanding of the First World War in art, poetry and literature, the 'poor nerve-wracked boy' will inevitably dominate. He perfectly encapsulates our emotional responses to the war, and he is an effective and moving literary figure.

Yet surely we need to recognize the mentally wounded soldier in all his complexity: he was not simply a cipher for all that was bad or unjust about the First World War.

This is not just about retelling the shell-shock story, although that in itself is long overdue. This reconceptualization of the shell-shocked soldier is also part of a necessary process whereby we reconsider the First World War. It was terrible in many ways, but it was not a unique event.[16] In the early nineteenth century Carl Von Clausewitz wrote that war 'is an act of violence intended to compel our opponent to fulfil our will'.[17] That now reads like a sensational statement rather than a simple description of the fact: under no circumstances would a Minister of Defence characterize British military action in such terms. Yet war is an act of violence. The savagery of the First World War was not an aberration and to treat it as such is sadly to mistake the nature of war. As I write this, British troops are engaged in 'Operation Panther's Claw', a major offensive against the Taliban in Helmand province, and there is much public concern about the number of casualties.[18] It is yet another war. Technological, political and cultural changes ensure that there are many different types of warfare, but its essential nature remains the same. As Clausewitz observed, 'War is always the shock of two hostile bodies in collision.'[19]

This shock, the shock of war, affects all men who fight although it does not affect all of them in the same way. Some mentally broken men never recovered from the First World War; others did. We cannot generalize about the shell-shock experience either during the war or after it. Yet we can say that most mentally broken men wanted their injuries to be seen as honourable war wounds and they wanted effective treatment; they did not want to be seen as the tragic victims of a hapless war. Blomfield's words provide a fitting conclusion here. He began his war memoirs by announcing that 'if there is anything in this yarn which appears as strange the reader can put it down to the effects of shell shock'.[20] Like many men, Blomfield simply wanted the long-lasting effects of shell shock to be acknowledged, but he also wanted to tell his story and remake his life.

Notes

Notes to Introduction

1   Gray, P. and K. Oliver (eds) (2004), *The Memory of Catastrophe*. Manchester: Manchester University Press, p. 4.
2   Owen, W., in R. Wohl, (1980), *The Generation of 1914*. London: Weidenfeld and Nicholson, p.105.
3   http://news.bbc.co.uk/1/hi/uk/7720601.stm (accessed 11 November 2008).
4   Sheffield, G. (2002), *Forgotten Victory the First World War: Myths and Realities*. London: Hodder; Bond, B. (2002), *The Unquiet Western Front*. Cambridge: Cambridge University Press; Todman, D. (2005), *The Great War: Myth and Memory*. London: Hambledon and London.
5   Gregory, A. (2008), *The Last Great War: British Society and the First World War*. Cambridge: Cambridge University Press, p. 294.
6   Ibid., p. 5.
7   Wessely, S. (September 2006), 'The life and death of Private Harry Farr', *Journal of the Royal Society of Medicine*, 99, 442. Simon Wessely is Professor of Epidemiological and Liaison Psychiatry at King's College, London.
8   Cooter, R. (1999), 'Malingering in modernity: psychological scripts and adversarial encounters during the First World War', in R. Cooter, M. Harrison and S. Sturdy (eds), *War, Medicine and Modernity*. Stroud: Sutton, pp. 125–48.
9   Blair, J. G. S. and A. C. Ticehurst (1998), *RAMC, 1898–1998. Reflections of One Hundred Years of Service*. Dundee: RAMC.
10 Bourke, J. (1999), *An Intimate History of Killing: Face to Face Killing in Twentieth Century Warfare*. London: Granta Books, p. 244.
11 Jones, E. and S. Wessely (2005), *Shell Shock to PTSD: Military Psychiatry from 1900 to the Gulf War*. Hove, New York, NY: Psychology Press, p.1.
12 Jones, E., I. Palmer and S. Wessely (2002), 'War pensions (1900–1945): changing models of psychological understanding', *The British Journal of Psychiatry*, 180, 375.
13 I would like to thank Professor Gavin Edwards for drawing my attention to the letters of Watkin Tench.
14 Tench, W. in G. Edwards (ed.) (2001), *Letters from Revolutionary France*. Cardiff: University of Wales Press, 2001, p. 6.
15 Ibid., p.6.
16 Sterne, L. (1998), *The Life and Opinions of Tristram Shandy, Gentleman*. Oxford: Oxford University Press, (first published in 1759). Sterne's Uncle Toby was clearly based on his own experiences of growing up in a military family.
17 BBC Radio 4, *Today*, 28 February 2009.

18   Beharry VC, Lance Corporal Johnson, Interview with the *Independent,* 28 February 2009.
19   Ibid.
20   Ibid.
21   For detailed analyses of shell shock during the First World War see Babington, A. (1997), *A History of the Changing Attitudes to War Neurosis.* London: Leo Cooper; Binnevald, H. (1997), *From Shell Shock to Combat Stress: A Comparative History of Military Psychiatry.* Holland: Amsterdam University Press; Bourke, J. (1996), *Dismembering the Male: Men's Bodies, Britain and the Great War.* London: Reaktion; Jones, E. and S. Wessely (2005), *Shell Shock to PTSD: Military Psychiatry from 1900 to the Gulf War.* Hove and New York, NY: Psychology Press; Leed, E. (1979), *No Man's Land: Combat and Identity in World War One.* Cambridge: Cambridge University Press; Leese, P. (2002), *Shell Shock: Traumatic Neurosis and the British Soldiers of the First World War.* London: Palgrave MacMillan; Shephard, B. (2000), *A War of Nerves.* London: Jonathon Cape.
22   Barham, P. (2004), *Forgotten Lunatics of the Great War.* New Haven, CT: and London: Yale University Press.
23   Falls, C. (1930), *War Books: A Critical Guide.* London: Peter Davies, p. vii.
24   The war poets, especially Sassoon, Owen and Gurney, are renowned for expressing their war anxieties through poetry. These poems should not be ignored but cannot be seen as representative of the ordinary soldier's wartime experience.
25   The Ex-Services' Welfare Society is now known as Combat Stress. See http://www.combatstress.org.uk (accessed 6 October 2009).
26   Winter, J. M. (2000), 'Shell shock and the cultural history of the Great War', *Journal of Contemporary History,* 35, (1), 8.
27   Leese, P. (1989), 'A social and cultural history of shell shock, with particular reference to the experience of British soldiers during and after the Great War'. (Unpublished PhD thesis, Open University).

Notes to Chapter 1: Shell Shock and Weak Nerves

1   Dahl, R. (1984), *Boy: Tales of Childhood.* London: Penguin, pp. 109–10.
2   The *Optimist,* 11 November 1929.
3   Ibid.
4   Ibid.
5   Combat Stress Archives (CSA), undated.
6   Ibid.
7   For a discussion of the current role of PTSD sufferers as involuntary commemorators of war see Stanley, J. (2006), 'Involuntary commemorations: post-traumatic stress disorder and its relationship to war commemoration', in T. Ashplant, G. Dawson and M. Roper (eds), *The Politics of Memory: Commemorating War.* London: Cassell, pp. 240–59.
8   For a refutation of the 'futile war' myth see Bond, B. (2002), *The Unquiet Western Front.* Cambridge: Cambridge University Press; and Todman, D. (2005), *The Great War: Myth and Memory.* London: Hambledon and London.
9   Young, A. (1995), *The Harmony of Illusions: Inventing Post-Traumatic Stress Disorder.* Princeton, NJ and Chichester: Princeton University Press, p. 50.

10   Gregory estimates that at the end of the war there were approximately 4.5 million bereaved close relatives in Britain, roughly 10 per cent of the population. (Gregory, A. (2008), *The Last Great War: British Society and the First World War*. Cambridge: Cambridge University Press, p. 252.) When referring to those who 'suffered' during the war, I am obviously referring to a far wider group.

11   There is vast literature on this subject. For example, see: Delaporte, S. (1996), *Les Gueules Cassées: les blessés de la face de la Grande Guerre*. Paris: Noêsis.

12   See Shephard, B. (2000), *A War of Nerves*. London: Jonathon Cape; Jones, E. and S. Wessely (2001), 'Psychiatric battle casualties: an intra- and interwar comparison', *The British Journal of Psychiatry*, 178, 242–7; and Jones, E. (2004), 'Doctors and trauma in the First World War: the response of British military psychiatrists', in P. Gray and K. Oliver (eds), *The Memory of Catastrophe*. UK: Manchester University Press, pp. 91–105.

13   Oram, G. (1998), *Worthless Men: Race, Eugenics and the Death Penalty in the British Army during the First World War*. London: Francis Bouttle; and Brooks, R. (1999), *The Stress of Combat, the Combat of Stress*. Brighton: The Alpha Press.

14   Lerner, P. and M. S. Micale (2001), 'Trauma, psychiatry and history: a conceptual and historiographical introduction', in M. S. Micale and P. Lerner (eds), *Traumatic Pasts: History, Psychiatry and Trauma in the Modern Age*. Cambridge, Cambridge University Press, pp. 1–27; Showalter, E. (1980), *The Female Malady: Women, Madness and English Culture, 1830–1980*. London: Virago, pp. 168–72; and Bourke, J. (1996), *Dismembering the Male: Men's Bodies, Britain and the Great War*. London: Reaktion, pp. 107–23.

15   For commentary on the 'Pardons' campaign, its motivation and history see Corns, C. and J. Hughes, (2001), *Blindfold and Alone British Military Executions in the Great War*. London: Cassell, especially Chapters 36–38.

16   For some of the problems associated with PTSD as a diagnostic category see Shephard, B. (2008), 'Why the psychiatry of war is too important to be left to psychiatrists'. Wellcome Collection (Deutsche Hygiene-Museum), Dresden, *War and Medicine* (Black Dog Publishing: London, pp. 166–79).

17   In particular, see Bond, B. (2002), *The Unquiet Western Front*. Cambridge: Cambridge University Press; and Todman, D. (2005), *The Great War: Myth and Memory*. London: Hambledon and London.

18   Winter, J. (1999), 'Forms of kinship and remembrance in the aftermath of the Great War', in J. Winter and E. Sivan (eds), *War and Remembrance in the Twentieth Century*. Cambridge: Cambridge University Press, p. 60.

19   *The Guardian*, 5 November 2008; and BBC *10 O'clock News*, 20 May 2009.

20   Sayers, D. (1937), *Busman's Honeymoon*. London: Victor Gollancz.

21   Orwell, G. (1984), *Down and Out in Paris and London*. London: Penguin 1984, (first published London: Victor Gollancz, 1933).

22   MacPherson, W. G., W. P. Herringham and T. R. Elliott (1923), *History of the Great War Based on Official Documents: Medical Services Diseases of the War*, (vol. II). London: HMSO, p. 8.

23   Mitchell, T. J. and G. M. Smith (1931), *History of the Great War Based on Official Documents: Medical Services: Casualties and Medical Statistics of the Great War*. London: HMSO, pp. 320–21.

24   Mott, F. W. and H. W. Kaye, (21 October 1920), *Special Committee to Enquire into Shell Shock; House of Lords Official Report*. The National Archives (TNA), Kew, WO/32/4747.

25 Knutsford, Lord, in *The Times,* 31 January 1916.

26 Elliot Smith, G. and T. H. Pear, (1918), *Shell Shock and its Lessons.* Manchester: University Press; and London: Longmans, Green and Co., p. 2.

27 Babington, A. (1997), *A History of the Changing Attitudes to War Neurosis.* London: Leo Cooper. See Chapter 2 for a discussion on the long history of war neuroses.

28 Ibid,. p. 35.

29 Dible, Captain J. H. (6 February 1915), *First World War Account of Captain James Henry Dible.* Imperial War Museum (IWM), London, Con Shelf.

30 Showalter, E. (1980), *The Female Malady: Women, Madness and English Culture, 1830–1980.* London: Virago.

31 *Encyclopaedia Britannica* (11th edn, 1910), p. 211.

32 Micale, M. S. (1995), *Approaching Hysteria: Disease and Its Interpretations.* Princeton, NJ and Chichester: Princeton University Press, p. 223.

33 HMSO (1911), *RAMC Training Manual.* HMSO: Military Books, p.128.

34 This theme will be explored in greater depth in the following chapter.

35 Knutsford Wellcome Library(WL), London, RAMC Muniments Collection, RAMC/ 446/7/17/20 July 1916 (no precise date).

36 Babington, A. (1997), *A History of the Changing Attitudes to War Neurosis.* London: Leo Cooper, p. 81.

37 Terraine, J. (1993), *Impacts of War 1914 and 1918.* London: Leo Cooper, p. 13.

38 Braybon, G. (ed.) (2003), *Evidence, History and the Great War Historians and the Impact of 1914–1918.* New York and Oxford: Berghahn Books, pp. 1–29.

39 Elliot Smith, G. and T. H. Pear, (1918), *Shell Shock and its Lessons.* Manchester: University Press; and London: Longmans, Green and Co, pp. 24–5.

40 Micale, M. S. (October 1990), 'Charcot and the idea of hysteria in the male: gender, mental science, and medical diagnosis in late nineteenth-century France', *Medical History,* 34 (4), 365–6.

41 Lerner, P. and M. S. Micale (2001), 'Trauma, psychiatry and history: a conceptual and historiographical introduction', in M. S. Micale and P. Lerner (eds), *Traumatic Pasts: History, Psychiatry and Trauma in the Modern Age.* Cambridge, Cambridge University Press, p. 12.

42 Shephard, B. (2000), *A War of Nerves.* London: Jonathon Cape, p. 28.

43 *The Times,* 8 July 1915.

44 *The Times,* 2 January 1915; and 8 July 1915.

45 *Labour Leader,* 15 May 1915.

46 *Labour Leader,* 30 September 1915.

47 *Labour Leader,* 21 October 1915.

48 *The Times,* 17 March 1915.

49 Ibid.

50 John Collie was the Chief Medical Officer of the Metropolitan Water Board; during the First World War he became a temporary Colonel in the Army Medical Services.

51 *The Times,* 27 January 1915.

52 Ibid.

53 Ibid.

54 Elliot Smith, G. and T. H. Pear, (1918), *Shell Shock and its Lessons.* Manchester: University Press; and London: Longmans, Green and Co, p. 30.

55 *The Times*, 1 March 1915.
56 *The Times*, 2 March 1915.
57 Collie, J. (April 1916), 'Malingering: examinations of the upper extremities', *Journal of the Royal Army Medical Corps,* 26, 85.
58 Buzzard, F. cited in R. Armstrong-Jones (July 1917), 'The psychology of fear and the effects of panic fear in war time', *Journal of Mental Science,* 63, 351.
59 Mott, F. W. (April 1918), 'War psychoses and neuroses', (paper presented to the Medico-Psychological Society), *Journal of Mental Science,* 64, 233.
60 *The Times,* 11 December 1914.
61 *The Times,* 18 January 1915.
62 *The Times,* 18 January 1915.
63 *The Times,* 3 March, 1915.
64 *The Times,* 8 July 1915.
65 West, B. (August–September1914), Unpublished diary. Imperial War Museum (IWM), London, B PP/MCR/335.
66 Gibbs, P. (1920), *Realities of War.* London: William Heinemann, p.140.
67 Wells, H. G. (1916), *Mr Britling Sees It Through.* London: Cassell and Company, p. 301.
68 Ibid., pp. 357–8.
69 For one example alongside many, see Sassoon, S. (1937), *The Complete Memoirs of George Sherston.* London: Faber and Faber, pp. 616–7.
70 Sayers, D. (1937), *Busman's Honeymoon.* London: Victor Gollancz.
71 *The Times,* 11 December 1914.
72 Gregory, A. (2008), *The Last Great War: British Society and the First World War* Cambridge: Cambridge University Press, p. 78.
73 *The Times,* 20 March 1915.
74 Mott, F. W. (1919), *War Neuroses and Shell Shock.* London: H. Frowde, and Hodder and Stoughton, p. 271.
75 Showalter, E. (1980), *The Female Malady: Women, Madness and English Culture, 1830–1980.* London: Virago, pp.168–72.
76 Shephard, B. (2000), *A War of Nerves.* London: Jonathon Cape, p. 149.
77 Anon. (31 July 1915), 'Parliamentary Intelligence, House of Lords, Monday 26 July, Treatment of nerve-shaken soldiers', *Lancet,* 261.
78 Dible, Captain J. H. (12 January 1915), *First World War Account of Captain James Henry Dible.* Imperial War Museum, London, Con Shelf.
79 RAMC (1920), *Ministry of National Service, 1917–1919 Report Vol. 1 Physical Examination of Men of Military Age by National Service Medical Boards 1 November 1917 – October 31 1918.* London: HMSO, p. 4, WL RAMC/739/18.
80 RAMC (1920), *Ministry of National Service, 1917–1919 Report Vol. 1 Physical Examination of Men of Military Age by National Service Medical Boards 1 November 1917 – October 31 1918.* London: HMSO, p. 24, WL RAMC/739/18. For a full analysis of these figures, see Winter, J. M. (April 1980), 'Fitness and civilian health in Britain during the First World War'. *Journal of Contemporary History,* 15 (2), 211–44.
81 Anon. (5 February 1916), 'A discussion on shell shock', (held at the Royal Society of Medicine on 25 and 27 January 1916), *Lancet,* 306.
82 Mott, F. W. (26 February 1916), 'Lettsomian Lecture on the effects of high explosives upon the central nervous system', *Lancet,* (part II), 448.

83   Burton-Fanning, F. W. (16 June 1917), 'Neurasthenia in soldiers of the home forces', *Lancet*, 907–11.

84   Henderson, D. K. (April 1918), 'War Psychoses: an analysis of 202 cases of mental disorder occurring in home troops', *Journal of Mental Science*, 64, 165–89.

85   Esplin, W. D. (undated). The National Archives, London, Memo PIN 15/2503 40B.

86   Rutherford, Jeffrey, G. (April 1920), 'Some points of interest in connection with the psychoneuroses of war', *Journal of Mental Science*, 66, 132.

87   *Labour Leader*, 6 May 1915.

88   *Labour Leader*, 10 June 1915.

89   *Labour Leader*, 10 June 1915.

90   Latham, P. cited in R. Porter (1995), '"Perplx't with tough names": the uses of medical jargon', in R. Porter and Peter Burke (eds), *Languages and Jargons: Contributions to a Social History of Language*. Cambridge: Polity Press, p. 42.

91   Jones, E. and S. Wessely (2005), *Shell Shock to PTSD: Military Psychiatry from 1900 to the Gulf War*. Hove and New York, NY: Psychology Press, p. 21.

92   Myers, C. S. (13 February 1915), 'A contribution to the study of shell shock. Being an account of three cases of loss of memory, vision, smell and taste admitted into the Duchess of Westminster's War Hospital, Le Toucquet', *Lancet*, 316–20.

93   Ibid., p. 320.

94   There was much discussion on this subject in the *Lancet* throughout 1915. For example, 'Shell explosions and the special senses', 27 March 1915, 663; and 'Nervous injuries due to shell shock explosions', 2 October 1915, 766.

95   Editorial (19 August 1922), '"Shell" shock and "cowardice"', *Lancet*, 399.

96   Head, H. cited in Anon. (5 February 1916), 'A discussion on shell shock', (held at the Royal Society of Medicine on 25 and 27 January 1916), *Lancet*, 306.

97   Mott, F. W. (11 March 1916), 'Lettsomian Lecture on the effects of high explosives upon the central nervous system', *Lancet*, (part III), 553.

98   Porter, R. (1995), '"Perplx't with tough names": the uses of medical jargon', in Roy Porter and Peter. Burke (eds), *Languages and Jargons: Contributions to a Social History of Language*. Cambridge: Polity Press, p. 49.

99   Ibid., p.46 .

100 I would like to thank Dr Brian Ireland for his comments on this issue.

101 Thomson, M. (1999), 'Status, manpower and mental fitness: mental deficiency in the First World War', in R. Cooter, M. Harrison and S. Sturdy (eds), *War, Medicine and Modernity*. Stroud: Sutton, p. 154.

102 Babington, A. (1997), *A History of the Changing Attitudes to War Neurosis*. London: Leo Cooper, pp. 62–3.

103 Stone, M. (1985), 'Shell shock and the psychologists', in W. F. Bynum, R. Porter and M. Shephard (eds), The *Anatomy of Madness*. London: Tavistock, p. 255.

104 Elliot Smith, G. (15 April 1916), 'Shock and the soldier', *Lancet*, 813.

105 Wiltshire, H. (17 June 1916), 'Contribution to the aetiology of shell shock', *Lancet*, 1207.

106 War Office (1922), *Report of the War Office Committee of Enquiry into 'Shell Shock'*. The National Archives, WO 32/4748, p. 4.

107 Rushdie, S. cited by J. Winter and E. Sivan (1999), 'Setting the framework', in J. Winter and E. Sivan (eds), *War and Remembrance in the Twentieth Century*. Cambridge: Cambridge University Press, pp. 6–39.

108 Winter, J. M. (2000), 'Shell shock and the cultural history of the Great War', *Journal of Contemporary History*, 35, (1), 10.

109 War Office (15 April 1921), *Special Committee to Enquire into Shell Shock House of Lords official Report*. The National Archives, WO/32/4747.

110 Butler, A. G. (1940), *The Australian Army Medical Services in the War of 1914–1918*. Canberra: Australian War Memorial, p. 72.

111 Ibid., p. 270.

112 *Reveille* (formerly *Recalled to Life*), September 1917, 43.

113 BMJ Publishing Group (1917), *British Medicine in the War, 1914–1917*. London: BMA, p. iv.

114 Aldren-Turner, W. (27 May 1916), 'Arrangements for the care of cases of nervous and mental shock coming from overseas', *Lancet*, 1073–5.

115 *The Times*, 27 July 1915.

116 *The Times*, 24 April 1915.

117 *The Times*, 27 July 1915.

118 Babington, A. (1997), *A History of the Changing Attitudes to War Neurosis*. London: Leo Cooper, p. 81.

119 Williams, K. cited in Lerner, P. (2000), 'Psychiatry and casualties of war in Germany, 1914–18', *Journal of Contemporary History*, 35, (1), 27.

120 *The Times*, 4 November 1914.

121 *The Times*, 4 November 1914.

122 *The Times*, 9 January 1915.

123 *The Times*, 18 January 1915; and 17 February 1915.

124 *The Times*, 26 May 1915.

125 Babington, A. (1997), *A History of the Changing Attitudes to War Neurosis*. London: Leo Cooper, p. 55.

126 *The Times*, 9 January 1915.

127 *The Times*, 25 May 1915.

128 *The Times*, 1 January 1916; and 4 January 1916.

129 *The Times*, 18 January 1915.

130 *The Times*, 6 February 1915.

131 Shephard, B. (1996), '"The Early Treatment of Mental Disorders": RG Rows and Maghull 1914–1918', in H. Freeman and G. E. Berrios (eds), *150 Years of British Psychiatry*. London: Athlone, p. 450.

132 *The Times*, 4 January 1916.

133 Brooks, R. (1999), *The Stress of Combat, the Combat of Stress*. Brighton: The Alpha Press, p. 11.

134 Fussell, P. (1975), *The Great War and Modern Memory*. New York and London: Oxford University Press, p. 74.

135 Hewitt, Private L. J. (recorded 1973), Imperial War Museum Sound Archive, 41/4, reel 1.

136 *The Times*, 11 January 1916.

137 Stone, M. (1985), 'Shell shock and the psychologists', in W. F. Bynum, R. Porter and M. Shephard (eds), The *Anatomy of Madness*. London: Tavistock, p. 245.

138 For a full discussion of these issues see Stone, M. (1985), 'Shell shock and the psychologists', in W. F. Bynum, R. Porter and M. Shephard (eds), The *Anatomy of Madness*. London: Tavistock, pp. 242–71; and Bogacz, T. (1989), 'War neurosis and cultural change in England,

1914–1922: the work of the War Office committee of enquiry into "shell shock", *Journal of Contemporary History*, 24, 227–56.

139 Kutek, A. (2000), 'Warring opposites', in E. Christopher and H. McFarland Soloman, (eds), *Jungian Thought in the Modern World*. London and New York, NY: Free Association Books, p. 92.

140 Editorial, (October 1915),'Table showing the number of those on the staff of asylums in the UK, exclusive of medical officers, who have joined the military or naval service during the present war up to the middle of July 1915', *Journal of Mental Science*, 61, 514–17.

141 Myers, C. S. (1940), *Shell Shock in France, 1914–1918*, (based on a war diary kept by Charles Myers). Cambridge, Cambridge University Press, p. 83.

142 *The Times*, 25 May 1915.

143 *The Times*, 27 November 1916.

144 Mercier, C. in *The Times, 17* January 1916.

145 Bourke, J. (2000), 'Effeminacy, ethnicity and the end of trauma: the sufferings of "shell shocked" men in Great Britain and Ireland, 1914–1939', *Journal of Contemporary History*, 35(1), 57–69.

146 Hurst, A. (1917), *Medical Diseases of the War*. London: E. Arnold, p. 1.

147 Steen, R. H. (October 1917), 'Book review of Eder (1917), *War Shock*. London: William Heinemann', *Journal of Mental Science, 63*, 592.

148 MacPherson, W. G., W. P. Herringham and T. R. Elliott (1923), *History of the Great War based on Official Documents: Medical Services Diseases of the War*, (vol. II). London: HMSO, p.341.

149 Boyle, H. (April 1914), 'Some observations on early nervous and mental cases with suggestions as to possible improvement in our methods of dealing with them', *Journal of Mental Science, 60*, 382.

150 McDowall, C. (January 1918),'Mutism in the soldier and its treatment', *Journal of Mental Science, 64*, 55; and Mott, F. W. (April 1918),'War psychoses and neuroses', (paper presented to the Medico-Psychological Society), *Journal of Mental Science, 64*, 231.

151 This topic is explored in greater detail in the following chapter.

152 Kaye, Captain H. W. (12 March 1916), Unpublished War Diary. The Wellcome Library (WL), London, WL RAMC/739.

153 Bourke, J. (1999), *An Intimate History of Killing: Face to Face Killing in Twentieth Century Warfare*. London: Granta Books, p. 244; and Ferguson, N. (1998), *The Pity of War*. London: Allen Lane, pp. 339–349.

154 Brown, T. (1984),'Shell shock in the Canadian Expeditionary Force, 1914–1918: Canadian psychiatry in the Great War', in C. G. Roland (ed.), *Health, Disease and Medicine*. Canada: The Hannah Institute for the History of Medicine, p. 322.

155 Thomson, M. (1999),'Status, manpower and mental fitness: mental deficiency in the First World War', in R. Cooter, M. Harrison and S. Sturdy (eds), *War, Medicine and Modernity*. Stroud: Sutton, p. 149.

156 Winter, J. (1999),'Forms of kinship and remembrance in the aftermath of the Great War', in J. Winter and E. Sivan (eds), *War and Remembrance in the Twentieth Century*. Cambridge: Cambridge University Press, p. 54.

157 Mott, F. W. (October 1917),'Chadwick Lecture: mental hygiene in shell shock during and after the war', *Journal of Mental Science, 63*, 478.

158 Porter, R. (2001), *Body Politics: Disease, Death and Doctors in Britain, 1650–1900*. Great Britain: Reaktion, p. 24.

159   Anon. (11 September 1915), 'Emotional shock as a restorative', *Lancet*, 630.

Notes to Chapter 2: Encountering Shell-Shocked Men

1   Collie, J. (September 1917), 'The management of neurasthenia and allied disorders contracted in the army', lecture delivered at the Royal Institute of Public Health, June 1917, *Recalled to Life*, 240.
2   Leed, E. (1979), *No Man's Land: Combat and Identity in World War I*. Cambridge: Cambridge University Press, p. 169.
3   Leese, P. (1989), 'A social and cultural history of shell shock, with particular reference to the experience of British soldiers during and after the Great War'. (Unpublished PhD thesis, Open University).
4   Walt Whitman, 'War', cited in the *Labour Leader*, 30 March 1916.
5   Porter, R. (2001), *Body Politics: Disease, Death and Doctors in Britain, 1650–1900*. London: Reaktion, pp. 256–7.
6   *Lancet*, 1823. See http://www.thelancet.com/about (accessed 6 October 2009).
7   Shephard, B. (2000), *A War of Nerves*. London: Jonathon Cape, p. 23.
8   Gabriel, R. and K. Metz (1992), *A History of Military Medicine from Renaissance through Modern Times*. London, New York, NY and Westport, CT: Greenwood Press, p. 217.
9   RAMC (19 August 1903), *Advisory Board for Army Medical Services*. Wellcome Library, London, RAMC Muniments Collection, RAMC/446/1/1.
10 Lovegrove, P. (1951), *Not Least in the Crusade: A Short History of the Royal Army Medical Corps*. Aldershot: Gale and Polden, pp. 29–30.
11 *The Times*, 27 January 1915.
12 Brereton, F. S. (1919), *The Great War and the RAMC*. London: Constable and Co., pp. 2–5.
13 Hutchinson, W. (1919), *The Doctor in War*. London, Cassell and Co., pp. 1–2.
14 Schuster, A. (11 September 1915), 'A presidential address on the common aims of science and humanity', *Lancet*, 592.
15 *Labour Leader*, 16 September 1915.
16 Wells, H. G. (1916), *Mr Britling Sees It Through*. London: Cassell and Company, p. 291.
17 For a discussion of German atrocities and propaganda see Gregory, A. (2008), *The Last Great War: British Society and the First World War*. Cambridge: Cambridge University Press, pp. 40–69.
18 Osler, William (9 October 1915), 'Science and war', *Lancet*, 801.
19 RAMC (1918), *Hints for RAMC Officers*. Edinburgh: William Bryce; and Beggs, S. T. (1916), *RAMC Training in First Aid and Nursing*. London: The Scientific Press.
20 Hutchinson, W. (1919), *The Doctor in War*. London, Cassell and Co, pp. 11–12.
21 Ibid., p. 109.
22 Norgate, R. H. (March 1920), 'The effects of the war on the mental condition of the citizens of Bristol', *Bristol-Medico-Chirurgical Journal*, XXXVII, 103.
23 Myers, C. S. (1940), *Shell Shock in France, 1914–1918* (based on a war diary kept by Charles Myers). Cambridge: Cambridge University Press, p. 25.
24 See, for example, Turner, W. A. (1916), 'Arrangements for the care of cases of nervous and mental shock coming from overseas', *Journal of the Royal Army Medical Corps*, 27, 619–22;

and Milligan, E. T. C., (RAMC), (1917), 'Shell shock, a method of treatment', *Journal of the Royal Army Medical Corps,* 28, 272–3.

25 Southborough, Lord (28 April 1920), The National Archives, Kew, London, WO/32/4742, p. 1096.

26 Kaye, Captain H.W. (12 February 1916), Unpublished War Diary, Wellcome Library, London, RAMC Muniments Collection, RAMC/739.

27 Mitchell, A. (1978), *Medical Women and the Medical Services of the First World War.* Limited edition Festschrift for Kenneth Fitzpatrick Russell, p. 1.

28 BMJ Publishing Group (1917), *British Medicine in the War, 1914–1917.* London: BMA, p. iv.

29 *The Times,* 20 January 1915.

30 Mitchell, A. (1978), *Medical Women and the Medical Services of the First World War.* Limited edition Festschrift for Kenneth Fitzpatrick Russell, p. 1.

31 *The Times,* 12 February 1916.

32 Leese, P. (2002), *Shell Shock: Traumatic Neurosis and the British Soldiers of the First World War.* London: Palgrave MacMillan, p. 53.

33 Lovegrove, P. (1951), *Not Least in the Crusade: A Short History of the Royal Army Medical Corps.* Aldershot: Gale and Polden, p. 37.

34 Correspondence: Lee to Kitchener (12 October 1914). Wellcome Library, London, RAMC Muniments Collection, RAMC/446/7/7.

35 Barrett, J. W. (1919), *A Vision of the Possible. What the RAMC Might Become.* London: HK Lewis, pp. 146–7.

36 Lovegrove, P. (1951), *Not Least in the Crusade: A Short History of the Royal Army Medical Corps.* Aldershot: Gale and Polden, p. 37.

37 Moran, C. (1945), *The Anatomy of Courage.* London: Constable, p. 197.

38 Kaye, Captain H. W. (2 November 1915), Unpublished War Diary, Wellcome Library, London, RAMC Muniments Collection, RAMC/739.

39 Ibid., 12 February 1916.

40 Ibid., 2 November 1915.

41 Terraine, J. (1993), *Impacts of War 1914 and 1918.* London: Leo Cooper, p. 28.

42 Lankford, N .D. (1980), 'The Victorian medical profession and military practice: army doctors and national origins', *Bulletin of the History of Medicine,* 54, (4), 516.

43 Barrett, J. W. (1919), *A Vision of the Possible. What the RAMC Might Become.* London: HK Lewis, p. viii.

44 Stagg, L. J., (British Nursing Orderly, RAMC), Imperial War Museum (IWM) Sound Archive 8764/7, reel 7 (recorded 1985); and Private W. G. Cook, IWM Sound Archive 9352/19, reel 4, (recorded 1986).

45 Kaye, Captain H. W. (12 February 1916), Unpublished War Diary. Wellcome Library, London, RAMC Muniments Collection, RAMC/739.

46 Ibid., 7 February 1916.

47 Ibid., 20 February 1916.

48 Dible, Captain J. H. (27 September 1914), *First World War Account of Captain James Henry Dible.* Imperial War Museum (IWM), London, Con Shelf.

49 Ibid., 27 September 1914; and 21 November 1914.

50 Esler, Captain M. S. (undated), Private Papers. Imperial War Museum, London, MS74/102/1.

51 Kaye, Captain H. W. (21 June 1915), Unpublished War Diary. Wellcome Library, London, RAMC Muniments Collection, RAMC/739.

52 Webster, Captain W. F. (October 1915). Wellcome Library, London, RAMC Muniments Collection, RAMC/384; and Esler, Captain M. S., IWM Sound Archive 378/3, (recorded 1974).

53 Whitehead, I. (1996), 'Not a doctor's work? The role of the British Regimental Medical Officer in the field', in H. Liddle and P. Liddle (eds), *Facing Armageddon: the First World War Experienced*. London: Leo Cooper, p. 472.

54 *The Times,* 4 October 1916.

55 Whitehead, I. (1996), 'Not a doctor's work? The role of the British Regimental Medical Officer in the field', in H. Liddle and P. Liddle (eds), *Facing Armageddon: the First World War Experienced*. London: Leo Cooper, p. 469.

56 Bosanquet, N. (1996), 'Health systems in khaki: the British and American medical experience', in H. Liddle and P. Liddle (eds), *Facing Armageddon: the First World War Experienced*. London: Leo Cooper, p. 462.

57 *The Times,* 19 February 1916.

58 Harding, Private G. (5 October 1914–6 June 1915), Personal Campaign Diary. National Army Museum (NAM), Chelsea, 2008-07-13.

59 Whitehead, I. (1996), 'Not a doctor's work? The role of the British Regimental Medical Officer in the field', in H. Liddle and P. Liddle (eds), *Facing Armageddon: the First World War Experienced*. London: Leo Cooper, pp. 471–2.

60 Grant, Dr A. R., Private Papers. NAM, 2000-09-62.

61 Dible, Captain J. H. (6 February 1915), *First World War Account of Captain James Henry Dible.* (IWM), London, Con Shelf.

62 Editorial, (6 January 1917), 'An ideal for the New Year', *Lancet,* 23.

63 Collective authorship (1935), *Tales of a Field Ambulance, 1914–1918,* (told by the personnel). Southend-on Sea: printed for private circulation, Preface pp.13–14.

64 Barrett, J. W. (1919), *A Vision of the Possible. What the RAMC Might Become.* London: HK Lewis, p. 170.

65 *Report of the War Office Committee of Enquiry into 'Shell Shock* (1922) London: HMJ, p. 122.

66 Collective authorship (1935), *Tales of a Field Ambulance, 1914–1918,* (told by the personnel). Southend-on Sea: printed for private circulation, p. 38.

67 Stagg, L. J., (British Nursing Orderly, RAMC). Imperial War Museum (IWM), Sound Archive 8764/7, reel 1.

68 Lovegrove, P. (1951), *Not Least in the Crusade: A Short History of the Royal Army Medical Corps.* Aldershot: Gale and Polden, p. 37.

69 Myers, C. S. (1940), *Shell Shock in France, 1914–1918* (based on a war diary kept by Charles Myers). Cambridge: Cambridge University Press, p. 84.

70 Ibid.

71 Dible, Captain J. H. (24 August 1914), *First World War Account of Captain James Henry Dible.* Imperial War Museum (IWM), London, Con Shelf.

72 Stagg, L. J. (British Nursing Orderly, RAMC). Imperial War Museum (IWM), Sound Archive 8764/7, reel 5.

73 Dible, Captain J. H. (24 August 1914; 27 September 1914), *First World War Account of Captain James Henry Dible.* Imperial War Museum (IWM), London, Con Shelf.

74 Barrett, J. W. (1919), *A Vision of the Possible. What the RAMC Might Become.* London: HK Lewis, p. 156.

75 Ibid., p.156.

76 Moran, C. (1945), *The Anatomy of Courage.* London: Constable, p. 190; and *John Bull,* 26 August 1916.

77 Esler, Captain M. S. (undated), Private Papers. Imperial War Museum, London, MS74/102/1.

78 Esler, Captain M. S., Imperial War Museum (IWM), Sound Archive 378/3, reel 2.

79 Babington, A. (1983), *For the Sake of Example.* London: Leo Cooper, p. x.

80 Stagg, L. J., (British Nursing Orderly, RAMC). Imperial War Museum (IWM), Sound Archive 8764/7, reel 4.

81 Loughran, T. (September 2007), 'Evolution, regression and shell-shock: emotion and instinct in theorist of the war neuroses c.1914–1918', *Manchester Papers in Economic and Social History,* 58, 1.

82 Myers, C. S. (1940), *Shell Shock in France, 1914–1918* (based on a war diary kept by Charles Myers). Cambridge: Cambridge University Press, p. 17.

83 Ibid., p. 90.

84 Jones, E. (2004), 'Doctors and trauma in the First World War: the response of British military psychiatrists', in Gray, P. and K. Oliver (eds), *The Memory of Catastrophe.* Manchester: Manchester University Press, p. 102.

85 Myers, C. S. (1940), *Shell Shock in France, 1914–1918* (based on a war diary kept by Charles Myers). Cambridge: Cambridge University Press, p. 140.

86 Forsyth, D. (12 April 1932), 'The place of psychology in the medical curriculum', *Proceedings of the Royal Society of Medicine,* 1200.

87 Ibid., p. 1202.

88 Mercier, cited in ibid., p. 1201.

89 Elliot Smith, G. and T. H. Pear, (1918), *Shell Shock and its Lessons.* Manchester: University Press; and London: Longmans, Green and Co., p. 126.

90 Rivers, W. H., cited in Shephard, B. (1996), '"The Early Treatment of Mental Disorders": RG Rows and Maghull 1914–1918', in H. Freeman and G. E. Berrios (eds), *150 Years of British Psychiatry.* London: Athlone, p. 444.

91 *Report of the War Office Committee of Enquiry into 'Shell Shock* (1922) London: HMJ, pp. 122–3.

92 Myers, C. S. (1940), *Shell Shock in France, 1914–1918* (based on a war diary kept by Charles Myers). Cambridge: Cambridge University Press, p. 120.

93 Parkes Weber, F. (25 December 1914), Personal Papers. Wellcome Library, London, PP/FPW/B163.

94 Correspondence: Townshend to F. Parkes Weber (1917, no precise date given). Wellcome Library, London, PP/FPW/B163.

95 Parkes Weber, F. (undated), Personal Papers. Wellcome Library, London, PP/FPW/B163.

96 *Report of the War Office Committee of Enquiry into 'Shell Shock* (1922) London: HMJ, pp. 49–50.

97 Strictly confidential memo from HQ (37th Division)(7 December 1917) Imperial War Museum (IWM), London, 97/37/1.

98 Esler, Captain M. S. Imperial War Museum (IWM), Sound Archive 378/3, reel 1.

99 Stagg, L. J., (British Nursing Orderly, RAMC). Imperial War Museum (IWM), Sound Archive 8764/7, reel 5.

100 Hewitt, L. J. Imperial War Museum (IWM), Sound Archive 41/4, reel 1.

101 Haigh, R. W. and P. W. Turner (eds) (1970), *The Long Carry: the Journal of Stretcher Bearer Frank Dunham, 1916–1918.* Oxford: Pergamon Press, p. 102.

102 Ibid., p. 166.

103 *Report of the War Office Committee of Enquiry into 'Shell Shock* (1922) London: HMJ, p. 9.

104 Stagg, L. J., (British Nursing Orderly, RAMC). Imperial War Museum (IWM), Sound Archive 8764/7, reel 3.

105 Oxley, H., (NCO, Battalion Gas Instructor), (recorded 1975). Imperial War Museum (IWM), Sound Archive 716/8, reel 8.

106 Esler, Captain M. S. Imperial War Museum (IWM), Sound Archive 378/3, reel 2.

107 Hewitt, L. J. Imperial War Museum (IWM), Sound Archive 41/4, reel 1.

108 Stagg, L. J., (British Nursing Orderly, RAMC). Imperial War Museum (IWM), Sound Archive 8764/7, reel 3.

109 Moran, C. (1945), *The Anatomy of Courage.* London: Constable, p. 22.

110 Oxley, H., (NCO, Battalion Gas Instructor), (recorded 1975). Imperial War Museum (IWM), Sound Archive 716/8, reel 8.

111 Oxley, H., (NCO, Battalion Gas Instructor), (recorded 1975). Imperial War Museum (IWM), Sound Archive 716/8, reel 8.

112 Moran, C. (1945), *The Anatomy of Courage.* London: Constable, p. 70.

113 Ibid., p. 25

114 Esler, Captain M. S., Imperial War Museum (IWM). Sound Archive 378/3, reel 2.

115 Wessely, S. (September 2006), 'The life and death of Private Harry Farr'. *Journal of the Royal Society of Medicine,* 99, 442.

116 Stagg, L. J., (British Nursing Orderly, RAMC). Imperial War Museum (IWM), Sound Archive 8764/7, reel 3.

117 Mott, F. W. (11 March 1916), 'Lettsomian Lecture on the effects of high explosives upon the central nervous system', *Lancet,* (part III), 549.

118 Moran, C. (1945), *The Anatomy of Courage.* London: Constable, p. 22.

119 RAMC (1918), *Hints for RAMC Officers.* Edinburgh: William Bryce, p. 26.

120 For a detailed debate on this issue see Thomson, M. (1999), 'Status, manpower and mental fitness: mental deficiency in the First World War', in R. Cooter, M. Harrison and S. Sturdy (eds), *War, Medicine and Modernity.* Stroud: Sutton, pp. 149–66.

121 Cited in Anon. (5 August 1916), 'Medico-Psychological Association of Great Britain and Ireland. Mental disabilities for war services', *Lancet,* 234.

122 Lovegrove, P. (1951), *Not Least in the Crusade: A Short History of the Royal Army Medical Corps.* Aldershot: Gale and Polden, p. 38.

123 Cooter, R. (1999), 'Malingering in modernity: psychological scripts and adversarial encounters during the First World War', in R. Cooter, M. Harrison and S. Sturdy (eds), *War, Medicine and Modernity.* Stroud: Sutton, pp. 125–48 (p. 129).

124 Myers, C. S. (1940), *Shell Shock in France, 1914–1918* (based on a war diary kept by Charles Myers), Cambridge: Cambridge University Press, p. 11.

125 Gabriel, R. and K. Metz (1992), *A History of Military Medicine from Renaissance through Modern Times.* London, New York, NY and Westport, CT: Greenwood Press, p. 237.

126 Stagg, L. J., (British Nursing Orderly, RAMC). Imperial War Museum (IWM), Sound Archive 8764/7, reel 3.

127 Ibid.

128　Lewis, T. H. (1935), 'Crossing overseas', in collective authorship, *Tales of a Field Ambulance, 1914–1918*, (told by the personnel). Southend-on Sea: printed for private circulation, p. 61.

129　Ibid., p. 63.

130　Esler, Captain M. S. Imperial War Museum (IWM), Sound Archive 378/3, reel 2.

131　Grant, A. R. (23 February 1918), Private Papers. National Army Museum, Chelsea, 2000-09-62.

132　Barnett, C. (1970), *Britain and her Army 1509–1970*. London: Allen Lane, p. 391.

133　Haigh, R. W. and P. W. Turner (eds) (1970), *The Long Carry: the Journal of Stretcher Bearer Frank Dunham, 1916–1918*. Oxford: Pergamon Press, p. 6.

134　Kaye, Captain H. W. (1916, no precise date given), Notes from the post-mortem room of a Casualty Clearing Station. Wellcome Library, London, RAMC Muniments Collection, WL RAMC/739/11.

135　Gabriel, R. and K. Metz (1992), *A History of Military Medicine from Renaissance through Modern Times*. London, New York, NY and Westport, CT: Greenwood Press, p. 248.

136　Shephard, B. (1996), '"The Early Treatment of Mental Disorders": RG Rows and Maghull 1914–1918', in H. Freeman and G. E. Berrios (eds), *150 Years of British Psychiatry*. London: Athlone, p. 441.

137　Brooks, R. (1999), *The Stress of Combat, the Combat of Stress*. Brighton: The Alpha Press, p. 8.

138　Correspondence: Elliott to Captain H. W. Kaye (3 January 1917). Wellcome Library, London, RAMC Muniments Collection, WL RAMC/739/11/5.

139　Haigh, R. W. and P. W. Turner (eds) (1970), *The Long Carry: the Journal of Stretcher Bearer Frank Dunham, 1916–1918*. Oxford: Pergamon Press, p. 19.

140　Kaye, Captain H. W. (5 March 1916), Unpublished War Diary. Wellcome Library, London, RAMC Muniments Collection, WL RAMC/739.

141　Ibid., (20 May 1916; and 7 July 1916).

142　Stagg, L. J., (British Nursing Orderly, RAMC). Imperial War Museum (IWM), Sound Archive 8764/7, reel 5.

143　*Report of the War Office Committee of Enquiry into 'Shell Shock'* (1922) London: HMJ, pp. 88–90.

144　Webster, Captain W. F. (October 1915). Wellcome Library, London, RAMC Muniments Collection, RAMC/384 (October 1915) [no precise date given].

145　Carrington, C. E. (1929), *A Subaltern's War: being a memoir of the Great War from the point of view of a romantic young man, with candid accounts of two particular battles, written shortly after they occurred, and an essay on militarism*. London: Peter Davies Ltd, pp. 65–6.

146　Rudy, C. (November 1918), 'Concerning Tommy'. *The Contemporary Review*, 546.

Notes to Chapter 3: Lest We Forget

1　Lord Southborough, House of Lords, (28 April 1920). The National Archives (TNA), Kew, London, WO/32/4742.

2　Two obvious exceptions to this general rule include Barbusse, H. (1916), *Le Feu, Journal d'un escouade*. Paris; and Herbert, A. P. (1919), *The Secret Battle*. London: Methuen.

3　Wells, H. G. (1916), *Mr Britling Sees It Through*. London: Cassell and Company, p. 339.

4　Lawrence, D. H. (1979), *The Ladybird*. London: Penguin, p. 29, (first published by Martin Secker, 1923).

5   Showalter, E. (1980), *The Female Malady: Women, Madness and English Culture, 1830–1980.* London: Virago, p. 188.
6   Woolf, V. (1992), *Mrs Dalloway.* London: The Hogarth Press, (first published by Hogarth, 1925); Meyer, J. (2004), '"Not Septimus Now": wives of disabled veterans and cultural memory of the First World War in Britain'. *Women's History Review,* 13, (1), 117–38.
7   West, R. (1918), *Return of the Soldier.* London: Nisbet and Co.
8   Falls, C. (1930), *War Books: A Critical Guide.* London: Peter Davies, p. 282.
9   Herbert, A. P. (1919), *The Secret Battle.* London: Methuen.
10 Gibbs, P. (1920), *Realities of War.* London: William Heinemann, p. 31.
11 *The Times,* 18 March 1918.
12 *The Times,* 22 March 1918.
13 *The Times,* 28 March 1918.
14 *The Times,* 29 September 1917.
15 Orr, D. (pathologist), cited in Shephard, B. (1996), '"The Early Treatment of Mental Disorders": RG Rows and Maghull 1914–1918', in H. Freeman and G. E. Berrios (eds), *150 Years of British Psychiatry.* London: Athlone, p. 441.
16 Silver, Lieutenant Colonel J. P. (December 1919), Personal papers. Wellcome Library, London, RAMC Muniments Collection, WL RAMC/542/15.
17 *Daily Herald,* 1 October 1920.
18 Collie, J. (September 1917), 'The management of neurasthenia allied disorders contracted in the army', lecture delivered at the Royal Institute of Public Health, June 1917, *Recalled to Life,* 234–53.
19 Ibid., p. 248.
20 Draper, W. (April 1918), 'Village centres for cure and training', *Recalled to Life,* 346.
21 *The Times,* 15 July 1919.
22 Norgate, R. H. (March 1920), 'The effects of the war on the mental condition of the citizens of Bristol', *Bristol-Medico-Chirurgical Journal,* XXXVII, 107.
23 O'Brien, F. J. (August 1918), 'Treat shell shock in quiet hospitals', *Medical World,* 304–5.
24 Fenton, N. (1926), *Shell Shock and its Aftermath.* London: Henry Kimpton, p. 139.
25 Lerner, P. (2000), 'Psychiatry and casualties of war in Germany, 1914–18'. *Journal of Contemporary History,* 35, (1), 20.
26 Mosse, G. (1990), *Fallen Soldiers: Re-Shaping the Memory of the World Wars.* Oxford and New York: Oxford University Press, pp. 107–9.
27 Mott, F. W. (April 1922), 'The neuroses and psychoses in relation to conscription and eugenics', *Eugenics Review,* XIV, (1), 16.
28 *The Times,* 20 August 1920.
29 Barham, P. (2004), *Forgotten Lunatics of the Great War.* New Haven, CT and London: Yale University Press, p. 233; for key comments on the commission see also Bogacz, T. (1989), 'War neurosis and cultural change in England, 1914–1922: the work of the War Office committee of enquiry into "shell shock"', *Journal of Contemporary History,* 24, 227–56.
30 *Minutes of the Government Committee of Enquiry into Shell Shock* (hereafter GCOESS Minutes), 8 December 1921. The National Archives (TNA), Kew, London, WO/32/4742.
31 *Daily Herald,* 28 October 1919.
32 Southborough, House of Lords, (28 April 1920).TNA, WO/32/4742
33 Ibid.
34 *The Times,* 18 January 1918.

35 Haldane, Viscount, House of Lords, (28 April 1920). TNA, WO/32/4742. For full details of the executions see Corns, C. and J. Hughes-Wilson, (2001), *Blindfold and Alone: British Military Executions in the Great War.* London: Cassell.

36 *Report of the War Office Committee of Enquiry,* p. 3.

37 Lord Horne, House of Lords (28 April 1920). TNA, WO/32/4742.

38 Lord Southborough, House of Lords (28 April 1920). TNA, WO/32/4742.

39 GCOESS Minutes, 4 November 1920.

40 Ex-Services' Welfare Society Executive Committee Minutes (hereafter ESWS Minutes), 27 January 1919. Combat Stress Archives (CSA), Leatherhead.

41 Medical notes. TNA, PIN 26/16542

42 GCOESS Minutes, 22 September 1921.

43 *Draft Report of the War Office Committee of Enquiry.* TNA, WO 32/4748 1A, p. 83.

44 Haldane, House of Lords, (28 April 1920). TNA, WO/32/4742.

45 GCOESS Minutes, 7 September 1920.

46 GCOESS Minutes, 27 October 1921.

47 GCOESS Minutes, 21 October 1920.

48 GCOESS Minutes, 22 September 1921.

49 GCOESS Minutes, 7 September 1920.

50 *Draft Report of the War Office Committee of Enquiry,* p. 72.

51 *The Times,* 20 August 1920.

52 GCOESS Minutes, 4 November 1920.

53 Correspondence: H. S. Jeudwine to Lord Southborough (14 January 1921). TNA, WO/32/4742.

54 Correspondence: Lord Southborough to H. S. Jeudwine; H. S. Jeudwine to Lord Southborough (14–27 January 1921). TNA, WO/32/4742.

55 Correspondence: C. S. Myers to Lord Southborough (9 October 1921). TNA, WO/32/4742.

56 GCOESS Minutes, 10 February 1921.

57 War Office Committee of Enquiry (1922). *Questions for the Guidance of Witnesses Giving Evidence Before the War Office Committee of Enquiry on 'Shell Shock'.* TNA, WO/32/4742.

58 GCOESS Minutes, 10 February 1921.

59 GCOESS Minutes, 13 April 1922.

60 War Office Committee of Enquiry (1922). *Questions for the Guidance of Witnesses Giving Evidence Before the War Office Committee of Enquiry on 'Shell Shock'.* TNA, WO/32/4742.

61 Correspondence: Admiralty to Southborough (12 October 1920). TNA, WO/32/4742.

62 MacPherson, J. (14 November 1921). TNA, WO/32/4747.

63 GCOESS Minutes, 18 November 1921.

64 Becker, A. (2002), 'Remembering and forgetting the First World War in Western Europe', in M. Spierring and M. Wintle (eds), *Ideas of Europe Since 1914.* Basingstoke: Palgrave Macmillan, p. 89.

65 Mosse, G. (1990), *Fallen Soldiers: Re-Shaping the Memory of the World Wars.* Oxford and New York, NY: Oxford University Press, p. 6.

66 Moriarty, C. (1997), 'Private grief and public remembrance: British First World War memorials', in M. Evans and K. Lunn (eds), *War and Memory in the Twentieth Century.* Oxford and New York, NY: Berg, p. 126.

67 Ibid., p. 139.

68   Ibid.

69   *Draft Report of the War Office Committee of Enquiry,* p. 43.

70   Winter, J. (1995), *Sites of Memory, Sites of Mourning.* Cambridge: Cambridge University Press, p. 2.

71   Sassoon, S. (1983), 'To One Who was With Me in the War', in *The War Poems.* London: Faber and Faber, p .141, (first published March 1926).

72   Rivers, W. H. R. (2 February 1918), 'An address on the repression of war experience', delivered before the Section of Psychiatry, Royal Society of Medicine, 4 December 1917, *Lancet,* 173.

73   *The Times,* 25 February 1919.

74   For a detailed consideration of psychiatric casualties from the First and the Second World Wars see Jones, E., I. Palmer and S. Wessely (2002), 'War pensions (1900–1945): changing models of psychological understanding', *The British Journal of Psychiatry,* 180, 374–9.

75   Medical notes. TNA, PIN 26/16532.

76   *John Bull,* 9 March 1918; and 16 March 1918.

77   *Labour Leader,* 17 November 1921.

78   Graham, S. (1923), 'The ex-service mind of Europe', *Contemporary Review,* 123, 290–300.

79   Cook, Private W. G. Imperial War Museum (IWM) Sound Archive 9352/19, reel 4 (recorded 1986).

80   Ibid.

81   Rudy, C. (November 1918), 'Concerning Tommy', *The Contemporary Review,* 546.

82   Pederson, S. (1990), 'Gender, welfare and citizenship in Britain during the Great War', *American Historical Review,* 95, (4), 983–1006.

83   Haig, in *The Times,* 2 July 1919.

84   *Morning Post,* 5 April 1922.

85   *Morning Post,* 27 April 1922.

86   Ibid.

87   Digby, A. (1996), 'Poverty health and the politics of gender in Britain, 1870–1948', in A. Digby and J. Stewart (eds), *Gender, Health and Welfare.* London and New York, NY: Routledge, p. 75.

88   Galsworthy, J. (August 1918), 'The gist of the matter', *Reveille* (formerly *Recalled to Life*), 14.

89   *Labour Leader,* 7 April 1921.

90   Galloway, J. (committee chairman), *Report upon the Physical Examination of Men of Military Age by National Service Medical Boards from 1 November, 1917–31 October, 1918,* vol. I, p. 4.

91   Barham, P. (2004), *Forgotten Lunatics of the Great War.* New Haven, CT and London: Yale University Press, p. 33.

92   Thane, P. (1996), 'Gender, welfare and old age in Britain, 1870s–1940s', in A. Digby and J. Stewart (eds), *Gender, Health and Welfare.* London and New York, NY: Routledge, p. 190.

93   Pederson, 'Gender, welfare and citizenship', 983–1006 (p. 985).

94   A. Keogh (June 1917), 'Treatment of the disabled', *Recalled to Life,* 6–40 (p. 6).

95   For war as a test of masculinity see Showalter, E. (1980), *The Female Malady: Women, Madness and English Culture, 1830–1980.* London: Virago; and Mosse, G. (1990), *Fallen Soldiers: Re-Shaping the Memory of the World Wars.* Oxford and New York, NY: Oxford University Press.

96   Editorial (June 1917), *Recalled to Life*, 3.
97   Anon. (June 1917), 'Good news for the disabled sailor or soldier', *Recalled to Life*, 67.
98   'Soldiers' Pensions. Provision for future, iii.–The human note', *The Times*, 20 February 1919.
99   Ibid.
100 *Morning Post*, 27 April 1922.
101 *Daily Herald*, 28 October 1919.
102 MOP Report (5 November 1919). TNA, PIN 15/421.
103 Birmingham Citizens' Committee (3 October 1919). TNA, PIN 15/421.
104 Portsmouth Local Committee (3 October 1919). TNA, PIN 15/421.
105 Ibid.
106 *The Times*, 20 February 1919.
107 *The Times*, 4 September 1917.
108 Collie, J. (2 February 1918). TNA, PIN 15/1230.
109 Soldiers' Award Branch Circular, 26 March 1918. TNA, PIN 15/1230.
110 *Labour Leader*, 9 March 1922.
111 Cameron, B. (c.1920), undated letter. TNA, PIN 26/16387.
112 Barham, P. (2004), *Forgotten Lunatics of the Great War*. New Haven, CT and London: Yale University Press, p. 226.
113 Anon. (June 1917), 'Care of disabled soldiers – preliminary arrangements', *Recalled to Life*, 105.
114 Anon. (June 1917), 'Care of disabled soldiers – preliminary arrangements', *Recalled to Life*, 126.

Notes to Chapter 4: Lunatics and Lunacy Reform

1   *The Times*, 27 July 1915.
2   Owen, W. (1977), 'Mental Cases' in *The Collected Poems of Wilfred* Owen London: Chatto and Windus (first published 1920 but written in 1917 or 1918).
3   The Shot at Dawn Campaign did not seek pardons for those soldiers executed for murder during the First World War. Leaving aside the unproven – and unprovable – assumption that all deserters were mentally wounded, this approach runs the risk of pardoning only those men who presented one specific (and to most modern observers, one very attractive) symptom of mental breakdown.
4   'Pour M. Sarkozy, les fusillés de 14–18 "n'avaient pas été des lâches"', *Le Monde*, 11 November 2008.
5   Barker, P. (1996), *The Regeneration Trilogy*. London: Viking.
6   Faulks, S. (1994), *Birdsong*. London: Vintage.
7   The work of the ESWS at this stage has already been acknowledged. See Jones, E. (2004), 'Doctors and trauma in the First World War: the response of British military psychiatrists', in P. Gray and K. Oliver (eds), *The Memory of Catastrophe*. Manchester: Manchester University Press, p. 98; Barham, P. (2004), *Forgotten Lunatics of the Great War*. New Haven, CT and London: Yale University Press, p. 296; Jones, E. and S. Wessely (2005), *Shell Shock to PTSD: Military Psychiatry from 1900 to the Gulf War*. Hove and New York, NY: Psychology Press, pp. 61–4.

NOTES TO PAGES 102–108

8   Anon. (June 1917), 'The care of disabled soldiers – the present system', *Recalled to Life*, 128.
9   Correspondence: Tyron to Butcher (27 September 1923). The National Archives, Kew, London, PIN 15/2499 3A.
10 Kipling, R. (1919), 'My Mother's Son', in ESWS campaign literature. CSA.
11 *The Times*, 31 March 1920.
12 *The Times*, 10 August 1920.
13 *The Times*, 23 September 1922.
14 *The Times*, 11 March 1920.
15 ESWS Minutes, 2 April 1919. Combat Stress Archives (CSA), Leatherhead. These early intentions were not always maintained. In 1925 the committee was quite opposed to providing support for a man suffering from GPI.
16 *Draft Report of the War Office Committee of Enquiry*. The National Archives (TNA), Kew, London, WO 32/4748 1A, p. 148.
17 Barham, P. (2004), *Forgotten Lunatics of the Great War*. New Haven, CT and London: Yale University Press, p. 270.
18 ESWS Minutes, 4 December 1918. CSA.
19 Barham, P. (2004), *Forgotten Lunatics of the Great War*. New Haven, CT and London: Yale University Press, pp. 169–74.
20 Addison, C. (January 1921), 'Parliamentary news', *Journal of Mental Science*, 67, 136.
21 Elliot Smith, G. and T. H. Pear, (1918), *Shell Shock and its Lessons*. Manchester: University Press; and London: Longmans, Green and Co, pp. 84–5.
22 Steen, R. H. (January 1920), 'Notes and news', *Journal of Mental Science*, 66, 71.
23 Jones, G. (1986), *Social Hygiene in Twentieth Century Britain*. London: Croom Helm, p. 81.
24 Robinson, W. (January 1921), 'The future of Service patients in mental hospitals', *Journal of Mental Science*, 67, 47.
25 Jones, K. (1960), *Mental Health and Social Policy, 1845–1956*. London: Routledge and Kegan Paul, pp. 95–6.
26 Ibid., pp. 98–9.
27 *Daily Herald*, 1 September 1919; and 9 October 1924.
28 *John Bull*, 5 August 1922.
29 Editorial, *The Times*, 6 September 1919.
30 Ibid.
31 *Morning Post*, 25 April 1922.
32 *The Times*, 27 September 1922.
33 Nicoll, M. and J. A. M. Alcock (April 1918), 'Neuroses of war', *Recalled to Life*, 254.
34 For an analysis of the physical culture movement in inter-war Britain see Zweiniger-Bargielowska, I. (2006), 'Building a British superman: physical culture in interwar Britain', *Journal of Contemporary History*, 41, (4), 595–610.
35 Standwell, T. W. (24 January 1920), 'Are you a potential post-war criminal?', *Health and Strength*, 62.
36 Ibid.
37 *Daily Herald*, 15 October 1920.
38 *Draft Report of the War Office Committee of Enquiry*, pp. 32–4.
39 Robinson, W. (January 1921), 'The future of Service patients in mental hospitals', *Journal of Mental Science*, 67, 40–8.
40 Norgate, R. H. (March 1920), 'The effects of the war on the mental condition of the citizens of Bristol', *Bristol-Medico-Chirurgical Journal*, XXXVII, 107.

41   *John Bull*, 9 February 1918.
42   TNA, PIN 26/16457 (17 May 1920–11 October 1921).
43   Douglas, R. (September 1972), 'The National Democratic Party and the British Workers' League', *The Historical Journal*, 15, (3), 539.
44   Ibid., p. 534.
45   Loseby, C. (9 November 1921), 'Report on House of Commons public meeting'. ESWS. CSA.
46   Ibid.
47   ESWS Minutes, 31 October 1921.
48   Leese, P. (2002), *Shell Shock: Traumatic Neurosis and the British Soldiers of the First World War*. London: Palgrave MacMillan, p. 133.
49   Graves, R. (1960), *Goodbye to All That*. London: Penguin, pp. 91–2, (first published by Jonathon Cape, 1929).
50   Lumsden, T., 'Medical referee for pensions', in *The Times*, 22 August 1917.
51   MacPherson, W. G. (January 1922), 'Parliamentary news', *Journal of Mental Science*, 68, 108.
52   Loseby, C. (9 November 1921), 'Report on House of Commons public meeting'. ESWS. CSA.
53   Loseby, C. (9 November 1921), 'Report on House of Commons public meeting'. ESWS. CSA.
54   MacPherson, W. G. (9 November 1921), 'Report on House of Commons public meeting'. ESWS. CSA.
55   Loseby, C. (9 November 1921), 'Report on House of Commons public meeting'. ESWS. CSA.
56   ESWS Minutes, 5 April 1924. CSA.
57   MacPherson, W. G. (January 1922), 'Parliamentary news', *Journal of Mental Science*, 68, 107.
58   Loseby, C. (9 November 1921), 'Report on House of Commons public meeting'. ESWS. CSA.
59   Lomax, M. (1921), *The Experiences of an Asylum Doctor with Suggestions for Asylum and Lunacy Law Reform*. London: George Allen and Unwin.
60   Lomax, M. (9 November 1921), 'Report on House of Commons public meeting'. ESWS. CSA.
61   Ibid.
62   Ibid.
63   Ibid.
64   Raw, N. (January 1921), 'Parliamentary news', *Journal of Mental Science*, 67, 137.
65   Raw, N. (9 November 1921), 'Report on House of Commons public meeting'. ESWS. CSA.
66   Roberts, F. O. (9 November 1921), 'Report on House of Commons public meeting'. ESWS. CSA.
67   *The Times*, 11 November 1921.
68   ESWS Correspondence: Waite to C. Loseby (10 November 1921). CSA .
69   ESWS Minutes, 17 March 1922. CSA.
70   ESWS Minutes, 7 July 1925. CSA.
71   ESWS Minutes, 15 February 1924. CSA.
72   ESWS Minutes, 3 June 1924. CSA.

73   *The Times,* 10 November 1923.

74   *The Times,* 10 November 1923.

75   *The Times,* 17 November 1923.

76   *Morning Post,* 24, 25 and 26 April 1924.

77   *Morning Post,* 24 April 1924.

78   *Morning Post,* 26 April 1924.

79   ESWS Minutes, 6 May 1924. CSA.

80   Memo: G. Chrystal and L. Webb to MPs and others (15 November 1924). TNA, PIN 15/2499 21A.

81   *The Times,* 11 November 1924.

82   *The Times,* 11 November 1924.

83   ESWS Minutes, 2 December 1924. CSA.

84   *St Columba's Church of Scotland Magazine,* December 1924, 176. CSA.

85   *The Times,* 25 January 1918.

86   TNA, WO 32/4747 22A; 29A.

87   ESWS Correspondence: A. Hunter-Weston to A. Fleming (22 December 1924). CSA.

88   ESWS Correspondence: E. Howard to A. Fleming (7 January 1925). CSA.

89   ESWS Correspondence: E. Howard to A. Fleming (10 March 1925). CSA.

90   Wiltshire, H. (17 June 1916), 'Contribution to the aetiology of shell shock', *Lancet,* 1207.

91   ESWS Correspondence: E. Howard to A. Fleming (10 March 1925). CSA.

92   Loseby, C. in *John Bull,* 1 July 1922.

93   ESWS Correspondence: E. Howard to A. Hunter-Weston (no date, but posted May 1925). CSA.

94   ESWS Correspondence: E. Howard to A. Fleming (7 January 1925). CSA.

95   ESWS Correspondence: E. Howard to A. Fleming (10 March 1925). CSA.

96   Lomax, M. (1921), *The Experiences of an Asylum Doctor with Suggestions for Asylum and Lunacy Law Reform.* London: George Allen and Unwin, pp. 124–8.

97   *John Bull,* 15 July 1922.

98   Orwell, G. (1984), *Down and Out in Paris and London.* London: Penguin 1984, (first published London: Victor Gollancz, 1933).

99   ESWS Correspondence: A. Fleming to E. Howard (17 April 1925). CSA; A. Hunter-Weston to E. Howard (28 March 1925). CSA.

100 ESWS Correspondence: W. Colfox to A. Milner (26 June 1925). CSA.

101 ESWS Correspondence: W. Colfox to E. Howard (30 July 1925). CSA.

102 ESWS Correspondence: W. Colfox to A. Milner (30 July 1925). CSA.

103 ESWS Minutes, 7 July 1925; ESWS Correspondence: A. Milner to W. Colfox (14 November 1925). CSA .

104 ESWS Correspondence: W. Colfox to A. Milner (18 November 1925). CSA.

105 Correspondence: G. Chrystal to G. Tyron (12 August 1925). TNA, PIN 15/749.

106 *Daily Herald,* 15 November 1924.

107 ESWS Minutes, 16 December 1924. CSA.

108 *Daily Herald,* 15 November 1924.

109 ESWS Correspondence: Ronald Bowes Lyon (Lieutenant-Commander, Equerry) on behalf of Prince George to A. Milner (9 December 1924), CSA.

110 Tyron, G., House of Commons, (11 December 1924).TNA, PIN 15/2500 2A .

111 ESWS Minutes, 6 January 1925. CSA.

112 ESWS Correspondence: E. Howard to *The Times* (16 December 1924, unpublished). CSA.

113 ESWS Minutes, 29 August 1923. CSA.

114 ESWS Correspondence: E. Howard to A. Fleming (22 December 1924). CSA .

115 ESWS Minutes, 28 February 1919. CSA.

116 Prost, A. (1992), *In the Wake of War: Les Anciens Combattants and French Society.* Providence and Oxford: Berg; Cohen, D. (2003), 'The war's returns: disabled veterans in Britain and Germany, 1914–1939', in R. Chickering and S. Förster, *The Shadows of Total War.* Cambridge: Cambridge University Press, p. 124.

117 Winter, J. M. (2000), 'Shell shock and the cultural history of the Great War', *Journal of Contemporary History,* 35, (1), 8.

118 ESWS Correspondence: C. Loseby to E. Howard (16 September 1925). CSA.

119 ESWS Correspondence: A. Milner to E. Howard (7 February 1925). CSA .

120 ESWS Correspondence: A. Milner to E. Howard (26 January 1925). CSA.

121 ESWS Correspondence: Milner to E. Howard (26 January 1925). CSA.

122 ESWS Minutes, 6 January 1925. CSA.

123 ESWS Minutes, 14 April, 1925. CSA.

124 Jones, E. (2004), 'Doctors and trauma in the First World War: the response of British military psychiatrists', in P. Gray and K. Oliver (eds), *The Memory of Catastrophe.* Manchester: Manchester University Press, p. 98.

125 ESWS Minutes, 9 June, 1925. CSA.

126 Correspondence: E. Mapother to A. Lisle Webb (17 June 1925). TNA, PIN 15/2501 1A.

127 *Daily Graphic,* 1 November 1925.

128 ESWS Minutes, 24 November 1925. CSA.

129 *Daily Graphic,* November 13–26, 1925.

130 ESWS Minutes, 22 July 1926. CSA.

Notes to Chapter 5: No Longer 'Nerve-Wracked Boys'

1 Ruskin, John, cited by A. K. Watson, ESWS *Annual Report,* 1929, p. 23. Combat Stress Archives (CSA), Leatherhead.

2 Terraine, J. (1993), *Impacts of War 1914 and 1918.* London: Leo Cooper, p. 4.

3 ESWS Minutes, 6 December 1928. CSA.

4 ESWS Minutes, 16 February 1922. CSA.

5 ESWS Minutes, 23 May 1922. CSA.

6 Evans, H. (August 1918), 'Development of the work', *Reveille,* 237.

7 *The Times,* 4 September 1917.

8 ESWS Minutes, 5 November 1920; and 1 July 1921. CSA.

9 The Pignall inventions were small hand-made novelties or gadgets. Mr Pignall was an amateur inventor who had placed several of his inventions at the disposal of the ESWS committee. He hoped that people would buy his inventions to support ex-servicemen, and that eventually the demand would be so great that the ESWS would establish a factory for large-scale manufacture.

10 ESWS Minutes, 2 April 1919. CSA.

11 ESWS Minutes, 28 February 1919. CSA.

12 Correspondence: Circular from Frederick Milner to George Robertson (10 July 1924). The

National Archives (TNA), PIN 15/2499 4C.

13　Correspondence: Helena Laurie to MOP (12 November 1924). TNA, PIN 15/2500 16C.

14　Correspondence: A. Daniel, Medical Superintendent of Hanwell Mental Hospital to ESWS (18 November 1924). TNA, PIN 15/2500 16B.

15　Ministry of Pensions (November 1924), *MOP Report.* TNA, PIN 15/2499 21B.

16　Ibid.

17　Ibid.

18　ESWS Publicity Photographs (undated, c.1929), Eden Manor Lounge. CSA.

19　ESWS Ladies' House Committee (ESWS LHC) Minutes, 5 July 1926. CSA.

20　ESWS Publicity Photographs (undated, c.1929), Eden Manor Garden. CSA.

21　18C Memo. E. C. Price for the Charity Organisation Society, TNA, PIN 15/2502. (25 April 1927).

22　*Swindon Advertiser,* 16 November 1928. TNA, PIN 15/2503 54A.

23　Correspondence: Eve Fairfax (F. Milner's niece) to Mrs Baldwin, (12 October 1928). TNA, PIN 15/2503 53B.

24　Leese, P. (1997), 'Problems returning home: the British psychological casualties of the Great War', *Historical Journal,* 40, (4), 1056.

25　*Recalled to Life,* April 1918, p. 589.

26　ESWS, *Annual Report,* October 1927, p. 10. CSA.

27　ESWS Minutes, 31 October 1921. CSA.

28　*Daily Herald,* 1 September 1919.

29　Petter, M. (1994), '"Temporary gentlemen" in the aftermath of the Great War: rank, status and the ex-officer problem', *Historical Journal,* 37, (1), 127.

30　ESWS Minutes, 9 February 1920. CSA.

31　ESWS Minutes, 2 April 1919. CSA.

32　*The Times,* 24 August 1920.

33　ESWS Minutes, 18 December 1922. CSA.

34　ESWS Minutes, 15 August 1923. CSA.

35　Correspondence: Dr Mapother to Lisle Webb (17 June 1925). TNA PIN 15/2501 1A.

36　ESWS Minutes, 19 July 1922. CSA.

37　Digby, A. and J. Stewart (1996), 'Welfare in context', in A. Digby and J. Stewart (eds), *Gender, Health and Welfare.* London and New York, NY: Routledge, p. 9.

38　ESWS Minutes, 4 September 1919. CSA.

39　ESWS Minutes, 19 July–14 August 1922. CSA.

40　ESWS Minutes, 29 September 1922. CSA.

41　ESWS LHC Minutes, 16 January 1925. CSA.

42　ESWS Minutes, 8 July 1929. CSA.

43　Collie, J. (January–December 1918), 'The management of neurasthenia and allied disorders contracted in the army', *Journal of State Medicine,* XXVI, 10.

44　Brock, A. J. (23 March 1918), 'The war neurasthenic: a note on methods of re-integrating him with his Environment', *Lancet,* 436.

45　Hotchkis, R. D. (April 1917), 'Renfrew District Asylum as a war hospital for mental invalids: some contrasts in administration with an analysis of cases admitted during the first year', *Journal of Mental Science,* 63, 242.

46　ESWS *Annual Report,* October 1929, p. 23. CSA.

47　ESWS Minutes, 13 November 1920. CSA.

48   ESWS Minutes, 12 April 1923. CSA.
49   ESWS Minutes, 26 October 1923. CSA.
50   ESWS publicity leaflet (1924). TNA, PIN 15/2499 14E; ESWS Finance Committee Minutes, 26 August 1925. CSA.
51   ESWS Minutes, 6 January 1925. CSA.
52   ESWS Minutes, 24 November 1925. CSA.
53   Interview with ESWS: MOP Minutes, 12 June 1926. TNA, PIN 15/749 75A.
54   ESWS Minutes, 2 September 1926. CSA.
55   ESWS Minutes, February–May 1927. CSA.
56   Correspondence: Tyron to Butcher (27 September 1923). TNA, PIN 15/249 3A.
57   Correspondence: Tyron to Sir Laming Worthington Evans (5 April 1927). TNA, PIN 15/2502 14A.
58   Metropolitan Police Report on ESWS (9 November 1926). TNA, HO 45/12492.
59   ESWS, *Annual Report,* October 1927, p. 8. CSA.
60   Ibid, p. 14.
61   ESWS, *Annual Reports,* October 1926–October 1930. CSA.
62   ESWS, *Annual Report,* October 1926, p. 11; October 1927, p. 16. CSA.
63   ESWS Minutes, 15 December 1925. CSA.
64   ESWS, *Annual Report,* 1926–1930. CSA.
65   Metropolitan Police Report on ESWS (9 November 1926). TNA, HO 45/12492.
66   ESWS, *Annual Report,* 1928 p. 9. CSA.
67   ESWS, *Annual Report* October 1930 p. 9. CSA.
68   The neurological hospital at Saltash was closed in 1927.
69   ESWS Minutes, 2 July 1924. CSA.
70   ESWS Minutes, 2 July 1924. CSA.
71   ESWS, *Annual Report,* October 1928, p. 13. CSA.
72   ESWS, *Annual Report,* October 1929, p. 5. CSA.
73   Correspondence relating to Fahey (14 June 1940). TNA, CO 295 621/5 914.
74   Correspondence relating to Fahey (May–June 1940). TNA, CO 295 621/5.
75   Correspondence: Waite to Loseby (10 November, 1921). CSA.
76   ESWS, *Annual Report,* October 1928, pp. 10–11. CSA.
77   *The Times,* February–March 1927.
78   Tyron, (16 September 1928). TNA, PIN 15/750 16A.
79   ESWS Minutes, 1 December 1925. CSA.
80   ESWS Minutes, 1 December 1925. CSA.
81   ESWS Minutes, 6 October 1925. CSA.
82   ESWS, *Annual Report,* 1928, p. 3. CSA.
83   ESWS, *Annual Report,* 1927, p. 7. CSA.
84   ESWS, *Annual Report,* October 1930, p. 25. CSA.
85   *The Optimist,* 11 November 1929.
86   ESWS Minutes, 1 September 1927. CSA.
87   ESWS Minutes, 1 September 1927. CSA.
88   Mosse, G. (1990), *Fallen Soldiers: Re-Shaping the Memory of the World Wars.* New York, NY and Oxford: Oxford University Press, pp. 63–64.
89   Details of Stanley's case can be found in *The Times,* 1 November 1917 and *Labour Leader,* 8 November 1917. In both cases he was referred to as 'the late private No A/6730 2 Battalion, Royal Scots Fusiliers'. His name was withheld.

90   *The Times,* 1 November 1917; and *Labour Leader,* 8 November 1917.

91   *Labour Leader,* 8 November 1917.

92   Showalter, E. (1980), *The Female Malady: Women, Madness and English Culture, 1830–1980.* London: Virago, p. 172.

93   Ibid., p. 8.

94   MacCurdy, J. (1918), *War Neuroses.* SI: Cambridge University Press, p. 268.

95   Wilson, L. (January 1921), 'Parliamentary news', *Journal of Mental Science,* 67, 142.

96   Somerville, H. (April 1923), 'The war anxiety neurotic of the present day: a clinical sketch', *Journal of Mental Science,* 69, 175.

97   Ibid., p. 174.

98   ESWS Minutes, 7 December 1923. CSA.

99   ESWS Finance Committee Minutes, 10 December 1925. CSA.

100 Correspondence: E. Howard to A. Fleming (10 March 1925). CSA.

101 Correspondence: E. Howard to W. Colfox (22 July 1925). CSA.

102 Correspondence: W. Colfox to E. Howard (30 July 1925). CSA.

103 MOP Minutes, 14 April 1926. TNA, PIN 15/749 50.

104 Kipling, R. (1919), 'My Mother's Son', in ESWS Campaign literature. CSA.

105 ESWS Minutes, 16 February 1922. CSA.

106 Somerville, H. (April 1923), 'The war anxiety neurotic of the present day: a clinical sketch', *Journal of Mental Science,* 69, 173.

107 Collie, J. (January–December 1918), 'The management of neurasthenia and allied disorders contracted in the army', *Journal of State Medicine,* XXVI, 11.

108 Elliot Smith, G. and T. H. Pear, (1918), *Shell Shock and its Lessons.* Manchester: University Press; and London: Longmans, Green and Co, p. 51.

109 'The sleep bath', in the *Daily Herald,* 25 October 1919.

110 Commissioner of Medical Services, West Midlands region, (10 October 1920). TNA, PIN 15/1230.

111 Correspondence: Medical Officer, John Leigh Memorial Hospital to Director General of Medical Services (10 October 1920). TNA, PIN 15/1230.

112 ESWS, *Annual Report,* October 1930, p. 22. CSA.

113 MOP Minutes (12 June 1926), Interview with ESWS. TNA, PIN 15/749 75A.

114 ESWS Minutes, 4 December 1918. CSA.

115 ESWS Minutes, 24 November 1927. CSA.

116 ESWS, *Annual Report,* October 1926, p. 11. CSA.

117 Correspondence: C. E. Thwaites to S. Thompson (8 January 1925). PIN 15/2500 42C.

118 ESWS Minutes, 1 December 1925. CSA.

119 ESWS Minutes, 5 May 1925. CSA.

120 ESWS Minutes, 6 October 1925. CSA.

121 *The Times,* 31 March 1920.

122 ESWS LHC Minutes, 3 December 1926. CSA.

123 MOP Minutes (12 June 1926), Interview with ESWS. TNA, PIN 15/749 75A.

124 Barr, N. (2005), *The Lion and the Poppy: British Veterans, Politics and Society 1921–1939.* Westport, Connecticut: Praeger Publishers, p. 4.

125 ESWS Articles of Association, 26 September 1927. CSA.

126 ESWS Minutes, 24 November 1927. CSA.

127 ESWS, *Annual Report,* October 1927, p. 13. CSA.

128   ESWS, *Annual Report*, October 1926, p. 10. CSA.
129   ESWS Minutes, 16 June 1927. CSA.
130   Ibid.
131   ESWS Publicity Photographs for their Appeal (c.1928). CSA.
132   ESWS Publicity Photographs (c.1926). CSA.
133   ESWS Minutes, 20 October 1927. CSA.
134   Barham, P. (2004), *Forgotten Lunatics of the Great War.* New Haven, CT and London: Yale University Press, Illustrations 9 and 10.
135   ESWS Minutes, 7 March 1929. CSA.
136   ESWS Minutes, 4 October 1928 and 7 March 1929. CSA.
137   ESWS Publicity Photographs, ESWS stand at the *Daily Mail* Ideal Home Exhibition, Olympia, 1929. CSA.
138   ESWS Minutes, 19 April 1928. CSA.
139   ESWS Publicity Photographs (1929), Thermega Workshop. CSA.
140   ESWS Minutes, 6 December 1928. CSA.

Notes to Chapter 6: Shell Shock and Veterans' Voices

1   Blomfield, Private E. (1931), 'A true war yarn', (unpublished memoir). National Army Museum, 2006-11-38.
2   The history of madness and the treatment of madness is a vast topic. For a good introduction see Porter, R. (1987), *A Social History of Madness: The World Through the Eyes of the Insane.* New York, NY: Weidenfeld and Nicolson.
3   ESWS (1928), *Annual Report*, p. 14. CSA.
4   ESWS (1928), Armistice Day literature. The National Archives, PIN 15/2502.
5   Hankey, D. (1918), *A Student in Arms.* London: Andrew Melrose, p. 242. I would like to thank Professor Andy Smith for drawing my attention to the published work of Donald Hankey.
6   Esplin's story is told in Chapter 1.
7   Blomfield, Private E. (1931), 'A true war yarn', (unpublished memoir). National Army Museum, 2006-11-38, pp. 1–20.
8   *Draft Report of the War Office Committee of Enquiry*, The National Archives, WO32/4748 1A. pp. 89–91.
9   Ibid., p. 39.
10   Hewitt, L. J., Imperial War Museum, Sound Archive 41/4.
11   Falls, C. (1930), *War Books: A Critical Guide.* London: Peter Davies, p.xi.
12   Holmes, R. (2004), *Acts of War: The Behaviour of Men in Battle.* London: Cassell Military Paperbacks, p. 9.
13   Gray, P. and Oliver, K. (eds), *The Memory of Catastrophe.* Manchester: Manchester University, pp. 1–4.
14   Lloyd George, D. (1942), *War Memoirs of David Lloyd George.* London: Odhams Press Limited, p. 32.
15   Badsey, S., cited in Sheffield, G. (2002), *Forgotten Victory the First World War: Myths and Realities.* London: Hodder, p. xx.

16   For a discussion on the problems associated with treating the First World War as a unique
     cultural event see Sheffield, G. (2002), *Forgotten Victory the First World War: Myths and
     Realities.* London: Hodder, pp. xxii–xxiv.
17   Clausewitz, C. (1997), *On War.* Ware: Wordsworth, p. 5, (first published 1832).
18   http://news.bbc.co.uk (accessed 10 July 2009).
19   Clausewitz, C. (1997), *On War.* Ware: Wordsworth, p. 8, (first published 1832).
20   Blomfield, Private E. (1931), 'A true war yarn', (unpublished memoir). National Army
     Museum, 2006-11-38, p. 1.

Bibliography

SECONDARY SOURCES: BOOKS, ESSAYS, THESES

Ashplant, T., G. Dawson and M. Roper (eds) (2006), *The Politics of Memory: Commemorating War*. London: Cassell, pp. 240–59.

Babington, A. (1983), *For the Sake of Example*. London: Leo Cooper.

—(1997), *A History of the Changing Attitudes to War Neurosis*. London: Leo Cooper.

Barham, P. (2004), *Forgotten Lunatics of the Great War*. New Haven, CT and London: Yale University Press.

Barr, N. (2005), *The Lion and the Poppy: British Veterans, Politics and Society 1921–1939*. Westport, CT: Praeger Publishers.

Barnett, C. (1970), *Britain and her Army, 1509–1970*. London: Allen Lane.

Becker, A. (2002), 'Remembering and forgetting the First World War in Western Europe', in M. Spierring and M. Wintle (eds), *Ideas of Europe Since 1914*. Basingstoke: Palgrave Macmillan, pp. 89–103.

Binnevald, H. (1997), *From Shell Shock to Combat Stress: A Comparative History of Military Psychiatry*. Holland: Amsterdam University Press.

Blair, J. G. S. and A. C. Ticehurst (1998), *RAMC, 1898–1998. Reflections of One Hundred Years of Service*. Dundee: RAMC.

BMJ Publishing Group (1917), *British Medicine in the War, 1914–1917*. London: BMA.

Bond, B. (2002), *The Unquiet Western Front*. Cambridge: Cambridge University Press.

Bosanquet, N. (1996), 'Health systems in khaki: the British and American medical experience', in H. Liddle and P. Liddle (eds), *Facing Armageddon: the First World War Experienced*. London: Leo Cooper, pp. 452–66.

Bourke, J. (1996), *Dismembering the Male: Men's Bodies, Britain and the Great War*. London: Reaktion.

—(1999), *An Intimate History of Killing: Face to Face Killing in Twentieth Century Warfare*. London: Granta Books.

Braybon, G. (ed.) (2003), *Evidence, History and the Great War Historians and the Impact of 1914–1918*. New York, NY and Oxford: Berghahn Books, pp.1–29.

Brooks, R. (1999), *The Stress of Combat, the Combat of Stress*. Brighton: The Alpha Press.

Brown, T. (1984), 'Shell shock in the Canadian Expeditionary Force, 1914–1918: Canadian psychiatry in the Great War', in C. G. Roland (ed.), *Health, Disease and Medicine*. Canada: The Hannah Institute for the History of Medicine, pp. 308–32.

Cohen, D. (2003), 'The war's returns: disabled veterans in Britain and Germany, 1914–1939', in R. Chickering and S. Förster, *The Shadows of Total War*. Cambridge: Cambridge University Press, pp. 113–28.

Cooter, R. (1998), 'Malingering in modernity: psychological scripts and adversarial encounters during the First World War', in R. Cooter, M. Harrison and S. Sturdy (eds), *War, Medicine and Modernity*. Stroud: Sutton, pp.125–48.

Corns, C. and J. Hughes-Wilson, (2001), *Blindfold and Alone: British Military Executions in the Great War*. London: Cassell.

Digby, A. (1996), 'Poverty health and the politics of gender in Britain, 1870–1948', in A. Digby and J. Stewart (eds), *Gender, Health and Welfare*. London and New York, NY: Routledge, pp. 67–90.

Digby, A. and J. Stewart (1996), 'Welfare in context', in A. Digby and J. Stewart (eds), *Gender, Health and Welfare*. London and New York, NY: Routledge, pp. 1–31.

Delaporte, S. (1996), *Les Gueules Cassées: les blessés de la face de la Grande Guerre*. Paris: Noêsis.

Ferguson, N. (1998), *The Pity of War*. London: Allen Lane.

Fussell, P. (1975), *The Great War and Modern Memory*. New York, NY and London: Oxford University Press, p. 74.

Gabriel, R. and K. Metz (1992), *A History of Military Medicine from Renaissance through Modern Times*. London, New York, NY and Westport, CT: Greenwood Press.

Gray, P. and K. Oliver (eds) (2004), *The Memory of Catastrophe*. Manchester: Manchester University Press.

Gregory, A. (2008), *The Last Great War: British Society and the First World War*. Cambridge: Cambridge University Press.

Holmes, R. (2004), *Acts of War: The Behaviour of Men in Battle*. London: Cassell Military Paperbacks.

Jones, E. (2004), 'Doctors and trauma in the First World War: the response of British military psychiatrists', in P. Gray and K. Oliver (eds), *The Memory of Catastrophe*. Manchester: Manchester University Press, pp. 91–105.

Jones, E. and S. Wessely (2005), *Shell Shock to PTSD: Military Psychiatry from 1900 to the Gulf War*. Hove and New York, NY: Psychology Press.

Jones, G. (1986), *Social Hygiene in Twentieth Century Britain*. London: Croom Helm.

Jones, K. (1960), *Mental Health and Social Policy, 1845–1956*. London: Routledge and Kegan Paul.

Kutek, A. (2000), 'Warring opposites', in E. Christopher and H. McFarland Soloman, (eds), *Jungian Thought in the Modern World*. London and New York: Free Association Books, pp. 87–104.

Lovegrove, P. (1951), *Not Least in the Crusade: A Short History of the Royal Army Medical Corps*. Aldershot: Gale and Polden.

Leed, E. (1979), *No Man's Land: Combat and Identity in World War I*. Cambridge: Cambridge University Press.

Leese, P. (1989), 'A social and cultural history of shell shock, with particular reference to the experience of British soldiers during and after the Great War'. (Unpublished PhD thesis, Open University).

—(2002), *Shell Shock: Traumatic Neurosis and the British Soldiers of the First World War*. London: Palgrave MacMillan.

Lerner, P. and. Micale, M. S (2001), 'Trauma, psychiatry and history: a conceptual and historiographical introduction', in M. S. Micale and P. Lerner (eds), *Traumatic Pasts: History, Psychiatry and Trauma in the Modern Age*. Cambridge, Cambridge University Press, pp. 1–27.

Micale, M. S. (1995), *Approaching Hysteria: Disease and Its Interpretations*. Princeton, NJ and Chichester: Princeton University Press.

Mitchell, A. (1978), *Medical Women and the Medical Services of the First World War*. Author's offprint from Festschrift for Kenneth Fitzpatrick Russell.

Moriarty, C. (1997), 'Private grief and public remembrance: British First World War memorials', in M. Evans and K. Lunn (eds), *War and Memory in the Twentieth Century*. Oxford and New York, NY: Berg, pp. 125–142.

Mosse, G. (1990), *Fallen Soldiers: Re-Shaping the Memory of the World Wars*. Oxford and New York, NY: Oxford University Press.

Oram, G. (1998), *Worthless Men: Race, Eugenics and the Death Penalty in the British Army during the First World War*. London: Francis Bouttle.

Porter, R. (1995), '"Perplx't with tough names": the uses of medical jargon', in Roy Porter and Peter Burke (eds), *Languages and Jargons: Contributions to a Social History of Language*. Cambridge: Polity Press, pp. 42–63.

—(1987), *A Social History of Madness: The World Through the Eyes of the Insane*. New York: Weidenfeld and Nicolson.

—(2001), *Body Politics: Disease, Death and Doctors in Britain, 1650–1900*. Great Britain: Reaktion.

Prost, A. (1992), *In the Wake of War: Les Anciens Combattants and French Society*. Providence, RI and Oxford: Berg.

Sheffield, G. (2002), *Forgotten Victory the First World War: Myths and Realities*. London: Hodder.

Shephard, B. (1996), '"The Early Treatment of Mental Disorders": RG Rows and Maghull 1914–1918', in H. Freeman and G. E. Berrios (eds), *150 Years of British Psychiatry*. London: Athlone, pp. 434–64.

—(2000), *A War of Nerves*. London: Jonathon Cape.

—(2008), 'Why the psychiatry of war is too important to be left to psychiatrists'. Wellcome Collection (Deutsche Hygiene-Museum, Dresden), *War and Medicine*. London: Black Dog Publishing.

Showalter, E. (1980), *The Female Malady: Women, Madness and English Culture, 1830–1980*. London: Virago.

Simpson, K. (1996), 'Dr James Dunn and shell shock', in H. Liddle and P. Liddle (eds), *Facing Armageddon: the First World War Experienced*. London: Leo Cooper, pp. 502–20.

Stanley, J. (2006), 'Involuntary commemorations: post-traumatic stress disorder and its relationship to war commemoration', in T. Ashplant, G. Dawson and M. Roper (eds), *The Politics of Memory: Commemorating War*. London: Cassell, pp. 240–59

Stone, M. (1985), 'Shell shock and the psychologists', in W. F. Bynum, R. Porter and M. Shephard (eds), *The Anatomy of Madness*. London: Tavistock, pp. 242–71.

Terraine, J. (1993), *Impacts of War 1914 and 1918*. London: Leo Cooper.

Thane, P. (1996), 'Gender, welfare and old age in Britain, 1870s–1940s', in A. Digby and J. Stewart (eds), *Gender, Health and Welfare*. London and New York: Routledge, pp. 67–90.

Thomson, M. (1999), 'Status, manpower and mental fitness: mental deficiency in the First World War', in R. Cooter, M. Harrison and S. Sturdy (eds), *War, Medicine and Modernity*. Stroud: Sutton, pp. 149–66.

Todman, D. (2005), *The Great War: Myth and Memory*. London: Hambledon and London.

Whitehead, I. (1996), 'Not a doctor's work? The role of the British Regimental Medical Officer in the field', in H. Liddle and P. Liddle (eds), *Facing Armageddon: the First World War Experienced*. London: Leo Cooper, pp. 466–74.

Winter, J. (1995), *Sites of Memory, Sites of Mourning*. Cambridge: Cambridge University Press.

Winter, J. and E. Sivan (1999), 'Setting the framework', in J. Winter and E. Sivan (eds), *War and Remembrance in the Twentieth Century*. Cambridge: Cambridge University Press, pp. 6–39.

Winter, J. (1999), 'Forms of kinship and remembrance in the aftermath of the Great War', in
    J. Winter and E. Sivan (eds), *War and Remembrance in the Twentieth Century.* Cambridge:
    Cambridge University Press, pp. 40–60.
Wohl, R. (1980), *The Generation of 1914*. London: Weidenfeld and Nicholson.
Young, A. (1995), *The Harmony of Illusions: Inventing Post-Traumatic Stress Disorder.*
    Princeton, NJ and Chichester: Princeton University Press.

SECONDARY SOURCES: JOURNAL ARTICLES

Bogacz, T. (1989), 'War neurosis and cultural change in England, 1914–1922: the work of the
    War Office committee of enquiry into "shell shock"', *Journal of Contemporary History,* 24,
    227–56.
Bourke, J. (2000), 'Effeminacy, ethnicity and the end of trauma: the sufferings of "shell
    shocked" Men in Great Britain and Ireland, 1914–1939', *Journal of Contemporary History,* 35,
    (1), 57–69.
Douglas, R. (September 1972), 'The National Democratic Party and the British Workers'
    League', *The Historical Journal,* 15, (3), 533–52.
Jones, E. and S. Wessely (2001), 'Psychiatric battle casualties: an intra- and interwar
    comparison', *The British Journal of Psychiatry,* 178, 242–7.
Jones, E., I. Palmer and S. Wessely (2002), 'War pensions (1900–1945): changing models of
    psychological understanding', *The British Journal of Psychiatry,* 180, 374–9.
Lankford, N .D. (1980), 'The Victorian medical profession and military practice: army doctors
    and national origins', *Bulletin of the History of Medicine,* 54, (4), 511–28.
Leese, P. (1997), 'Problems returning home: the British psychological casualties of the Great
    War', *Historical Journal,* 40, (4), 1055–67.
Lerner, P. (2000), 'Psychiatry and casualties of war in Germany, 1914–18', *Journal of
    Contemporary History,* 35, (1), 13–28.
Loughran, T. (September 2007), 'Evolution, regression and shell-shock: emotion and instinct
    in theorist of the war neuroses c.1914–1918', *Manchester Papers in Economic and Social
    History,* 58, 1–24.
Meyer, J. (2004), '"Not Septimus Now": wives of disabled veterans and cultural memory of the
    First World War in Britain', *Women's History Review,* 13, (1), 117–38.
Micale, M. S. (October 1990), 'Charcot and the idea of hysteria in the male: gender, mental
    science, and medical diagnosis in late nineteenth-century France', *Medical History,* 34, (4),
    363–411.
Pederson, S. (1990), 'Gender, welfare and citizenship in Britain during the Great War',
    American Historical Review, 95, (4), 983–1006.
Petter, M. (1994), '"Temporary gentlemen" in the aftermath of the Great War: rank, status and
    the ex-officer problem', *Historical Journal,* 37, (1), 127–52.
Wessely, S. (September 2006), 'The life and death of Private Harry Farr', *Journal of the Royal
    Society of Medicine,* 99, 440–3.
Winter, J. M. (April 1980), 'Fitness and civilian health in Britain during the First World War',
    Journal of Contemporary History, 15, (2), 211–44.
—(2000), 'Shell shock and the cultural history of the Great War', *Journal of Contemporary
    History,* 35, (1), 7–11.
Zweiniger-Bargielowska, I. (2006), 'Building a British superman: physical culture in interwar
    Britain', *Journal of Contemporary History,* 41, (4), 595–610.

LITERARY SOURCES

Barbusse, H. (1916), *Le Feu, Journal d'un escouade*. Paris: Flammarion.

Barker, P. (1996), *The Regeneration Trilogy*. London: Viking.

Butler, S. (1996), *Erewhon*. Ware: Wordsworth Classics, (first published by Trübner and Co., 1872).

Dahl, R. (1984), *Boy: Tales of Childhood*. London: Penguin.

Carrington, C. E. (1929), *A Subaltern's War: being a memoir of the Great War from the point of view of a romantic young man, with candid accounts of two particular battles, written shortly after they occurred, and an essay on militarism*. London: Peter Davies Ltd.

Graves, R. (1960), *Goodbye to All That*. London: Penguin, (first published by Jonathon Cape, 1929).

Falls, C. (1930), *War Books: A Critical Guide*. London: Peter Davies.

Faulks, S. (1994), *Birdsong*. London: Vintage.

Herbert, A. P. (1919), *The Secret Battle*. London: Methuen.

Lawrence, D. H. (1979), *The Ladybird*. London: Penguin, (first published by Martin Secker, 1923).

Owen, W. (1977), 'Mental Cases' in *The Collected Poems of Wilfred Owen*. London: Chatto and Windus (first published 1920)

Orwell, G. (1984), *Down and Out in Paris and London*. London: Penguin, (first published London: Victor Gollancz, 1933).

Remarque, E. M. (1980), *All Quiet on the Western Front*. London: Putnam, (first published 1929).

Sassoon, S. (1937), *The Complete Memoirs of George Sherston*. London: Faber and Faber.

—(1983), 'To One Who was With Me in the War', in *The War Poems*. London: Faber and Faber.

Sayers, D. (1937), *Busman's Honeymoon*. London: Victor Gollancz.

Sterne, L. (1998), *The Life and Opinions of Tristram Shandy, Gentleman*. Oxford: Oxford University Press, (first published 1759).

Tench, W. in G. Edwards (ed.) (2001), *Letters from Revolutionary France*. Cardiff: University of Wales Press, 2001.

Tolstoy, L. (2001), *War and Peace*. London: Wordsworth (first published 1865–69).

Wells, H. G. (1916), *Mr Britling Sees It Through*. London: Cassell and Company.

West, R. (1918), *Return of the Soldier*. London: Nisbet and Co.

Woolf, V. (1992), *Mrs Dalloway*. London: The Hogarth Press, (first published by Hogarth, 1925).

CONTEMPORARY MILITARY AND MEDICAL TEXTS: JOURNAL ARTICLES

Addison, C. (January 1921), 'Parliamentary news', *Journal of Mental Science*, 67, 136.

Anon. (June 1917), 'Good news for the disabled sailor or soldier', *Recalled to Life*, 61–8.

—(June 1917), 'Care of disabled soldiers – preliminary arrangements', *Recalled to Life*, 100–28.

—(June 1917), 'The care of disabled soldiers – the present system', *Recalled to Life*, 111–28.

—(31 July 1915), 'Parliamentary intelligence, House of Lords, Monday 26 July, Treatment of nerve-shaken soldiers', *Lancet*, 261.

—(11 September 1915), 'Emotional shock as a restorative', *Lancet*, 630.

—(October 1915), 'Table showing the number of those on the staff of asylums in the UK, exclusive of medical officers, who have joined the military or naval service during the present war up to the middle of July 1915', *Journal of Mental Science,* 61, 514–17.

—(5 February 1916), 'A discussion on shell shock', (held at the Royal Society of Medicine on 25 and 27 January 1916), *Lancet,* 306–7.

—(5 August 1916), 'Medico-Psychological Association of Great Britain and Ireland. Mental disabilities for war services', *Lancet,* 234.

Turner, W. A. (1916), 'Arrangements for the care of cases of nervous and mental shock coming from overseas', *Lancet,* 1073–5.

Armstrong-Jones, R. (July 1917), 'The psychology of fear and the effects of panic fear in war time', *Journal of Mental Science,* 63, 346–89.

Boyle, H. (April 1914), 'Some observations on early nervous and mental cases with suggestions as to possible improvement in our methods of dealing with them', *Journal of Mental Science,* 60, 381–98.

Brock, A. J. (23 March 1918), 'The war neurasthenic: a note on methods of re-integrating him with his environment', *Lancet,* 436.

Burton-Fanning, F. W. (16 June 1917), 'Neurasthenia in soldiers of the home forces', *Lancet,* 907–11.

Buzzard, F. cited in R. Armstrong-Jones (July 1917), 'The psychology of fear and the effects of panic fear in war time', *Journal of Mental Science,* 63, 346–89.

Clausewitz, C. (1997), *On War.* Ware: Wordsworth, (first published 1832).

Collie, J. (April 1916), 'Malingering: examinations of the upper extremities', *Journal of the Royal Army Medical Corps,* 26, 85–91.

—(September 1917), 'The management of neurasthenia and allied disorders contracted in the army', lecture delivered at the Royal Institute of Public Health, June 1917, *Recalled to Life,* 234–53.

Draper, W. (April 1918), 'Village centres for cure and training', *Recalled to Life,* 346.

Editorial, (October 1915), 'Table showing the number of those on the staff of asylums in the UK, exclusive of medical officers, who have joined the military or naval service during the present war up to the middle of July 1915', *Journal of Mental Science,* 61, 514–17.

Editorial, (6 January 1917), 'An ideal for the New Year', *Lancet,* 23.

—(19 August 1922), '"Shell" shock and "cowardice"', *Lancet,* 399.

Evans, H. (August 1918), 'Development of the work', *Reveille,* 237.

Elliot Smith, G. (15 April 1916), 'Shock and the soldier', *Lancet,* 813–17.

Forsyth, D. (12 April 1932), 'The place of psychology in the medical curriculum', *Proceedings of the Royal Society of Medicine,* 1200–12.

Galsworthy, J. (August 1918), 'The gist of the matter', *Reveille* (formerly *Recalled to Life*), 14.

Graham, S. (1923), 'The ex-service mind of Europe', *Contemporary Review,* 123, 290–300.

Henderson, D. K. (April 1918), 'War psychoses: an analysis of 202 cases of mental disorder occurring in home troops', *Journal of Mental Science,* 64, 165–89.

Hotchkis, R. D. (April 1917), 'Renfrew District Asylum as a war hospital for mental invalids: some contrasts in administration with an analysis of cases admitted during the first year', *Journal of Mental Science,* 63, 242.

Keogh, A. (June 1917), 'Treatment of the disabled', *Recalled to Life,* 6–40.

MacPherson, W. G. (January 1922), 'Parliamentary news', *Journal of Mental Science,* 68, 107–8.

Milligan, E. T. C., (RAMC), (1917), 'Shell shock, a method of treatment', *Journal of the Royal Army Medical Corps,* 28, 272–3.

McDowall, C. (January 1918), 'Mutism in the soldier and its treatment', *Journal of Mental Science,* 64, 54–64.

Mott, F. W. (1916), 'Lettsomian Lecture on the effects of high explosives upon the central
    nervous system', *Lancet,* (part I), 12 February 1916, 331–8; (part II), 26 February 1916;
    441–9; (part III), 11 March 1916, 545–53.
—(October 1917), 'Chadwick Lecture: mental hygiene in shell shock during and after the war',
    Journal of Mental Science, 63, 467–88.
—(April 1918), 'War psychoses and neuroses', a paper presented to the Medico-Psychological
    Society, *Journal of Mental Science,* 64, 230–5.
—(April 1922), 'The neuroses and psychoses in relation to conscription and eugenics', *Eugenics
    Review,* XIV, (1), 14–22.
Myers, C. S. (13 February 1915), 'A contribution to the study of shell shock. Being an account
    of three cases of loss of memory, vision, smell and taste admitted into the Duchess of
    Westminster's War Hospital, Le Toucquet', *Lancet,* 316–20.
Nicoll, M. and J. A. M. Alcock (April 1918), 'Neuroses of war', *Recalled to Life,* 252–8.
Norgate, R. H. (March 1920), 'The effects of the war on the mental condition of the citizens of
    Bristol', *Bristol-Medico-Chirurgical Journal,* XXXVII, 94–108.
O'Brien, F. J. (August 1918), 'Treat shell shock in quiet hospitals', *Medical World,*
    304–5.
Osler, William (9 October 1915), 'Science and war', *Lancet,* 795–801.
Rivers, W. H. R. (2 February 1918), 'An address on the repression of war experience', delivered
    before the Section of Psychiatry, Royal Society of Medicine, 4 December 1917, *Lancet,* 173–7.
Robinson, W. (January 1921), 'The future of Service patients in mental hospitals', *Journal of
    Mental Science,* 67, 40–8.
Rudy, C. (November 1918), 'Concerning Tommy'. *The Contemporary Review,* 545–52.
Rutherford, Jeffrey, G. (April 1920), 'Some points of interest in connection with the
    psychoneuroses of war', *Journal of Mental Science,* 66, 131–42.
Schuster, A. (11 September 1915), 'A presidential address on the common aims of science and
    humanity', *Lancet,* 587–95.
Somerville, H. (April 1923), 'The war anxiety neurotic of the present day: a clinical sketch',
    Journal of Mental Science, 69, 171–80.
Standwell, T. W. (24 January 1920), 'Are you a potential post-war criminal?', *Health and
    Strength,* 62.
Steen, R. H. (October 1917), 'Book review of Eder (1917), *War Shock.* London: William
    Heinemann', *Journal of Mental Science,* 63, 592.
—(January 1920), 'Notes and news', *Journal of Mental Science,* 66, 71.
Turner, W. A. (1916), 'Arrangements for the care of cases of nervous and mental shock coming
    from overseas', *Journal of the Royal Army Medical Corps,* 27, 619–22.
Wilson, L. (January 1921), 'Parliamentary news', *Journal of Mental Science,* 67, 142.
Wiltshire, H. (17 June 1916), 'Contribution to the aetiology of shell shock', *Lancet,* 1207–12.

CONTEMPORARY MEDICAL AND MILITARY TEXTS: BOOKS

BMJ Publishing Group (1917), *British Medicine in the War, 1914–1917.* London: BMA.
Collective authorship (1935), *Tales of a Field Ambulance, 1914–1918,* (told by the personnel).
    Southend-on Sea: printed for private circulation.
Encyclopaedia Britannica (11th edn, 1910).
Report of the War Office Committee of Enquiry into 'Shell Shock (1922) London: HMJ.

Barrett, J. W. (1919), *A Vision of the Possible. What the RAMC Might Become.* London: HK Lewis.

Beggs, S. T. (1916), *RAMC Training in First Aid and Nursing.* London: The Scientific Press.

Butler, A. G. (1940), *The Australian Army Medical Services in the War of 1914–1918.* Canberra, ACT: Australian War Memorial..

Brereton, F. S. (1919), *The Great War and the RAMC.* London: Constable and Co.

Elliot Smith, G. and T. H. Pear, (1918), *Shell Shock and its Lessons.* Manchester: University Press; and London: Longmans, Green and Co.

Fenton, N. (1926), *Shell Shock and its Aftermath.* London: Henry Kimpton.

Ford, A. P. and W. Denoon (1935), 'Early days at Chelsea', in *Tales of a Field Ambulance, 1914–1918,* (told by the personnel). Southend-on Sea: printed for private circulation, pp.13–38.

Galloway, J. (1918), *Report upon the Physical Examination of Men of Military Age by National Service Medical Boards from 1 November, 1917–31 October, 1918,* (vol. I). London, HMSO.

Gibbs, P. (1920), *Realities of War.* London: William Heinemann.

Haigh, R. W. and P. W. Turner (eds) (1970), *The Long Carry: the Journal of Stretcher Bearer Frank Dunham, 1916–1918.* Oxford: Pergamon Press.

Hankey, D. (1918), *A Student in Arms.* London: Andrew Melrose.

Hurst, A. (1917), *Medical Diseases of the War.* London: E. Arnold.

Hutchinson, W. (1919), *The Doctor in War.* London: Cassell and Co.

Lewis, T. H. (1935), 'Crossing overseas', in *Tales of a Field Ambulance, 1914–1918* (told by the personnel). Southend-on Sea: Printed for private circulation, pp. 45–71.

Lloyd George, D. (1942), *War Memoirs of David Lloyd George.* London: Odhams Press Limited.

Lomax, M. (1921), *The Experiences of an Asylum Doctor with Suggestions for Asylum and Lunacy Law Reform.* London: George Allen and Unwin.

MacCurdy, J. (1918), *War Neuroses.* Cambridge: Cambridge University Press.

MacPherson, W. G., W. P. Herringham and T. R. Elliott (1923), *History of the Great War based on Official Documents: Medical Services Diseases of the War,* (vol. II). London: HMSO.

Mitchell, T. J. and G. M. Smith (1931), *History of the Great War based on Official Documents: Medical Services: Casualties and Medical Statistics of the Great War.* London: HMSO.

Moran, C. (1945), *The Anatomy of Courage.* London: Constable.

Mott, F. W. (1919), *War Neuroses and Shell Shock.* London: H. Frowde, and Hodder and Stoughton.

Myers, C. S. (1940), *Shell Shock in France, 1914–1918,* (based on a war diary kept by Charles Myers). Cambridge: Cambridge University Press.

RAMC (1911), *RAMC Training Manual.* Military Books, London: HMSO.

—(1918), *Hints for RAMC Officers.* Edinburgh: William Bryce.

CONTEMPORARY NEWSPAPERS AND JOURNALS

Daily Graphic
Daily Herald
John Bull
Labour Leader
Optimist
The Times
Morning Post

WEBSITES, NEWSPAPERS, RADIO

http://news.bbc.co.uk/1/hi/uk/7720601.stm (accessed 11 November 2008).
http://www.thelancet.com/about (accessed 02 June 2009).
BBC, *10 O'clock News* 20 May 2009.
BBC Radio 4, *Today*, 28 February 2009.
Beharry VC, Lance Corporal Johnson, Interview with the *Independent,* 28 February 2009.
Le Monde
The Guardian

ARCHIVES AND COLLECTIONS

COMBAT STRESS ARCHIVES, COMBAT STRESS, LEATHERHEAD

ESWS *Annual Reports,* 1926–1930.
ESWS Executive Committee Minutes, 1919–1930.
ESWS campaign literature and publicity leaflets, 1919–1930.
ESWS correspondence, 1919–1930.
ESWS Ladies' House Committee Minutes, 1925–1928.

IMPERIAL WAR MUSEUM (IWM), LONDON

Dible, Captain J. H. (6 February 1915), *First World War Account of Captain James Henry Dible.*
    IWM, Con Shelf.
Esler, Captain M. S., Private Papers. IWM, MS74/102/1.
West, B., Unpublished Diary. IWM, B PP/MCR/335.

Sound Archive
Esler, Captain M. S., 378/3.
Hewitt, L. J., 41/4.
Oxley, H., 716/8.
Stagg, L. J., 8764/7.

THE NATIONAL ARCHIVES (TNA), KEW, LONDON

CO 295 621/5
HO 45/12492
PIN 15/249
PIN 15/421
PIN 15/749
PIN 15/750
PIN 15/1230
PIN 15/2499
PIN 15/2500
PIN 15/2501
PIN 15/2502

PIN 15/2503
PIN 26/16387
PIN 26/16532
PIN 26/16542
PIN 26/16457
WO/32/4742
WO/32/4747
WO/32/4748

NATIONAL ARMY MUSEUM (NAM), CHELSEA

Blomfield, Private E. (1931), 'A true war yarn', (unpublished memoir). NAM, 2006–11–38.
Grant, A. R., Private Papers. NAM, 2000–09–62.
Harding, G., Personal Campaign Diary. NAM, 2008–07–13.

THE WELLCOME LIBRARY (WL), LONDON

Personal papers
Parkes Weber, F. Personal Papers, WL, PP/FPW/B163.

RAMC Muniments Collection
Kaye, Captain II. W., Unpublished War Diary. WL, RAMC/739.
Silver, Lieutenant Colonel J. P., Personal Papers. WL, RAMC/542/15.
Webster, Captain W. F., RAMC/384.
RAMC/446/1/1
RAMC/446/7/17/20
RAMC/446/7/7
RAMC/739/18

Index